Escaping Has Ceased to Be a Sport

Escaping Has Ceased to Be a Sport

A soldier's memoir of captivity and escape in Italy and Germany

Frank Unwin

Pen & Sword
MILITARY

First published in Great Britain in 2018 by
Pen & Sword Military
an imprint of
Pen & Sword Books Ltd
47 Church Street
Barnsley
South Yorkshire
S70 2AS

ISBN 978 1 52671 493 0

Printed and bound in England by TJ International Ltd, Padstow, Cornwall.

Pen & Sword Books Ltd incorporates the Imprints of Pen & Sword Archaeology, At-
las, Aviation, Battleground, Discovery, Family History, History, Maritime, Military,
Naval, Politics, Railways, Select, Transport, True Crime, Fiction, Frontline Books,
Leo Cooper, Praetorian Press, Seaforth Publishing, Wharncliffe and White Owl.

For a complete list of Pen & Sword titles please contact
PEN & SWORD BOOKS LIMITED
47 Church Street, Barnsley, South Yorkshire, S70 2AS, England
E-mail: enquiries@pen-and-sword.co.uk
Website: www.pen-and-sword.co.uk

Contents

Foreword   vii

Acknowledgements   xi

Part I   Italy   1

Chapter 1   Capture   3

Chapter 2   Laterina Prisoner of War Camp No. 82   15

Chapter 3   Borgo San Lorenzo Working Party   25

Chapter 4   The Tunnel   45

Chapter 5   Freedom   61

Chapter 6   I Leave My Companions   81

Chapter 7   Pietraviva   93

Chapter 8   My Introduction to Montebenichi   99

Chapter 9   Village Life   107

Chapter 10   A New Home, but Danger is Never Far Away   119

Chapter 11   The Decision to Leave   133

Chapter 12   Departure from Montebenichi   141

Chapter 13   La Fortezza da Basso   153

Chapter 14   The Transit Camp at Mantua   163

Chapter 15   Leaving Italy   167

Part II   **Germany**   173

Chapter 16   Stalag XIa, Altengrabow   175

Chapter 17   Jesabruch factory   181

Chapter 18   The *Lazarett*   191

Chapter 19   Anhalt Quarry   195

Chapter 20   More Thoughts of Escape   205

Chapter 21   Personalities and States of Mind   209

Chapter 22   Factory Jobs   213

Chapter 23   The Salt Mine   219

PART **III**   THE TIDE TURNS   221

Chapter 24   Welcome Glimmers of Hope   223

Chapter 25   The Long March to Freedom   225

Chapter 26   Home at Last   235

Epilogue   241

Foreword

In October 1938 war clouds were gathering and many men were volunteering to join the Territorial Army. My father, Frank Unwin, was unsuccessful in joining his father's regiment, the 6th Battalion of the King's Liverpool Regiment, because it had a full complement and a long waiting list. However, in April 1939 it became clear that war was inevitable. Frank was again refused by the 6th Battalion so he enlisted in his uncle's 59th Medium Artillery Regiment.

The 59th now had sufficient men to form a sister regiment, and Frank found himself in the 68th Medium Regiment. On the outbreak of war in September 1939 the regiment was mobilized. For a year they trained and later, when invasion was expected, they took up positions covering airfields for action against expected German parachute landings.

In September 1940 the regiment was set to be posted to Egypt. Frank was given two weeks' embarkation leave. At the same time his younger sister Betty, aged twelve, was selected for child evacuation to Canada. Together Frank and Betty visited friends saying their farewells. Then Frank returned to his unit. However, before the unit left England, Frank received a telegram with the devastating news: 'Betty torpedoed. Come home if possible.' Frank applied for leave, but embarkation was so imminent that he was refused. However, he felt that he had to be with his family and went absent without leave, hitchhiking through the night from High Wycombe to Liverpool, arriving home during a dawn air raid. The next day the family received the tragic news that Betty was not among the survivors. The following day, Frank felt that he could do no more so returned to his regiment, leaving his family home just before the Military Police arrived looking for him. Back at High Wycombe, Frank went before the battery commander. He was offered sympathy, and no punishment was handed out. The following day, the regiment was transported to Liverpool docks and sailed to Egypt.

After acclimatization in Cairo, Frank's regiment joined the Western Desert Forces to act as cover for the 6th Australian Division. The Italians were driven back into Libya as far as Benghazi, at which point the regiment's guns were no longer needed and his unit returned to Cairo.

Frank's unit then joined the ill-fated expedition to Greece, where 60,000 Allied troops were sent to support the Greek army. The eventual German invasion of Greece was sufficiently strong to overwhelm the Allied force and, with no air cover to defend them against the incessant Stuka dive bomber attacks, the Allies were forced to retreat to Athens. Eventually, with no more diesel available in Greece, the gun-towing lorries were of no further use; orders were received to spike the guns and drive all unnecessary vehicles into the sea. Using their remaining vehicles, the troops set off to Athens.

They were then evacuated by ship from a beach near Athens. Frank and half his unit landed on Crete and were transported to Heraklion, where they were equipped with light artillery guns which had been captured from the Italians in Libya. The Allied troops formed two bridgeheads, at Maleme and Heraklion. The Germans soon launched their offensive in the Battle of Crete, dropping a great force of parachutists. After ten days the Maleme bridgehead ran out of ammunition and became indefensible. The military authorities in Cairo decided at that point to evacuate all Allied troops to Egypt. Frank was picked up by a Royal Navy cruiser, HMS *Orion*. During the voyage to Egypt, after day-long attacks by Stukas, the *Orion* sustained colossal damage and heavy loss of life, but she eventually managed to reach port at Alexandria. After some months of rest, Frank's unit returned to the western desert, where they faced Rommel's *Afrika Korps*. In June 1942 the garrison at Tobruk was overwhelmed and Frank was captured.

Until now Frank's war had included a strange mixture of periods of inaction whilst waiting for attacks that didn't come, times of intense fear as he came under attack from Stuka dive bombers and Messerschmitt fighters, and surreal periods of relaxation as he enjoyed the bars, cinemas and night clubs during periods of acclimatization in Cairo and Alexandria.

Capture was to change everything. However, Frank's war was not yet over and would continue to be a mixture of those same extremes: tedium, fear, excitement and pleasure; but added to these would be periods of sustained hardship, difficult for anyone to imagine if they have not seen service in war.

From an early age Frank had been a resilient and independent child. Born in Liverpool in 1920, he was the eldest of four children. His father ran a grocery store in Kirkdale. Together with his brother and two sisters, Frank had a happy and adventurous childhood, playing with local children in the street and enjoying holidays on the Wirral and in North Wales with his family. He had the freedom of the countryside and consequently became very independent. From the age of six he frequently spent weekends with his Auntie Sis on the Wirral; unescorted, he took the tram bound for Liverpool Pier Head and then a ferry across the Mersey to Birkenhead and a bus to the village of Stoureton.

At eight years old Frank joined the Life Boys and at twelve transferred to the Boys' Brigade, in the evenings engaging in activities such as drills, first aid, wayfarers and gymnastics. In the Boys' Brigade he also took part in hiking, playing cricket and Sunday morning parades with the band. From the age of eleven to seventeen

Frank attended the Liverpool Collegiate School. He then worked with a firm who specialised in camping and outdoor equipment until he joined the Territorial Army, aged eighteen.

At the age of twenty-one, after almost two years in combat, Frank found himself taken prisoner. However, his upbringing in Liverpool had given him remarkable drive, initiative and independence, and a dogged resilience that he never lost. From the moment of capture he maintained a determination which stayed with him throughout the war to escape and, even as a PoW, to play his part in resisting the German war effort.

Escaping Has Ceased to be a Sport tells the story of how, during three years of captivity, Frank's whole focus would be on his escape plans, to the point where he came to treat escaping as a pastime, almost a sport. The constant plotting to seize any possible chance of escape, learning to speak Italian, stowing away food rations – all these kept him focussed, helped to maintain his sanity and played their part in getting him through the war. Despite terrible odds, his escape plans continued even during his imprisonment in Germany.

Ironically, it was immediately after Frank and his fellow would-be escape partner decided not to pursue any further escape plans that they saw a notice posted by the military authorities in Berlin, designed to deter all thoughts of escape and reading 'ESCAPING HAS CEASED TO BE A SPORT'. By that time, they found the notice rather amusing. That was in early spring 1945, weeks before Frank took part in the Long March, and before his eventual release by Allied forces on 12 April 1945.

Betty Merrick

If anyone who reads this book recognizes any person's name or location mentioned and would like to ask any questions or share their story with Frank and Betty, please feel free to contact Betty at bettymerrick4@gmail.com. Also, please feel free to look at (and join) the Facebook group 'Escaping Has Ceased to be a Sport', where details can be found about how to access Frank's other written accounts of his experiences in the Libyan campaigns, Greece and Crete and during the ill-fated evacuation of Crete, aboard HMS *Orion* in May 1941.

Acknowledgements

This book could not have been written without wonderful support over many years from my daughter, Betty. After an Italian historian, Enzo Droandi, asked me for an account of the escape tunnel at Laterina PoW camp, it was Betty who convinced me, when I was in my mid-seventies, that I could learn to use a computer. Then, with great patience, she taught me word processing.

It took another twenty years to complete this project, ten of them spent nursing my darling wife Marjorie through dementia until her death in 2005. Throughout that time Betty has been a constant source of support for myself and Marjorie, and following Marjorie's death she encouraged me to get back into my writing. She has spent many hours with me, reading and improving the text, and as my sight succumbed to macular degeneration, in recent years she has taken over the production and publication of the book.

Betty's husband Andy has given us much technical support with the computing and has scanned and enhanced all the illustrations, including tiny Kodak Brownie photos dating from 1940.

Thanks go also to my son Peter for encouraging me to continue beyond the original tunnel story for Droandi and to recount my entire time in captivity and escape.

I would also like to thank Peter's wife Maggie for all the loving care she has shown in looking after me in recent years.

Also worthy of thanks for all the help they have given me are my good friends Jan Whitehead and her partner David Lewis.

Finally, the bravery and love of the people of Montebenichi and surrounding farmsteads will always be with me. They risked their lives to look after me, and without them this story would not have been there to be told.

Part I

ITALY

Chapter 1

Capture

Capture came as a surprise. Soon after daybreak on 21 June 1942, German tanks overran the gun position of C Troop of 234 Battery, 68th Medium Regiment, Royal Artillery, a Liverpool Territorial Army unit, inside the Tobruk garrison on the Libyan coast. It was hard to accept after so many incidents and excitements in Libya, Greece and Crete, then back to the Libyan desert again, that we finally found ourselves, in the jargon of the day, 'in the bag'. I was three weeks short of my twenty-second birthday.

Apart from the hope of coming through a battle unscathed, there were three possible outcomes that a soldier considered. The first, being killed, was generally accepted by most men, even if uncomfortably so. The second, being wounded and possibly maimed, was the most feared of all. The third, capture, was seldom given a second thought. It was looked upon as something that could never happen, until we were suddenly overtaken by the classic German cry *'Für dich der Krieg vorbei'* ('For you the war is over') and it became a reality.

In November 1941, 234 Battery, comprising the four 155mm guns of C Troop and the four of D Troop, had gone into the Libyan desert for the second time, this time under the command of General Auchinleck. Battles were now to be fought against a much more daunting enemy than in our first spell in the desert in December 1940. At that time General Wavell's troops of British units supporting the 6th Australian division, known as the Western Desert Forces, or more familiarly as 'Wavell's 30,000', had overrun Mussolini's Italians. Now the battery was to find itself up against the might of General Rommel's *Afrika Korps*.

Initially, things went well, and when the regiment entered the western desert once again in November 1941, Sollum, a small port on the Egyptian side of the border, and the larger port of Bardia, across the border into Libya, were soon retaken. We then advanced to relieve the Australian and British forces that had held out successfully for many months under siege in a bridgehead at Tobruk. From there the advance progressed westwards into Libya. A line was established east of Tobruk, with its northern point at Gazala on the coast and extending south to Bir Hakeim in the desert. C Troop's gun position was in the northern sector of the line towards the coast, supporting a South African division.

The fighting on the Gazala line then became strangely static. Action for C Troop developed into occasionally taking a couple of guns forward at night and firing some rounds of harassing fire into enemy lines, before returning to the gun position before daylight. On one occasion the guns were taken down to Bir Hakeim for a few days to support the Free French in an action against enemy tanks, but this was never repeated. Living in a slit trench in a wilderness of sand, day after day for a long period of time, led to boredom creeping in.

Maintenance of equipment became one of the most important tasks. The ammunition on the gun position had to be protected, and this was done by burying the shells in small shallow trenches a little way behind the guns. About a dozen shells were buried in each trench, protected from rust by a layer of empty sandbags laid below and above them, and then covered with a layer of sand. They then had to be occasionally lifted and scrubbed with a wire brush as a further precaution. This task kept the gun crews busy.

On one occasion this process resulted in a tragic incident. Two gunners from one gun crew, Bob Barnwell and Arnold Segar, were crouching over a trench carrying out the work when an unexplained accident occurred: one of the shells being handled exploded, killing the two men instantly. The pair were two of the most popular men in the troop, and their loss affected the rest of the troop badly. The one consolation was that, although many men were in close proximity to the explosion, no one else was harmed.

One of the hardest things to tolerate was the shortage of water. The cookhouse supplied a very welcome mug of tea at each mealtime. Otherwise, the daily ration was scarcely more than one pint. This had to suffice for drinking water and for washing yourself and your clothes. Surprisingly, men managed to achieve this.

Blinding, day-long sandstorms were also hard to cope with. It was an awesome sight to see a dense wall of swirling sand approaching like angry clouds towering above us, only 100yds away and about to envelop the gun position. There was no escape. Very soon, sand penetrated our clothing to the skin, and our eyes, nostrils and lips were attacked by the stinging grains.

Daily life was thus pretty tough, but there was one possible break from the dull routine. A weekly draw was held, names being entered in pairs, with one lucky pair being awarded two weeks' leave in Cairo. As there were almost 100 men in the troop, this did not bring much consolation, except to the fortunate pair who won the draw each week. I was never lucky enough to have my number drawn.

*

As June 1942 arrived there was a feeling that the Allied command may have been considering an attack on Rommel's forces; but it was in fact Rommel who made the first move, and his attack took place towards the southern half of the Gazala line. The panzers broke through at a gap in our line of defences, so they then had the freedom of the desert and were able to attack Allied units in the Gazala line from the rear. At C Troop we were not aware of this and had not been involved in any action at all. Then came orders to fall back into Tobruk and its immediate surroundings, thus forming the same bridgehead as that which had been successfully defended by the Australians some months earlier. Our first gun position was at El Adem, which was on the southern sector facing the airfield. Almost at once we were moved to a different position on the western sector, facing Tmimi along the coast. We set about digging gun pits at once.

On 20 June the Germans attacked the bridgehead on its eastern sector and during the day gained a foothold inside it. A crest half a mile behind our gun position meant that we had no idea of the scene beyond that point. A quiet night followed, but early the following morning the action began again. German tanks rumbled into view over the crest behind us. Mobile artillery was following right behind them. Once those guns had us in their sights they opened up with airburst shells. As each shell burst above us, a cloud of black smoke appeared in the air and a shower comprising chunks of shrapnel rained down on the gun position.

With our guns dug down into gun pits, there was no way we could turn them to engage the tanks. With the enemy fast approaching, the command post received over the radio the order 'Destroy your guns'. Immediately, the gun crews rammed a shell down each end of the barrel of every gun. Then an extended lanyard was attached to the firing pin of each gun. The crews took shelter in nearby slit trenches and the guns were fired. The resulting explosions when the two shells met totally destroyed the gun barrels. It seemed a miracle that we sustained no casualties during this exercise.

Meanwhile, the panzers were grinding to a halt at our gun position. Our two officers, Gun Position Officer Captain Mike Leahy and Troop Leader Lieutenant Franklin-Briggs, emerged from the command post with hands raised and approached the leading tank to surrender. The tank commander, probably the Squadron Leader, standing in the turret of his tank, his face caked in a thick layer of sand, took off his peaked cap and cleared his goggles. Utterly oblivious to his appearance, he was the picture of a hard-bitten, triumphant soldier. Then he pointed backwards towards the crest and uttered the fateful words '*Für dich der Krieg vorbei*'. It was a moment of abject shame and dejection as we tramped towards the crest, accompanied by one German foot soldier, rifle slung across his shoulder. It was certainly the end of any military activity for us, but I was to learn that the war was by no means over yet.

It was galling to recall that eighteen months previously at Bardia, our very first battle, we had watched thousands of Italian prisoners tramping disconsolately across the desert in exactly these circumstances. Now we were the ones to suffer. Our destination proved to be an assembly point, where thousands of men were being gathered. There was no information or action of any kind, and we were just left to our own thoughts. It was midsummer's day in the desert and the sun was still rising. We had not eaten, and the only water available was the small amount in our water bottles. Without shade, the heat became almost intolerable, but there was no escape.

Eventually, relief arrived with darkness, and men tried to sleep. After the heat of the day, the desert sand proved to be a very cold bed during the night. My army greatcoat helped, but it was an uncomfortable and sleepless night. It was hard to believe, and even harder to accept, that I had become a prisoner of war. That was my deep-down feeling, and also that of my colleagues from C Troop.

Tobruk had fallen surprisingly quickly. The feeling amongst the troops, herded together on an area of sand, was that initially the attacking German forces had not been strong enough to warrant the garrison having fallen so fast. The German force seemed relatively small, but it was realized that even if the attack had been repulsed, the Germans would have been able to send strong reinforcements in to finish the task later. However, the Allied collapse should still not have been so rapid. There had been a total lack of air support for the garrison, and there were stories that tanks and anti-aircraft guns may have been withdrawn towards Egypt before the German troops had completely cut off the garrison.

The Army had always emphasized that, if captured, a soldier's duty was to try to escape. I felt that there was a great stigma attached to the fall of Tobruk, and in these early days the thought was born in me that the only way to wipe out the stigma was to escape. From then on, that was my firm intention.

*

The morning after capture, everybody was given a small amount of hard rations. A large water tanker enabled everybody to fill their bottles. Later, a fleet of large lorries arrived, and we were handed over to Italian forces. The lorries were open-backed and had sides little more than waist high. Every one was packed to capacity, with about forty men standing in each. Two Italian soldiers were in the cab, and a North African soldier, probably Libyan, armed with a rifle, sat on top.

Once the lorries were loaded, the convoy moved off and travelled west along the coast road. The journey was most uncomfortable, with everyone having to stand crushed against his neighbours. The Libyan soldier had spells of becoming wildly excited, with eyes rolling and his rifle waving threateningly over the heads of the men in front of him, all the time calling out loudly in his own language. There were one or two halts, when we were allowed to dismount for a short break. One halt I remember was at a large bay, the Gulf of Bomba, where a huge RAF Sunderland flying boat flew past towards the east, very low over the water, no doubt heading for its base in Egypt. I felt very forlorn thinking of the aircrew and how they would be relaxing in their mess that evening.

Our destination proved to be Derna, the next port along the coast. The lorry on which I was travelling made its way to an isolated compound, a bare patch of ground about 20yds square, surrounded by a high wire mesh fence. As we approached, it seemed to be just uneven sand. Once we had dismounted we were ushered into the compound and the gate was securely locked. Some sentries took up their posts around us. As soon as we were left to ourselves we surveyed our surroundings and soon realized that our circumstances were pretty terrible. What we had at first taken to be uneven sand was in fact an Arab graveyard. The bodies had been buried in shallow graves and the sand had just been shovelled back to cover them in a low heap. The thought of lying down to sleep suddenly became unpalatable. Another most unhygienic horror was that there were no toilet facilities. As there was a diagonal slope in the ground, it was agreed that the lowest corner should be the toilet area and we would sleep as far from it as possible.

It was a merciful relief when daylight arrived next morning. After being given a little food, we mounted the lorry and were soon travelling westwards along the coast road again. This time our destination was the town of Benghazi. There we pulled up in the open desert outside the town and joined a large number of men who had arrived earlier.

We were then marched some way to a very large compound. Enormous coils of barbed wire that were stretched out concertina-fashion formed two very large circles in the sand to act as compounds. The two circles came together for a distance of about twenty yards and for that short distance only one coil separated the compounds. This was to be of some significance later. Both compounds were soon filled with men, many thousands in all. Before entering the compound we were sorted into groups of fifty.

There were row upon row of low open-fronted tents in the compound, each sheltering five or six men. In my tent there was just one man I knew from the unit, Eric Sprawson from Oldham. I was to spend five or six weeks in this compound which was an extremely depressing period. It boiled down to just learning to survive. There was little good humour between men, and morale was very low.

We received a small daily ration of food, but water was a problem. Day after day the sun burned down, and there was seldom enough water for a satisfying drink. The water distribution left a lot to be desired. An enormous water bowser would be driven into the compound and left inside the gate. At the rear end of the tank there were three taps from which we could draw the water, which then fell into three very large basins placed below the taps. We only had our water bottles and army mess tins, and the scene was like a flock of vultures descending on a carcass.

Eventually, everybody would get some water, but an enormous amount was lost in spillage.

After some time in the compound I thought I really must clean my teeth. I had a toothbrush and toothpaste but no water. I had not cleaned them since being captured, so I spread some paste on the brush. As I took a good sweep at my teeth I recoiled in pain, which seemed to shoot from my mouth straight down to my boots. My mouth and throat must have been so dry that the toothpaste seemed to act like acid. The damage was done, and I had no water to rinse my mouth out. This painful condition persisted for some time until I next managed to get some water. Then I used the whole lot at once on swilling out my mouth and throat.

*

On one occasion I had a great stroke of luck. I was alongside the gate when a couple of Italians opened it, saying they wanted half a dozen men to carry out some jobs. The thought of getting out of the compound for a time was heavenly. I was lucky enough to get through the gate in the first half dozen, and we were taken to the nearby Italian camp. One chap collared me and took me with him. The destination proved to be the Italians' cookhouse. It was not a building but a system of waterproof groundsheets buttoned together to form a roof and propped up to ceiling height by poles, with more groundsheets hanging as occasional wall sections. It was shaded and cool, and an excellent shelter from the sun.

As I entered, there were four or five cooks preparing various meals. What caught my eye was an enormous cartwheel-shaped cheese on a nearby table. It was already half eaten, but six or seven fist-size chunks were lying on the table. The sight was too much for me. Without another thought I was at the table, picking up a chunk and biting into it ravenously. I had never heard of *parmigiano* cheese but I knew I was on to something good. I expected to be pulled off and maybe thumped, but the Italians were on my side. One said, 'Very good, *si?*', with a pleasant Italian accent. Another chap added, 'Evverrything issa good when you are hungry, *si?*' They did not know how true their words were. To this day I love parmesan cheese, but superb though the taste still is, it has never reached the height of those first bites in Benghazi.

The Italians were so friendly that I decided to chance my arm and I unbuttoned my khaki desert shirt and started stuffing chunks of cheese into it. I thought I might be stopped by the Italians, but when I had cleared the table, they began using a little dagger-like tool to break off more chunks for me until my shirt would hold no more. I stayed with them until the party was called to return to the compound. At the compound gate I was afraid the cheese might be confiscated. This did not happen, so I went back to my shelter to see exactly what I had brought.

I kept a good supply for myself and split the rest among the four or five men in the shelter. It had been an excellent exercise. I did not know what the other five men of the work party had done, but I had not been asked to do a stroke.

*

Finally, men started being taken from the camp, in groups of fifty. Periodically, many groups were ordered to be ready to march that evening. The parties always left after dark. We assumed this was to go to Benghazi harbour to board a ship bound for Italy. After a number of these departures the compound was much less crowded. This eased the water problem, making it much easier to draw supplies.

I learned that in the compound across the coil of wire there was one group of fifty that included many of my friends. Whenever I could contact them in the adjoining compound I used to enjoy our chats across the wire. I thought how good it would be if I were in that compound. Then one day I remembered how a Regimental Sergeant Major I had seen in a camp at Sidi Bishr, near Alexandria, in Egypt, when passing the coil of barbed wire that formed the camp boundary, had seen a cat stepping carefully through the tangle of wire. In true RSM fashion, he bellowed for the Orderly Sergeant. When the unfortunate fellow arrived, the RSM furiously pointed his stick at the offending cat, roaring, 'If a cat can get through it, a man can get through it. Get it fixed.' I thought about this and wondered if the RSM might have been right. So the next morning I thought I would explore the position. No sentry could get anywhere near that point because there was only the one coil of wire separating the two compounds. I found to my delight that, with a bit of a struggle, I could begin to make a path through the wire.

The next morning, together with another fellow who also wanted to change compounds, I started work in earnest. With no fear of sentries spotting us, we worked together, each pulling in opposite directions. It was not too long before there was a visible tunnel under the wire. We decided to try it, and I went first. It had looked quite clear, but although I was slim I must have got hooked on every barb. Levering my body through and trying to miss the barbs was both painful and difficult, but eventually I made it. I was exhausted.

Before long my companion was also through. When we reached my friends, it was wonderfully relaxing to sit chatting and swapping experiences. I explained the tunnel through the coil of wire and asked if anybody in the group wanted to swap compounds. We were delighted when two fellows volunteered to do so.

We said we would go back to collect our kit and return for the swap to take place later that day. We successfully negotiated the wire and were soon back in our own compound. During the afternoon we thought it best to go while it was still light, since disengaging snagged barbs would then be easier. This time it was more difficult, as we were bringing our kit. I went first, pushing my kit in front of me and prising it under the barbs. It took rather longer, but I made it. My companion followed, and I reached in and assisted him through with his gear. We were now in great spirits and went off to find the exchange pair. My arms and legs were bleeding and really sore with catching on the barbs, but I did not mind that. However, we were in for the most awful news. When we met the two exchangers they told us that they had changed their minds and no longer wanted to go. This was a shattering blow, but we could do nothing about it, and now we were faced with the task of returning through the wire.

I was most depressed at the thought of not joining my friends when success had seemed so sure: Bill Pople from Bristol, George Davies from Manchester, Tiffy Hunt from Portsmouth, our REME artificer who had been my dugout partner for the months at Gazala, and Ron Taylor from Lewes with whom I had spent a hectic leave in Cairo a year earlier. Ron Taylor's leg was always being pulled because he so often strummed his guitar and sang an elegiac song which started, 'Not a sound could be heard save the cry of the wild bird, as it flew o'er the dying soldier's head' and towards the end went, 'Tell my dear old mother, that I'm not coming home'. There were so many others in that group together with whom I had fought battles and shared good times, and from whom I would now be separated.

Back with my former group, I did not have long to dwell on my disappointment, as a few days later we were ordered to move that evening. It was confirmed that we were heading for Benghazi harbour to board a ship bound for Italy. When the time came to form up outside the compound it was found that a number of men were not fit to march anywhere. Conditions in the camp had brought these fellows down to a reduced state of health in the six weeks that we had been in Benghazi, and they were now in a very poor way. The unfit were left at the roadside to be brought along by vehicle, and the remainder set off on foot. Everybody had to carry their kit, which made the situation worse.

As we began to march, some men were dropping out at the roadside. It became apparent that they were not up to it. Progress was very slow. The heat of the day had gone, but even so it was hard to put one foot in front of the other. It was with enormous relief, when those of us who made it finally arrived, that we dropped to the ground exhausted.

*

Once in Benghazi harbour, we were ordered to form a queue alongside a ship moored at the quayside. After a while those at the front of the queue began being taken on board. When my turn came, I found myself walking across the deck to a hatch cover about 12ft square over the cargo hold. A small section of the cover had been removed to give access to a ladder leading down into the bottom of the hold. There were a number of Italian sailors and soldiers on the deck. Two or three German soldiers were also moving about and they seemed to be controlling things on board.

A couple of Italians were at the opening in the hatch cover, helping men on to the ladder. When I reached that point and looked over the edge I almost swooned. The ladder seemed to go down for ever and the two sides seemed to meet in infinity at the bottom. I have never had a head for heights, and now I was scared stiff. At once I protested to the Italians, but they made it plain that whatever my feelings, I was going down.

What made things seem worse was that about 10ft down into the hold there was a deck from side to side of the ship, except for the area immediately below the hatch cover. That area of deck had been filled almost to the edge by the first men down the ladder, and there was no room for any more men at that level. The only course was to go right down to the bottom. When I got on to the ladder I hung on for dear life and was almost too scared to take my hands from it. After some rungs I was passing the crowded intermediate deck. Once past that point, I knew it was a long way to the bottom of the hold. I had to cling desperately to the ladder, saying a prayer as I went down. It was with great relief that I eventually felt my boot touch the floor.

The floor was steel, cold and unyielding, and the space was already beginning to become crowded. More and more men were coming down, and soon it was difficult for newcomers to find room to sit. Even sitting was uncomfortable because the floor was cold and damp. I made myself as comfortable as I could, shutting my eyes and trying to close my mind to the surroundings. However, there was no escape from the noise that was amplified by strong echoes. Everybody was speaking or shouting, and every call seemed to be a different sort of protest. A few bright lights hung from the deck high above, but they were so far away that we were in semi-darkness.

I must have fallen asleep, because the noise of the ship's engines being started wakened me. At first the noise was fairly gentle but, as we left harbour and hit the open sea, it got worse. Crossing the Mediterranean was full of danger because Allied submarines were hunting by night and day. So the ship's captain sailed at full speed as much as he was able. This caused the ship to pitch and roll more than it would have done normally. She was just an old tramp steamer and hardly up to the work of troop transport.

The banging, clattering and creaking of the ship travelling under pressure became hardly bearable. Then water, which had seeped in from somewhere, made sitting, huddled on the cold steel floor, a most unpleasant experience. Men tried to stand in the semi-dark, but the ship's movement made it impossible and they simply fell on to their sitting neighbours. Sleep was impossible now; at best, you could lapse into semi-consciousness.

We had not been at sea for very long when another problem arose. The motion of the ship began to cause seasickness. One man after another fell victim, and it was not long before many were struck down. The unfortunate victims were retching on almost empty stomachs and the stench of vomit was overpowering. Nobody could do anything to look after themselves. Seasickness did not hit me, and I stayed clear of other men's misfortunes. However, just being there seemed almost enough to take away one's reason. Fortunately, when men who were standing against the ship's side succumbed and staggered forward, I was able to find a place to stand against it myself. This let me feel a little above and apart from the horrors happening all around me.

Even now we were to find that things could get worse. We had left the compound early the previous evening, and since then nobody had had access to a toilet. Now, down in the bottom of that hold, there were no facilities whatsoever. Men held on as best they could, but in the unfortunate state many were in they could hold on no longer.

It was now just a matter of waiting for daylight. Finally, we were able to see a small patch of light through the hole in the hatch cover high above us. Soon after dawn the Italians began lowering jerricans of water down on long ropes. As men saw these they crowded to a point below the cans, waiting impatiently for them to come within reach. By the time they were just above head-high, lots of men were leaping up to get a first hold on them. In all the fighting that went on much of the water was spilt.

As the day progressed a message came down that small parties would be allowed on deck for a spell. It meant climbing the ladder but, after the experiences of the night, I was prepared to do anything to get away for a short time from the atmosphere and the smell of the hold. When I started climbing the ladder there was one man immediately one rung above me and another one rung below me, all moving at the same rate, so somehow I did not feel the fear of the previous evening. It had seemed like Hell in the hold during the night, and to clamber out of the hatch cover on a warm sunny day and catch the sweet sea breeze was positively like an instant transfer to Heaven. The ship was an old one, but in the bright sunlight the deck looked clean and warm.

A line of toilets had been erected along the deck and there was an enthusiastic queue outside them. The Italian sailors were friendly. However, the German soldiers, looking very smart in their uniforms, were aloof with both sailors and prisoners. I was on deck for about half an hour before anyone suggested I should go below again. I think it was not so much a case of enjoying myself while I was up there but rather just of shedding the horrors of the night. I did not like the thought of going below again but now I was prepared to do so. When I reached the hold I just stood against the side again, closed my eyes and tried to close my mind as well.

Later in the day I was able to go back on deck. This time restrictions had been relaxed and I was able to stay on deck. The ship was now sailing very smoothly on a calm sea and I learned we were off the east coast of the heel of Italy. When the ship arrived at the port of Brindisi she anchored offshore, and lighters came out from the port to disembark us. It was early August 1942 and I was about to experience my introduction to Italy.

Chapter 2

Laterina Prisoner of War Camp No. 82

O n the quayside at Brindisi harbour lorries were waiting to ferry us to various destinations. I was with a party of about 100 that was taken to a grassed area surrounded by a brick wall. The description sounds mundane, but to eyes which for eight months had seen only the wastes of the Libyan desert it was like paradise. The grass was lush and the surrounding wall, with its well-worn red bricks and weathered mortar, reminded me of an enclosed orchard back home. The wall had just one small doorway in it, and nearby there was a tap. The smooth, untrodden grass and the mellow style of the old wall on a calm sunny day could well have been somewhere on the edge of a pretty English village.

After we had relished the setting for a little while and sunned ourselves on the grass, a delivery of bread arrived at the door. It was a pile of freshly baked 120gm buns, which was to be our standard daily bread ration in Italy. This was our first food for several days. Together with the tap water, which was a totally different commodity to the brackish liquid supplied by a water wagon in the desert, it was perfect. Relaxing under a tolerably warm sun with the water and the bread we had been given, men were as satisfied as any other possible meal could have made them.

Our stay on the outskirts of Brindisi was brief. We saw little of the town and its port, but it had been very pleasant. Later that day we were whisked to the railway station, where we found a line of goods wagons waiting. This at first seemed miserable accommodation, but the Italians had done us proud. Each wagon had benches installed so we could all be comfortably seated. The front half of a wagon had four benches facing backwards, almost from side to side. The rear half had four similar benches facing forward. The large sliding door on both sides was left open, and across each doorway was a waist-high viewing bar, so we were to travel both comfortably and enjoyably. There was one guard per wagon.

We set off not knowing what our destination was to be. The train travelled through the night and now our sleep was comfortable. We woke to a beautiful morning. As we passed a large city, the guard told us it was Naples. From there we travelled on north, passing through attractive, ever-changing landscape. Compared to the desert, this seemed a veritable Shangri-La.

*

The weather changed as we travelled north. As night fell, rain set in, so we closed the wagon doors. The trials of the previous days were still heavy on us, but on the reasonable seating we slept soundly. When we were wakened at our destination it proved to be the station for the small Tuscan town of Laterina.

It was about 3.00 am when we left the train. The night was very dark, and it was raining heavily. The camp lay about nine miles from the station. The Italians were unwilling to march us to the camp in such conditions because escape would have been too easy in the dark. The outcome was that we were shepherded into a nearby field, with sentries surrounding us. There we spent several uncomfortable hours standing in the rain, waiting for dawn.

It was a relief when we were able to get out on to the road and march off. The rain had stopped, and we were soon marching downhill into a narrow valley. At the bottom, we crossed a bridge over the River Arno. The valley floor was a very pleasant and picturesque place. We passed lots of vineyards and fields of maize, but the main crop seemed to be tobacco. There were a number of very large factory buildings for tobacco processing.

Then we saw the town of Laterina stretched along a ridge on the north side of the valley. The valley had narrowed to some hundreds of yards here. The south side was bounded by low cultivated hills, with the River Arno running at their foot. It was not a major river at this point. Our PoW camp was situated at the base of the hill below Laterina. It was a lovely setting, and we could not have asked for a nicer location, which was some consolation. In spite of this, my spirits were very low as I entered the camp gate.

*

Laterina prison camp was in the very early stages of development. The land had previously been a vineyard. The compound was surrounded by two parallel curtains of barbed wire about 7ft high and 4ft apart. These formed a corridor in which the sentries could patrol. Eight feet inside the barbed wire there was a trip wire. This was about 6ins above the ground. We were warned that any prisoner crossing this wire was liable to be shot. Outside one corner of the compound there was a machine gun tower. The only structures already built were an open-sided cookhouse and an administration building.

Once inside the compound, we were each issued with an Italian army waterproof cape. This was the type of groundsheet I had seen in the Italians' cookhouse at Benghasi. We were shown how eighteen of them could be buttoned together to form a ridge tent for eighteen men. The tent sites had already been marked out, and tent poles, guy ropes and pegs were available. We were left to get on with it. Later, each man was given two blankets and a palliasse, which he had to fill with straw. This was the end of our journey. We were now 'home', but after the night's rain at the station, not quite dry.

*

There were five officers and about 2,000 men in the camp. The officers were two medics and three padres, Protestant, Catholic and Jewish. The senior British non-commissioned officer in the camp was Regimental Sergeant Major Cockcroft of the South African army. He controlled internal matters in the camp and had a small office staff. A camp police squad was appointed, mainly from members of the Royal Military Police, as well as a team of cooks and one of latrine diggers. There were also other roles to fill, such as a few barbers.

The tented area was to one side of the compound, leaving a large area of open ground which was used for the daily morning roll call. The rows of vines which had occupied the site prior to our arrival had been cleared but not the trees that grew as supports along the rows. The lengths of wire stretching from tree to tree to support the vines had also been removed. The trees were 10ft apart in rows, and the rows were 20ft apart.

One immediate necessity was the provision of toilet facilities. The Italians had excavated one field latrine prior to our arrival, a pit about 33ft long, 3ft wide and more than 3ft deep. Each latrine had a timber roof and a waist-high timber wall back and front. Our latrine-digging team went into action immediately, digging several more. They were communal field toilets for the 2,000 men in the camp, and we soon had two or three in use at any one time. As a pit became redundant, the earth was carted by wheelbarrow from the new pit to the old one until it became solid ground again.

Most men were severely demoralized and in poor health after the first six weeks of captivity, spent mostly in atrocious conditions in the Libyan desert. The food rations we received at Laterina, though not plentiful, were sufficient. The daily ration was a ladle of pasta and a 120gm bun with a very small portion of cheese once a week. Twice a week there was a small amount of meat in the pasta. The rations were served to groups of twenty-one men and were quite simple to re-issue to individuals. There were occasional issues of minor items to each group which were a little more difficult to distribute, such as two onions and a plum, or two apples and a carrot. Such issues were difficult to divide between twenty-one hungry men. All men employed on any job in the camp received double rations.

*

One thing which improved morale was when the Italians erected a large marquee near the main gate to act as a concert pavilion. Men soon came forward to organize concerts, which reached a high standard. There were sufficient talented individuals who volunteered their skills to make for a good show. One popular turn was Jimmy Jones, a Manchester man from my unit, who did an exhibition dance act. It was a type of dance the audience had never seen before and was always eagerly awaited. Jimmy was ahead of his time, and his somewhat frenzied style became very popular after the war. Another chap had made a makeshift ATS uniform, as worn by women in the Army. He played the part of a feckless female called Georgina Stodge. This was always popular and drew many bawdy comments from the audience. There were also a number of good vocalists, groups, comedians and other acts. The shows were well managed and very popular. Some individuals gave lectures, usually about their professions. One was a professional golfer and another a professional jockey who had won the Brighton Cup.

An even bigger boost to morale came when Red Cross food parcels arrived from UK, together with tins of fifty Rothmans 555 cigarettes. The food parcels were packed and labelled from about ten different towns in the UK and there was also a parcel sent from Canada. The name of the town in which each UK parcel had been packed was printed on the parcel. The Canadian parcels were unanimously considered to be the best. Those from UK were very similar to each other, but most men had one particular town which they considered produced the best parcels. Each parcel, weighing 10lbs, contained a selection of foods chosen because they contained plenty of added extra vitamins. An average parcel would comprise things like bacon, salmon, spam, peaches, pineapples, creamed rice, condensed milk, cheese and butter, as well as packets of tea and sugar and a bar of Meltis chocolate.

An unusual item of food which arrived on one occasion was a consignment of large tins of pea soup, a gift from the Government of Argentina. Given the shortage of bowls and basins, there was a problem finding a way to dish it out. It also led to a very well received piece of parody at one of the camp concerts. During an enactment of the witches' scene from *Macbeth* a pot of green liquid was poured into the cauldron to the accompaniment of the chant:

Double, double, toil and trouble;
Fire, burn, and dixie bubble.
Now to make the mixture green,
A little pea soup from the Argentine.

The Red Cross parcels were said to be despatched for a weekly issue, but in practice they would arrive at intervals of up to four or five weeks. We never learned what happened to the missing ones. This long break between parcels led to men pairing up as 'parcel muckers', each drawing a parcel but sharing first one parcel before opening the second. This spread the food over a longer period. My parcel mucker was a fellow from my unit, Jack Devlin from Warrington. We proved to be a good match and had few disagreements about programming the menus.

*

After a while we became inured to the rigours of camp life, and general health improved. This boosted morale. Brick dormitory blocks, referred to as 'huts' and numbered 1 to 11, began to be built by the prisoners, with Italian work-men supervising. Gradually the tents were dispensed with as new huts became available. Every hut contained an ablution and toilet section at one end, and the sleeping quarters held a couple of hundred men. Inside the hut a system of walls divided it into partitions holding six three-tier bunks for eighteen men. This was convenient but was complicated by the fact that at meal times food was dished out for groups of twenty-one. The men in my tent were allocated to Hut 11, so we had several months to wait before we could leave our tents. A twelfth hut was later built for amenity purposes such as a barber's shop, and various storage rooms.

As winter came on there was much heavy rain and the ground became increas-ingly waterlogged, especially on the parade ground, where the daily roll call took place. On rainy days this area became a quagmire. This led to the guards flounder-ing in the mud, causing miscounts which in turn required a complete recount. It was a miserable experience, and so a storm trench was excavated behind the huts. At its start behind Hut 12 it was quite shallow, but it became much deeper as it passed behind Hut 1, leaving the camp at the nearby corner beneath the machine gun tower to drain into the River Arno just a few yards away. This improved the condition of the ground a great deal.

With the general improvement in health and morale, men settled down and began to exercise again. Groups of three or four would perambulate the trip wire for hours on end, conversing all the time. The many South Africans in the camp were particularly keen on trip wire perambulation. They spoke in Afrikaans and were obviously often discussing food since in mid-sentence they would come out with English phrases such as 'bacon and meat roll'. The main topic of conversation was invariably food, although when Red Cross parcels arrived and food was a little more plentiful, it would temporarily change to women.

*

I perambulated the trip wire very often, and by now thoughts of escape were occu-pying my mind. Two fellows had tried, one getting through the main gate somehow and the second being discovered hiding in a vehicle as it left. The first fellow was recaptured within an hour, illustrating the difficulty involved.

As we moved into November we lost the early morning mists in the valley which had always given way to bright sunshine. Every aspect of the weather was bad. It was cold with strong winds, heavy rain and sometimes fog. Life became altogether more miserable. We were awaiting the construction of Hut 11, so were still in tents. The tents were of such flimsy material that we had to spend much of our time under our blankets. Nobody ventured out for a cold water shower in the open air, and this led to an infestation of body lice. As we felt them crawling between the blankets and our bodies, the only recourse was to run a glowing cigarette along the seams of one's shirts and underclothes.

I bided my time, as yet having no escape plans. I thought that one essential preparation was first to learn Italian. There was no contact with any Italian civilians, but the camp was patrolled day and night by sentries who were always bored. I took every opportunity to converse with them so as to practise my Italian. I spent hours sitting by the trip wire just a few yards from the barbed wire corridor where the sentries were stationed. There were three or four of them along each side of the camp. They always welcomed the opportunity to relieve their boredom by chatting, even though conversation was difficult. A little flattery worked wonders, however, and they were always pleased to speak to somebody who was trying to learn their language. It started with signs, but soon a smattering of words came, then conversation began to flow. This was the first positive start of my escape plan. The very thought of it thrilled me and filled me with excitement.

*

Since the arrival of the 68th Medium Regiment in Egypt, in October 1940, when I was twenty years old, I had been posted as missing on one previous occasion, and my family had gone some time not knowing what had happened to me. That was in May 1941, after the battle of Crete and the ensuing evacuation voyage to Alexandria aboard HMS *Orion*, the battle cruiser on which so many men were so tragically lost. On that occasion I was able to write home again after arriving in Egypt.

The second time, which lasted much longer, followed my capture at Tobruk. That time, back in Liverpool, my family heard the good news that I was alive from the mother of my closest friend, Jimmy Moore. Mrs Moore was addicted to listening to the Vatican City radio station. Late each night the station broadcast a list of names of men who had been taken prisoner. One night she heard my name. At once she ran as fast as she could, arriving breathless at my father's shop to gasp out, 'I've just heard your Frank's a prisoner. He's alive!'

My mother at once made enquiries about what she could do to help me and learned that, apart from official Red Cross food parcels, families could send a personal parcel every three months. These could weigh up to 10lbs and could contain only clothes, chocolate and books. My mother acted quickly, and soon afterwards my first parcel arrived. I found myself with top quality shirts, underclothes, socks, enormous bars of chocolate and some books. The most valuable thing in the parcel was a Hugo's Italian pocket dictionary. This was a brilliant piece of thinking on my mother's part. The dictionary was of enormous value to me, helping me to learn Italian.

We also received a consignment of clothing and sports gear from the Red Cross in London. I received a battledress tunic and trousers, which made a great difference to my comfort. The sports gear was mostly just a supply of footballs, but they were invaluable. As soon as we had footballs, the game became the major activity in the camp. The parade ground for the daily count was comfortably large enough for an acceptably sized football pitch. The snag about it was that, although the vines had been removed, the small trees that had supported them were still in place. Trees, dotted in rows all over the pitch, made a mockery of any games we played. We approached the Italians for permission to remove the trees, but this was refused. There was no option but to play on the pitch as it was, but it was like playing football in a wood.

Then came a big surprise: when the camp wakened one morning, we found that every tree had been sawn down almost to ground level during the night. Who had done it remained a mystery to us; it might even have been the Italians who were the culprits. The outcome was that, as a collective punishment to the camp, fires were forbidden in the brewing area for seven days. This meant that we could not have a cup of tea for a week. At that point permission was given for the tiny stumps of the trees to be removed, and from then on football became of consuming interest to the whole camp.

Preparations were made to draw up a couple of leagues. Two teams, A and B, were formed from each of the eleven occupied huts, with two teams of extras added, to form two leagues of twelve teams each. Equipment began to appear like magic. The Italians gave us timber for goalposts. Some of the South African prisoners were fishermen and experts in net-making. They used the strong Red Cross parcel string to make excellent goal nets. Fixture lists were drawn up, and we were ready to go.

There was also a sufficient mixture of nationalities in the camp to have international matches. These were the highlight of the entertainment. There were teams from England, Scotland, Ireland, Wales and South Africa. Scotland was the best of the UK teams, but best of all were the South Africans. There was one professional referee named Pye, from an Essex league, and some professional players, one of whom was Buchan, a Scot who played for Blackpool and, I think, also for Scotland. However, men were not in the best physical condition, so matches lasted less than forty-five minutes each way.

The large marquee just behind the football pitch, originally erected as the concert pavilion, was perfectly sited to be used as a dressing room for the international football matches, and this became its principal use. Vests for the teams had been dyed in the national colours and everybody had khaki shorts. The two captains came out alongside each other, each carrying a ball, their team filing out behind them. They were greeted by a roar from around 2,000 chaps. It only needed the Edge Hill Railway Band forming up in the centre of the pitch playing the Post Horn Gallop before the game and countermarching on the pitch at half time to let me imagine I was back on the Spion Kop at Anfield, Liverpool's football ground, for a derby match against Everton. The Italians became as keen on these games as we were, and a stand was built near the cookhouse to accommodate around fifty Italian officers and other ranks.

A friend of my father, Bob Prole, was 'Ranger', the sports editor of the *Liverpool Echo*. He used to send me reports of the friendly games being played back at home. I enjoyed reading them, after which I pinned them on the board for all to see.

*

One sad event happened when a party of about fifty prisoners arrived at the camp from various PoW camps around Italy. The Red Cross and the Italian authorities had found their medical condition to be sufficiently serious to warrant repatriation, and they were assembled at Laterina prior to their journey home. The camp was already crowded, and finding places for these men was difficult. It was expected that their departure would be imminent, but this proved not to be so. As time passed, they became ever more depressed.

Eventually, disaster struck one morning when the roll call showed one prisoner short. The sentries carried out their usual drill and made a search of every building. A recount proved unnecessary because, sadly, one of the medical repatriatees was found hanging in the ablutions area of a hut. His funeral took place in Laterina cemetery a few days later with an escort party of prisoners. Two or three days after the funeral the party of repatriatees left the camp, bound for the UK. The unfortunate fellow had given up only days before release.

About this time I received worrying news when some new prisoners arrived at the camp: another prison ship sailing from Benghazi soon after the one I had been aboard had not been as fortunate as mine and had been intercepted and torpedoed by a British submarine during the crossing to Italy. I thought of the party of fifty men, many of them my friends, whom I had tried so hard to join in the compound at Benghazi. The conditions aboard my ship had been horrific, and to imagine being trapped in those circumstances and then to suffer a torpedo strike was more than I could bring myself to contemplate. I just hoped that my friends were not aboard that ship and that they had not suffered such a fate.

*

In January 1943 the weather improved dramatically. In the frosty early mornings the parade ground was frozen solid. But by 10.00 am the sun from a clear blue sky had melted the frozen mud and led to a beautiful crisp day. The Italians started a programme of walks around the valley. The men from each hut would, in turn, be taken for a walk, escorted by eight or nine guards and one officer. The walk was along the road to the end of the valley, returning to camp on a road along the other side of the valley. It must have been between one and two miles. The walks boosted morale, bringing a wonderful feeling of freedom, despite the presence of guards. There was plenty to see in the fields, with many peasants, including elderly ladies dressed entirely in black, busy at their seasonal pursuits.

I was on one of the walks, and everybody's spirits were really high. The whole company was walking along happily chatting, when suddenly chaos broke out. As we came alongside a grass meadow, one man broke ranks and went haring across the field. Immediately, the officer and guards went off in pursuit, firing their rifles as they chased him. He was dressed in a white T-shirt so made a perfect target. Our hearts were in our mouths as we watched. A lot of the rifles appeared to be tilted upwards, just firing in the air, while the officer led the men, brandishing his pistol and firing away. The escaper made the bushes at the far side of the field but found he had arrived at the River Arno.

His luck was out as he found a 6ft high bank on both sides of the river. With the guards only a few yards behind him, he wisely decided to raise his hands in surrender. He had broken from the rear of the column, and the officer had been leading the party so had been way over on the right of the action. It was only when the escaper was being brought back to the road that we saw that the officer was kneeling on the ground. When he rose he was holding a bloodstained handkerchief to his left hand. He had been struck by a bullet which could only have been fired by a guard. He was so far off the general line of fire that it seemed to have been a most unlikely accident, but the wound was there for all to see.

The officer was in a foul temper when he returned to the column. He had the escaper's hands bound behind his back, and the man was tied to a guard. When the return to camp began, the officer walked behind his prisoner and every few yards kicked him viciously behind the knees, bringing him to the ground. It had been a most useless exercise and was a classic demonstration of how not to attempt escape. Needless to say, to everyone's disappointment, the walks were stopped. I had been on two or three, and it was always exciting to be out of camp. That feeling itself brought out thoughts of escape, and this latest episode, foolish though it was, emphasized that it was time for me to give thought to my own plan.

*

The location of Laterina camp was beautiful. The valley was not many hundreds of yards wide, and the low hills to both north and south were very picturesque. The hill to the north was a long rather narrow ridge, and it was along this ridge that the town was built. The closely packed line of the very old buildings, topped by the bell tower of a church and another two or three ancient towers, made a striking skyline. With the added clumps of cypress, it was Tuscany at its best.

The hill to the south was devoted to agriculture, and in the warm weather which now prevailed a favourite pastime of many men in the camp was to just sit and watch the workers going about their tasks in the fields on the hillside. With no mechanical help, the men worked with pairs of white oxen. They would spend the day guiding the oxen in pulling a very primitive plough. It was surprising how they could operate, crossing and re-crossing fields on quite steep slopes. As the ploughing progressed, the landscape changed from a mosaic of green fields to one of brown, interspersed with small clumps of woodland and the black of the ubiquitous cypress trees. Oddly, there were no vineyards to be seen along that hillside. It was a memorable scene, and if a PoW camp had to be built, it could not have been located in a more pleasing environment.

Chapter 3

Borgo San Lorenzo Working Party

I spent much time gazing at the work being carried out on the hills, but whilst appreciating the scene my mind was firmly fixed on how I could get out there myself. Groups of prisoners were being sent from Laterina camp to work camps in the region. The Italians did not specify which prisoners should go to any particular camp. The system was that a sheet of paper was sent into the camp setting out the type of work and the number of men required for any particular posting. This was circulated around the camp, and men wishing to go added their names to the list.

Up to this point I had not signed up for any work camp, but the days were now pleasantly sunny and it was time to go. I had no interest in working for the Italians, but I felt sure that there would be more opportunity to escape from a work party, and the earlier I was at a work camp the sooner I would have a chance. I had made some close friends in Laterina and I would miss them unless some happened to come to the same camp. So the next time a list came round asking for volunteers, I added my name. A few days later it was confirmed that I was to join a work party.

So in early July 1943 I was among a party of about forty prisoners who arrived at Borgo San Lorenzo, a small town in the hills just north of Florence. The work camp was situated on what had been the town football ground. The large house at the roadside became the guards' quarters, with the prisoners' compound at the rear. The whole property was surrounded by a high brick wall, and the barbed wire of the compound followed the touchline of the football pitch. Surprisingly, at the far end of the pitch the wire did not turn to lie along the goal line but carried on to meet the boundary wall at two separate points, thus leaving about 10yds of wall as the compound boundary.

The purpose of the work camp was to complete the early stages of constructing a sugar beet factory. This brought me into close contact with Italian workers and occasionally even with farm families, so I had excellent opportunities to practise speaking Italian. My main job was on the construction of the boundary wall. It was built with trimmed white stone and was quite an interesting job. Part of the wall lay alongside the road, and I found that passers-by were only too interested to stop and chat with anybody who was able to get by in Italian.

Food rations at a work camp were twice those of the PoW camp, and we also received occasional Red Cross food parcels. So my health benefited, my morale blossomed and I prepared myself for the escape I had so long cherished. I had been hoarding suitable food, mainly chocolate and raisins. On that point, I remembered Cadbury's pre-war slogan that there was two hours' marching in a 2oz bar of their Dairy Milk Chocolate.

After I had been in the camp for about a month, the official Italian interpreter, Signor Papini, a hard man and a member of the Fascist Militia, was called away because of some family crisis. This led to my being given the job of interpreter. From that moment on, my smattering of Italian began to bloom.

I needed a companion for the escape, since I did not want to go out of camp and find myself entirely alone in the world. So I weighed up a few chaps who had spoken of escape. After some thought, I chose a chap from the Coldstream Guards who seemed to be genuinely interested in an attempt. He was a big fellow who I felt could be an asset at difficult moments. When I put the suggestion to him, he agreed immediately.

*

One occasion which was particularly pleasant and boosted my Italian was when I had the chance to join in with a local farming tradition. I had left my normal position on the boundary wall and was working on the other side of the site. There was a hedge behind my back and beyond the hedge was a farmyard. On that particular day the farmer was threshing his wheat in the farmyard. The local farmers were all peasants without a great deal of land or money and none of them owned equipment such as a thresher. So they took turns to rent the appliance, with four or five other farmers and their wives coming to help for the day. They all worked very hard, but it was both a happy day and a cheerful social occasion for them.

At lunchtime a line of tables was set up in the yard alongside the thresher, and the farmer's wife served up a scrumptious alfresco lunch. There was lots of Tuscan bread with a selection of salamis, followed by huge bowls of pasta and an assortment of chicken, rabbit and pigeon and lots of wine from the farmer's vineyard. It was all followed by sweet desserts and home-made *pecorino* ('little sheep'), a sheep's milk cheese which is a wonderful Tuscan speciality.

It was a perfect summer's day and everyone was in great form. The men were all talking at the top of their voices and guffawing away, while the wives sat more sedately at the table chatting among themselves. Their appetites proved to be gargantuan, and dish after dish was soon emptied. I had been watching them through a gap in the hedge, and when somebody spotted me, they called me into the yard and a place was made for me at the table. They wanted to know all about me, and when they learned I spoke Italian, I was home and dry. It was the best meal I had had in years. None of the guards bothered me. I had forged good relations with them through trying to learn Italian. I think they may have seen me and just left me to get on with it. The next day the farmyard was deserted and the happy little interlude was over. It had been a very enjoyable experience.

*

The property alongside the camp was a very large house with spacious grounds. The family had four daughters, three teenagers, Pina, Enrica and Maria, and one a little older, Fiorella. On their side of the wall some sort of platform had been built on to which the girls could climb and talk to us over the wall. Each day soon after we arrived back from work the girls appeared at the wall and we would chat and joke together. Both sides enjoyed the break, and soon the girls began to bring little goodies with them. Pina soon became not only a good friend but, without realizing it, also helped me greatly with my Italian. She was a pretty girl, and our friendship grew, even though it was hampered by the gap between the wire and the wall.

Between the barbed wire and the wall there was a corridor about 30ft wide. One of the two sentries on duty patrolled that section of the wire. When the girls began to bring little presents of food to pass to us, the collusion of the sentry was needed. The things were dropped down to him so that he could pass them to us through the wire. Not many of our fellows spoke Italian, and as I was streets ahead of them, almost all of Pina's presents came to me. I got splendid things such as a loaf, a couple of eggs, a flask of wine, fruit and various other goodies. I gave some of these to my escape partner but kept most for myself. I wanted to get myself as fit as possible and had no doubt that these little extras were helping me.

*

There was an incident about this time which was quite memorable; I am surprised I have never heard mention of it in reports of wartime events. It concerned an Italian radio broadcast and it brought all business to a sudden halt in Borgo San Lorenzo. If it had been on the national network and not just on a Tuscan regional station, I imagine it would have caused chaos all over Italy.

Every day the station broadcast a news bulletin at midday. There was always a gap of some minutes between the previous programme ending and the news bulletin starting. During that gap there was always silence. One particular day we were settling down to lunch on the work site when we realized there was much noise and excitement about. Moments later, the reason reached the ears of our guards. They immediately became deliriously happy and were dancing about, shouting, '*La guerra è finita, la guerra è finita*', meaning, of course, 'The war is over'.

Within moments, everybody was running about excitedly in the road, and the guards were embracing us like old friends. Guards were throwing their rifles in the air in their excitement. One came down to earth bayonet first and the bayonet snapped in two. The guards then invited prisoners to accompany them to a bar in town to celebrate. Quite a few of our party joined them, although, along with others, I decided that I would stay behind. It was more than I could take in to think that this was going to be the start of the freedom we had prayed for so fervently. It was even more astounding because it came so suddenly.

We learned that the source of the excitement had been a message given over the radio: an unknown station had come on air during the short interval of silence with a special announcement, to the effect that Mussolini had surrendered to the Allied forces and everyone should stand by for further news. Of course there was no further news. In any case, everybody was out in the street, excitedly celebrating. There was no way of knowing who had instigated the false announcement, but we suspected it was a clever propaganda ploy on the part of the BBC in London. Whoever did it, it caused a great amount of confusion and unrest amongst the people of Borgo San Lorenzo.

The Italian authorities needed only relatively few moments to organize themselves and come on air to denounce the announcement as a trick of enemy propaganda. The government of Mussolini, they claimed, was firm in its will to fight and the people should remember the dictum of *Il Duce*, stencilled in black paint on the walls of buildings in every town and village in Italy: '*Credere, Obbedire, Combattere*' ('Believe, Obey, Fight'). Of course, the official refutal of the announcement, even though made quickly, came too late, as the excited townspeople were already in the streets celebrating, while police and soldiers were making every effort to restore order and get the guards and prisoners back to the work site. In the latter task they were partly successful, but a considerable number of fellows managed to remain undiscovered in various bars. When they were eventually traced they were all in an advanced state of drunkenness, being quite unused to wine.

An elderly Italian gentleman was brought in to the work site to address us dressed in an immaculate white suit and a white Panama hat. He spoke good English with an engaging Italian accent. His message was that our unruly actions were totally unacceptable and that any similar riotous behaviour would be severely punished. He threatened that the punishment would be a return to the concentration camp at Laterina. He played on the similarity of the name Laterina and the English word latrine: 'You wouldn't like to be sent back and locked in the latrine, would you?' He was an avuncular sort of person and spoke in the manner of a father gently admonishing his children. It was so different from the usual manner of address we received that we warmed to him and chatted to him for a while.

Eventually, our group at the work site was formed up and marched back to the compound. When we entered the compound we found there had been as much celebration there as at the work site. This was evident when we got to the far end of the compound and saw that a hail of potatoes was being tossed over the camp wall from the far side and eagerly gathered up by men in the camp. It turned out that no action had been taken against a few chaps who had scaled the boundary wall and found a potato crop nearby on the other side of the wall. The spot inside the camp at which the potatoes were being picked up was the camp brewing-up area. As we arrived we found that small fires were already being fanned to boil potatoes for a welcome and unexpected meal.

I was sure that the two sentries on duty during the potato stealing incident cannot have reported the matter to their superiors. If they had done so it would have been apparent at once how simple it was to scale the wall, and steps would have been taken to re-align the barbed wire along the goal line of the football pitch. That would have scuppered our plans for escape.

*

The thought of those chaps going over the wall during a period of collapsed discipline set my mind to work. Could my colleague and I not use the same tactics that evening for a dummy run of our plan? We thought it over and decided to give it a try when all was quiet. We had already agreed on a routine for the escape itself and we decided to put that into effect for the dummy run. The strike point was to be at the spot where the barbed wire ran at right angles into the boundary wall, as shown in Sketch 1. The barbed wire was about 9ft high and the wall about 10ft. The wire consisted of horizontal strands about 8ins apart and the verticals were also 8ins apart. The horizontals virtually operated as a ladder, so the top of the wall could be reached in seconds.

There were always two sentries on duty, and their beats are shown in Sketch. To distract them both while the breakout took place, a number of fellows in the camp were to carry out diversions. A new hut had been built in anticipation of an extra group of prisoners not yet arrived. This hut obstructed one of the sentries' view of the escape point from the spot where we chatted with the girls. A group of fellows would arrange a brawl at that point; the sentries could never resist a ringside view of the occasional fight. Meanwhile, the other sentry controlled his side of the camp and also the entrance gate which was just around the corner from his beat. A group of fellows were to assemble at the gate and loudly raise some cooked-up complaint to entice him down to see what the fuss was all about. We spread news to everybody of our proposed dummy run that evening.

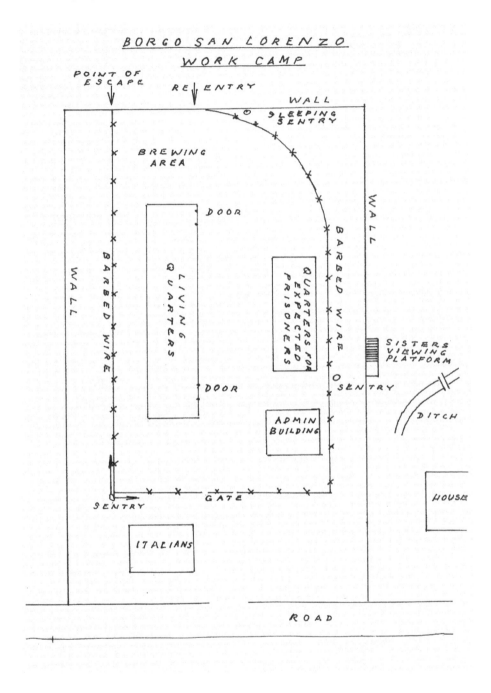

When my colleague and I decided to test the escape possibilities, I had Pina in mind, thinking that I could leave a little surprise packet for her over the wall. I decided to take a bar of chocolate from my escape rations and a bar of Red Cross parcel toilet soap to leave for her.

That evening, soon after dark, after we got the word that both diversions were in operation, we went into action. I went first. It was simple mounting the wire, sitting on the coping stone for a moment, swinging my legs over, then dropping down to the ground. My colleague followed moments later. It was surprising to find that we were standing, backs to the wall, in deep shadow. I was used to the lights beaming down on the inside of the camp wall but had never followed through with the thought that the outside would be in shadow. The series of high standards supporting the security lights were placed outside the wall but the horizontal section at the top of each standard cantilevered the lamp to a point inside the camp. This was fortunate, since the shadow in which we had landed gave us a breathing space to collect our thoughts and get over the excitement of being outside.

Weighing up our situation, we found there was a large area of orchard in front of us offering a quick method of getting away from the immediate area of the camp. That was useful to know but did not serve our purpose now as we were aiming for the neighbouring property, a big house alongside the camp. When we got to the corner of the camp wall we saw that the rear of the house was just an undeveloped grassy area with a narrow ditch running across it. A long flagstone lay across the ditch, acting as a footbridge. We also saw that steps led up to the viewing platform from which the girls were able to see over the wall and talk to us.

Our arrival at the house proved to be a disappointment. Although lights were on in the ground floor rooms, each window had a blind drawn which completely obscured our view. Worse was to come, since when we approached the house we heard sounds of laughter and loud chatter. To our dismay, when we listened outside the windows, we were able to distinguish the voices of some of the sentries. That put an immediate end to my hopes of meeting Pina. The best I could do then was to go back to the flagstone across the ditch. There I scribbled on a scrap of paper 'For Pina' and put it on the stone with the chocolate and soap.

We wanted to try the road but now we knew that sentries could be going back and forth between the gates of our camp and the big house, so we had to be careful. Across the road from the house was a track we used to use every morning on our way to work. We decided to take it. The track ran alongside a field of maize, and every day we used to grab a couple of cobs as we passed. Now we were without any escort we could enjoy it at our leisure, so we pushed in away from the edge of the crop and ate our fill. The young cobs were soft, sweet and really good to eat.

The track took us as far as the bank of a river. Every morning as we walked to work we turned right at that point and walked along the river bank, skirting the edge of the town until we reached the site of our sugar beet factory. Although it was quite dark on this evening and we could see no sign of people about, we decided not to follow the river but to return to the road. This time we thought we would try a stroll on the road. Cars were not a great danger as the blackout masks on their headlights dimmed them so much we would have plenty of time to take cover.

After a short distance on the road we thought that was enough and it was time to get back. We re-entered the grounds of the big house and quietly crept towards the camp wall. At this point I began to have qualms about getting back into the camp. Climbing the wire to get out had been an easy matter, but I had not paid any attention to the nature of the wall. If it was smooth and unclimbable we were sunk and would suffer the indignity of having to go to the guards' quarters to surrender. It was with trepidation that I approached the wall. To my intense relief, I saw that the mortar between every course of bricks had weathered and decayed for nearly an inch in between the bricks. There were finger and boot holds for its entire height.

We approached our climbing point very quietly. Scaling the wall was easy, and we reached the top and rested our forearms on the coping. We looked along the length of the barbed wire but could not see the sentry. Then we spotted that he was almost beneath us, a few yards to our left, fortunately some yards beyond the point at which the barbed wire met the wall. He was leaning with his back against the wall, obviously fast asleep, with his head drooping and his rifle resting against his stomach.

Opposite us, about 15yds away, was the gable end of our hut, with the door around the left-hand corner. On the door was a long metal bar which swivelled upwards like the handle on the doors of many theatres and cinemas. So we had to get to the door and make a right angle turn to enter. Whispering, we agreed that we would both jump on a mouthed 'one, two, three, go' system. We hit the ground together, running as we touched down. We reached the corner of the hut at full speed and, turning at the door, hit the bar so hard it struck the door with a loud crack like a rifle shot.

The noise wakened everybody in the hut, and we were undressing as we ran to our bunks. In seconds our boots were off, pyjamas were on and we were under the blankets. It was not long before the guards came rushing in, not quite knowing what they were looking for. They could not find anything amiss and eventually left us. We had found that it had been much harder to break back in than to break out. Our spell outside must have lasted around an hour.

The following morning, roll call took place as usual and no mention was made of the events of the night. Nobody was missing, and the Italians would never have even imagined that anyone would break out only to return later. In retrospect, it was an outrageously foolish act. I would have ruined my chances of escape if anything had gone wrong, for I would have been sent back to Laterina, with no chance of another work camp.

The next day I came in for a shock. My colleague told me that, on reflection, he did not think it a good idea to go and he was backing out. This was disappointing news. However, I consoled myself, it was better to have learned of his weakness before we set off on the real thing. It meant that although one good thing had come out of our dummy run, I was back where I started, looking for a partner.

*

Then an extraordinary situation arose. A sentry whom we called Bob, presumably Roberto, from Sicily, had been very co-operative in passing things from Pina to me and had become friendly towards me. One day he motioned me to move along the wire away from the group of chaps talking with the girls.

To my surprise, he asked me, 'Do you ever think of escaping?'

I replied, 'Why do you ask such a question?'

It emerged that he wanted to desert and join his family in Sicily, now in Allied hands. He was proposing that I should join him and he assured me that he could arrange my escape from the camp. He was confident he could move safely south through Italy, but he was frightened of getting through the Allied lines and wanted an Englishman with him at that time. It was a startling offer, and I told him I would think it over.

My first thought was that it was not a good recommendation for a man to have become a prison camp guard. At the same time, Bob seemed smarter and more intelligent than the other guards. One thing which seemed encouraging was that he claimed he wanted me to be with him at the very end of the project. This suggested he would be thinking of my welfare while we were travelling through Italy. I gave the matter a lot of thought, but in the end decided Bob's offer was much too risky to consider.

So I was left with the task of finding a new partner for my own venture. The most promising seemed to be a fellow named Danny, from the Hampshire Regiment. Unlike the guardsman, he was not tall but broad and stocky. Moreover, he already had a stock of suitable foods and we could soon boost it by bartering Red Cross parcel cigarettes. A number of other people were keen to join the project, but I thought two was the optimum number.

Soon afterwards we chose the date. We arranged for the same cover as on the dummy run break-out, and the timing would be similar, in mid-evening. Again the weather was fine. The exercise seemed more serious this time. The first effort had been carried out in the aftermath of the confusion following the false radio announcement. This time it was deadly serious. We also had to carry our haversacks, filled with rations, over the wall with us.

The atmosphere was a carbon copy of the previous time. The brewing area was right alongside our strike point, and now the same men were brewing a late cup of tea before retiring, just as they had been last time. The signal for the diversions had been given as before, and we heard the rumblings of noise becoming louder.

To many people it was just a normal evening in camp, although some were watching anxiously for our departure. Danny and I were standing with bated breath while we listened to the diversions. There were only two sentries, and they were both totally distracted from guard duties by the efforts of our fellow prisoners. So we knew we were safe on that point. We waited for confirmation and, on the order 'Go Go Go!' we grabbed our haversacks loaded with Red Cross goodies: chocolate, raisins, biscuits, all stuffed with extra vitamins and calcium, tins of bacon, salmon and cheese.

A last look back and then I shinned up the wire on to the coping on top of the wall. A quick look down and I leapt to the ground, knowing this time that I would be hidden in shadow. I pressed myself hard against the wall and moments later, looking up, saw Danny's legs swinging over the wall before he thudded down beside me. Breathlessly, we shook hands. My heart was pounding frantically. The realization that we were now outside and the plan was finally in operation made it the most exciting moment I had ever experienced.

Although we found ourselves in shadow, the ground in front of us was bathed in light from the high lamps surrounding the camp. It was no time to dawdle, and soon we were scurrying, half-crouched, through the orchard which lay behind the camp. We set out to put as much ground as possible between ourselves and the camp before we were missed at morning roll call. The euphoria of freedom was still with us and we found nothing more alarming as we strode along than the furious barking of dogs any time we came within the vicinity of a house or a farm. It brought home to us that we had no friends and emphasized how much on our own we were.

The perils of freedom became apparent when, from somewhere in the darkness ahead of us, the challenge '*Alt*' rang out. It was pitch dark, and we could see nothing ahead. The person calling must have heard our footsteps rather than seen us, but as the call rang out, we both flung ourselves into the roadside ditch. One voice had called, but we did not know how many there were in all. We slithered back along the ditch for some way as fast as we could and, when all seemed quiet, crawled up the bank alongside us into a field. In case a sentry was still on the prowl we decided to crawl across the field on our bellies. What we did not realize was that this field had been neglected for some time and, in the Italian fashion, the farmer re-cultivating it had burned all the growth. So we found ourselves pushing our faces through charred, sooty scrub.

After a few more fields we arrived at another road, which seemed deserted, with no sign of houses. It was edged by a rickety barbed wire fence, which we negotiated and got on to the road. We intended turning left but at that moment we heard the sound of a car engine approaching from our right. There was a bend in that direction and we could see nothing. We hopped smartly across the road and were once again confronted by the rickety wire fence. I found the top wire, felt lower down for the bottom one, stretched them apart and threw myself into the gap between. Unfortunately, there was a middle strand of barbed wire and, with the car approaching, I found my forehead impaled on one of the barbs. It was painful and bled a fair amount, but I dropped to the ground and let the car pass. The headlamps were blacked out except for a minute T-shape cut in a mask covering the headlamps. The light was so feeble the driver would hardly have seen the road, let alone us.

Roads seemed rather unlucky, so we decided to keep to the fields for a while. When we saw the first light of dawn we decided to find a safe place to lie up and happily came to a promontory of rock towering about thirty feet above us, with a small stream at its base. There was a fair covering of bushes near the rock, and the grassy ground across the stream sloped gently up for some way towards an area of woodland. It seemed ideal cover, and at once we relaxed. After drinking copiously from the stream we lay down on the grass, revelling in the sheer bliss of not being surrounded by barbed wire. Deep, dreamless sleep came immediately. One thing lurking in my mind, not exactly a black cloud on the horizon, but an assessment of our predicament, was the thought that we had set off from the camp without any idea whatsoever of the pitfalls we were likely to encounter.

*

When I woke, the sun was already up. I was in the shadow of the rock, and the stream was tinkling beside me. But any thought of our idyllic situation was shattered when I realized a man's voice was calling. It was probably this which had wakened me. I craned my neck a little and saw that he was standing at the edge of the rock above me and calling to a girl, who I then saw was down on our level but a little way off. She could not possibly have seen us, but I felt the man could not fail to spot something if he just dropped his gaze to where we and our haversacks were spread below his feet. However, fortune was with us, and soon he turned and disappeared.

I wakened Danny and, when we saw each other, we both burst out laughing. The previous night's crawl through the charred scrub had put a thick coating of soot on our faces and we were hardly recognizable. I had suffered worse, because the blood from my tangle with the barbed wire had run down and mingled with the soot. Of all the possessions I treasured and guarded at this time, the most prized was an oval, bevelled glass mirror with an ebony back and handle which I had taken from my mother's dressing table when I was mobilized at the outbreak of war. Never had it reflected a more bizarre sight than when I saw my face in it now.

The morning was warm, and we just stripped and lay in the stream and washed off all trace of the night's events. Even though there had been lots of opportunities to lie in the sun back at the camp, relaxing now in the lush grass in the warm sunshine seemed like a forgotten luxury. We ate sparingly of our rations and kept our water bottles filled with the fresh stream water. Hunger seemed to be the last thing to worry about, and we just wallowed in the contentment of being free.

Some months previously, an Italian tailor had been drafted in to Laterina camp. His task had been to cut two holes in the material of everybody's battledress, one on the left thigh and one on the right shoulder. Then over each hole he sewed a patch of red flannel about 5ins square. I regarded these as a positive stigma. Whatever had been the Italians' purpose in having them done, being bent on escape, I did not want such identification on me. So when I had inched along in the queue towards the tailor's table I had in my hand a good supply of Red Cross parcel cigarettes. Arriving at the table I put them down and said quietly, '*Non tagliare*' ('Don't cut'). Accustomed as he was to the abominable wartime Italian cigarettes, *Nazionale* or *Esportazione*, he acted like lightning. In moments I was carrying away my uncut battledress sporting two red flannel patches, while the tailor was unashamedly puffing away at a Rothman's 555.

Now that I was out of camp, it occurred to me that this was the moment to cut the flannel patches from my battledress and remove this stigma of prison camp life. Danny did not have that option as he would be left with two gaping holes in his battledress. When he saw what I was about to do he became embarrassed and began to cough and clear his throat. It was plain there was something wrong. He suggested that maybe I should not cut off the patches.

The atmosphere worsened as he said, 'We may have been very foolish in what we've done. Our parents at home think we're safe behind barbed wire for the duration of the war and instead we're wandering about and could be shot on sight.'

It became clear that Danny was now very frightened. He had lost his bottle and wanted out. Eventually, he announced that he was going to surrender. I saw no point in trying to change his mind. His nerve had gone and there was no way he could recover it. We had seen that there was a farmhouse not far away and that was where he would give himself up. He said he would leave his haversack with me. Although I was disgusted with him, in the circumstances the suggestion made sense, and the extra weight would not be too much for me.

There was just one thing I wanted from him. I asked, 'When I move off tonight will you lie low and keep your head down for twenty-four hours before giving yourself up?'

This would give me some chance of getting a reasonable distance from the spot before the hue and cry was raised. He agreed to do this and just kept one day's food with him. I learned later that when I left at nightfall he went off hotfoot to the farm almost before I was out of sight.

It had been a stroke of fortune that the first companion I had chosen decided to pull out before we committed ourselves. It was now a bitter pill to swallow that, in spite of the lesson I had learned on the dummy run, I had chosen a fellow of the same mould for the real escape. So now I found myself in the one scenario I had wanted to avoid. I was left entirely on my own and faced the daunting prospect of having no companion and not a soul in the world I could talk to.

*

The greatest difficulty was having to travel by night in this type of country. Daytime was far too dangerous as there was always someone not too far away. I was now among high hills, and none of the tracks I wanted to travel on seemed to take me over a summit. I spent some frustrating nights not making much progress. The days I found quite pleasant, even relaxing. It was early autumn and the weather was quite perfect, with sunny days which were not too hot, and a gentle breeze. There was no shortage of food in the fields, and I did not have to fall back too much on the rations I was carrying. Streams abounded in the hills and the water was beautifully cold and clear, so thirst was not a problem.

Tomatoes were plentiful, and on one occasion I was sitting in a large plot of tomato plants tucking in when an elderly peasant woman passed by. I was a little way from the track and my concentration must have lapsed. I gave a wave of my hand and a quiet '*Buon giorno*', hoping she would not cause trouble. She just gave an equally quiet '*Buon giorno*' and continued her very slow walk. There were also some crops of maize and again the cobs were small, sweet and lovely to eat. There were occasional fruit trees, and the fruit was just about ripe enough to eat.

Because the weather was good and without any prospect of rain, when I chose a place to lie up I did not bother trying to find a roof. I just found a safe place where I would not be seen. One morning I made a mistake in choosing a not very large clump of bushes, isolated some way down a sharply sloping hill, with a farm further down the slope. When I woke I realized I could not move for the rest of the day because the bushes were in full view of the farm. The family were moving in and out through the day, and there were a couple of dogs about. That day I ate some of my Red Cross food and, as my water bottle was full, I had no problem apart from feeling rather hemmed in.

The day holds one pleasant memory. My hillside was in a large deep valley. The far side sloped as sharply as it did on my side. At one point in the day I heard voices. I was worried about where they were coming from, but I realized they were distant and eventually I identified them. Across the valley, at a higher level than me, I made out a road sloping gently down and, quite a way along the road, were two children. I first spotted the brightly coloured dress of a little girl.

They were playing and dancing as they came along the road. The main voice was that of the girl singing. They were some hundreds of yards away, but her voice carried across the valley as clear as a bell. Her companion looked like a little boy. I watched and listened to the singing, quite spellbound. In the clear air of an Apennine valley on an early autumn day they were magic moments, and all my worries left me for that spell.

On another day, a Sunday, I had a fright which made me reconsider how I was trying to move about the countryside. I had decided to spend the day in a narrow gully in which a small brook was flowing alongside the grass. A short distance below me the gully reached a track going downhill at right angles. My cover seemed perfect and I was totally relaxed. During the day I decided to bathe in the brook and I stripped off and began to wash myself down. In the midst of doing this my gaze wandered down the gully. To my dismay, half a dozen young boys and girls were standing on the track, about 50yds below me. They seemed horrified and dumbstruck at seeing this figure, stark naked, standing in the stream. My reaction was instantaneous: I grabbed my clothes and haversacks as fast as I could and went galloping up the hill. This also broke the spell for the Italians, and I saw them scurrying down the track.

I knew that I must leave the small tracks and find a road along which I could make better progress. So I decided to change tactics and spent the afternoon heading downhill. After some time I was pleased to see that I was looking down on a road which was running through a narrow valley. At the foot of the hill there was first a railway track alongside the road and beyond that a river. Just beyond the river the hill on the far side of the valley began to climb and, curving up to the left, disappeared from view. I saw houses dotted alongside the road and it looked like the start of a small town. I decided to try to skirt the town, keeping at the same height above the road. For a time there were tracks which let me manage this. Then all tracks seemed to be taking me down into the valley. This brought me nearer the houses. The road was scarcely 50yds beyond the railway, and all the houses lay on the nearside of the road in a narrow strip of land. I could see no sign of any side streets. I knew that I would soon be at the road level and wondered what my next move should be.

Evening was coming on and the light was beginning to fade. I finally found myself on flat ground with the hedge bordering the railway immediately in front of me. I decided to sit under the hedge and wait for nightfall. Up to this point I had been thinking of tackling the town by going along the road. However, with the rail tracks just a few feet away, I decided to walk along the track to avoid any contact with villagers. So I sat and relaxed.

I had been rationing myself with cigarettes but now I felt good and decided to have one and then make my move. Five minutes later I was puffing away, totally relaxed, when I heard footsteps. I quickly stubbed out my cigarette and sat sphinx-like under the hedge. The footsteps were on the sleepers of the track and were now very near. It was too late to move in case I made a noise, so I sat still.

It proved to be two Italian soldiers, rifles slung over their shoulders. They passed just a yard or two from me, quite unaware of my presence. As they faded into the darkness, I knew my plan was scuppered. I could no longer use the railway track because the Italian soldiers were quite likely to settle down for a break and a smoke, just as I had. It seemed cruel luck that I had lost the railway, but I consoled myself with thinking that if the soldiers had been twenty minutes earlier they would have been on the track ahead of me without my knowing. If they had stopped for a smoke, I would have wandered right into them.

With the Italian soldiers ahead, my thoughts turned to the road. Immediately across the track in front of me an unlit path led away from the railway. I took the path, and after a short distance another path shot off to the left which I guessed would take me towards the road. This path was also narrow and unlit, with a high wall on each side. I came to a bend, only to hesitate in horror after two or three steps. I had barged into the large forecourt of the local bar-restaurant, and it was filled with locals at tables, enjoying their Sunday evening aperitif. A number must have seen me at once, but I could not see much interest in their glances. It was no use turning to run because I was still fairly heavily laden with rations and I was sure a number of them would have been after me like a shot. In any case, I had nowhere to run to. This all went through my mind in a flash. So almost without hesitation I carried on, making my way through the tables to the point on the far side which was obviously the main approach to the bar.

Although many lights were dimmed to comply with the blackout, there was a fair amount of illumination on the forecourt. My heart was in my mouth as I walked. But drinking and animated chatter continued as I wound my way between the tables. A number of waiters were weaving about among the tables, carrying trays of aperitifs. When my path was about to converge with a waiter the chap would hold back, tray held high, for me to pass. I could not believe it was happening and expected to be jumped on at any moment. Soon I was approaching the wide exit from the forecourt. My nerves were jangling wildly, but I had safely passed the last table.

When I reached the exit I found a road in front of me which sloped down for about 100yds and then seemed to run obliquely into the main road. There were no buildings along the left side of this road, but the right hand side had a pavement and a line of terraced houses. I was so relieved at getting through the restaurant forecourt that I gave no thought as to how best to approach the road. When I found myself at the pavement, I just started walking along the row of terraced houses.

At the very moment I was passing a house, the front door opened and a young boy of eleven or twelve appeared. For a moment I was bathed in light and I heard him gasp. Then the door slammed shut. This was terrible luck, and I knew that most likely I was in deep trouble. I was dressed in battledress, carrying two army haversacks and maybe looking a little scruffy, although I had smartened myself as best I could that afternoon. I thought that, after my having been spotted bathing earlier, there would probably be an alert for me in the neighbourhood. I feared that the young boy had rumbled me and now I really felt hunted. I knew I could not hurry back through the restaurant forecourt and I was apprehensive about the main road ahead.

There was no alternative but to carry on and hope that my fears were unwarranted. After a few moments I was reaching the end of this short road when my young spotter boy, together with a few friends, ran alongside me. Not saying a word, they just galloped around me for a while, buzzing me like fighter planes around a bomber. Then they sped rapidly out of sight ahead. I arrived at the main road, still worried about the boys.

My luck now went rapidly from bad to worse. Almost all the local young people were engaged in the ritual *passeggiata*, the evening stroll. Dressed in their Sunday best, they were ambling along in small groups walking in both directions, but mostly towards me, chatting and laughing, sometimes with *Mamma* acting as chaperone to the younger girls. It was a beautiful warm evening and there was a happy tone to the hubbub of chatter. I felt desperately lonely and had a sense of being in deep trouble.

My choice was between isolation on the left side of the road or mingling with the pack on the pavement. Choosing the pavement side, I crossed and joined the crowd, taking a line near the kerb, alongside the ornamental trees. Everybody seemed so intent on their own little group that no heed seemed to be paid to me at all. Despite this I was becoming ever more nervous and finding it difficult to breathe. The constant bumping into shoulders or stepping aside and the repeated mumbling of '*Scusi*' in the lowest of undertones became too much. So I stepped into the roadway and took a line fairly near the kerb, walking in as nonchalant a manner as I could. I still seemed to draw no attention from the people taking part in the *passeggiata*. I began to hope that I could make it. I was more relaxed and breathing slightly easier.

I still could see no end to the road, but there was no alternative but to keep walking. Then I realized that I could hear another pair of footsteps on the road behind me. I carried on without looking round, but soon the footsteps were right on my heels. Out of the blue the person behind me spoke.

'*Dove vai?*' ('Where are you going?')

My mind was racing and there did not seem any sensible answer to such a question but, without hesitation, I replied, '*Casa*' ('Home').

I kept my voice as calm as I could, but my tone probably sounded more wistful than cool.

The reply from the voice came straightaway: '*Brave parole*' ('Brave words').

As this short exchange ended, four or five *Carabinieri*, the military-style police, leapt out from a building on the left side of the road and thrust rifles into my midriff. I could not see my questioner but I knew this was the end of my Odyssey. I was thankful that the drama had been played out in the roadway, where I was alone, and not on the crowded pavement amongst all the young people. Clearly, the group of boys who had disappeared ahead of me had hurried to the police station to report their sighting and then the *Carabinieri* just waited for me. My shadow had attached himself as I approached the station.

*

This incident awoke the nearby *passeggiata* groups to the events, and a great crowd was immediately jostling around me. The *Carabinieri* frog-marched me into their station. Once inside, the atmosphere became relaxed, and nobody pressurized me at all. Now I knew it was all over, I slumped on a bench, totally exhausted. Very little questioning followed. I told them who I was, and my particulars were entered in the detention book. There were no other formalities. Although being retaken was the thing I had wanted to avoid beyond all else, there was now some sense of relief in being able to talk to somebody.

The *Brigadiere*, the chap in charge, told me that I would have to spend the night in a cell but that in the meantime I could stay in their room with them. This seemed better than immediate occupation of a cell, so I accepted. The resident housekeeper was called in and prepared me a meal, which proved to be most appetizing. However, I was completely exhausted and demoralized. Hardly able to eat, I just sat flopped on the bench.

The ceiling of the room was extremely high and the only window was in the wall opposite me at a height normally on the first floor level. After a while I heard giggling and looked up at the window. It seemed there must have been a catwalk outside at that level, because two or three young girls were kneeling down to peer through the open window. When they caught my eye they began to chant in English, in engaging Tuscan accents, 'I love you'. It was comforting to know the natives were friendly, and, in different circumstances I would have found it a very encouraging approach. Soon after that I fell asleep on the bench.

When I woke there were two *Carabinieri* in the duty room. I felt the second one was still there because of my presence. They told me I should go into the cell now, but when I asked if I could wash, they readily agreed. Before going to the cell I had to surrender my belt, bootlaces and haversacks, standard practice in case a prisoner wished to do himself harm. Then I was escorted along a corridor to my cell. My bed was just an iron frame hinged to the wall which could be lowered to a horizontal position. There was a thin hard mattress with it. The only other item in the cell was a little pot for my convenience. My escort was friendly and almost apologetic.

When he left, the door slammed shut. It was the first time I had heard a cell door slam from the inside. I do not think I had ever felt so forlorn. On leaving the cell, my escort opened the little spy window in the door. A little shaft of light entered as he called out, '*Buonanotte*'. I replied, but I was left with a heavy sense of being all alone. I did not undress but lay on the bed and was soundly asleep in moments.

Soon after I woke I was taken from the cell to the duty room, where a breakfast was waiting for me. The *Carabinieri* were friendly and seemed to enjoy having me there. When I had finished breakfast I was given back my belt and bootlaces, collected my haversacks and was told it was time to go. A couple of *Carabinieri* escorted me out of the station and there, to my surprise, a police car was waiting, surrounded by a large number of people waiting to see me. As I was ushered into the car there was no animosity shown towards me by the crowd; they were just looking on with curiosity.

I was unsure about where I was being taken – to the work camp at Borgo San Lorenzo or to the concentration camp at Laterina – so I lay back and let come what may. Our destination proved to be Borgo San Lorenzo *Carabinieri* station. When my particulars had been entered, I was again relieved of my belt, bootlaces and haversacks and was ushered into a cell. To my surprise, there was Danny waiting for me. On reflection, I felt this showed the Italians had been confident of recapturing me, because they held Danny at Borgo San Lorenzo until my arrival.

At first I felt somewhat hostile towards Danny but then I realized that we were again in the same boat together. The hostility soon dissolved, and I told him of my adventures. Soon after we were brought a meal, and our comradeship was by then warm again. We stayed the night there. Fortunately, there was a bed hinged to the wall on both sides of the cell, so neither of us had to endure the discomfort of sleeping on the stone floor.

As darkness fell and we were lying on our beds idly chatting in the dark, an incident occurred which illustrates the nervous tension from which we were both suffering. Danny was telling a few jokes. He told one about an Italian couple, setting it as a baker and his wife in some little southern Italian village. The baker was proud of his prowess as a lover, but his wife had an even more voracious appetite. One night, after he had performed manfully seven or eight times and had declined his wife's urgings to carry on, she lay quiet for a while and then whispered, '*Antonio, chi è l'altra donna?*' ('Antonio, who is the other woman?').

This seemed a pretty dull joke, but even before the end he was helpless with laughter and had difficulty finishing the story. I am not sure whether it was the joke

itself or just Danny's contagious laughter that got to me, but I found myself joining in. Whichever it was, we just howled uncontrollably with laughter, each of us
rolling about on our bed in the pitch dark. It was not just a short fit of laughter, it
went on and on without end. The Italians eventually became concerned and came
along to shine a beam of light through the spy window in the door. This only made
the situation worse, and we were now almost choking with laughter.

The Italians could no longer contain themselves and entered the cell. When we
still did not stop they shook us until we sobered up. They asked what had got into
us, so I related Danny's joke in Italian. It meant absolutely nothing to them. When
I explained that to Danny, it set the pair of us off again. When we were finally quiet
they took a pragmatic Italian view of the situation and asked how long it had been
since we had had a woman. I told them I had been in the desert and prison camps
for two years, and they grimaced in sympathy.

'*Due anni! Perbacco!*' ('Gosh, two years!').

They left us, expressing deep sympathy. We were by now in a sober state and
ready to drift off to sleep. My lonely, incident-packed week had left my nerves as
tight as they could be without actually snapping, but that experience in the cell had
relaxed them and from that point I felt calm. I do not think the *Carabinieri* station
can have known a night like it before or since.

The next day I was told I was being taken back to the work camp to collect the
kit I had abandoned on escape. Then Danny and I were to be returned to the concentration camp at Laterina. I appreciated the offer to return to the work camp to
collect my kit and walked the mile or so to the camp with two *Carabinieri* escorts.
When the rest of the chaps saw me approaching the gate they raised a cheer, but I
felt crestfallen at being marched ignominiously back. I packed my belongings and
was officially removed from the camp roll. The officer signing me off was warm in
his farewells.

During the day on which we had escaped, the four sisters had been at the wall
and said that two of them, Pina and Enrica, the youngest, were going to the hills on
their bicycles that day. There was much hilarity from the girls and especially from
the sentry who was standing by me when I added, '*Anch'io*' ('Me too').

Now, a week or so later, I was back collecting my belongings. As I walked back to
town along with my escorts, the road was deserted until I saw Pina walking towards
us on her way from town. When we met she had a half smile on her lips but wagged
her finger at me, saying, '*Cattivo Franco*' ('Naughty Franco'). I think the Italians
may have suspected that she was party to my escape and they had probably given
her a good grilling.

I rejoined Danny in the town. Escorted by three *Carabinieri*, all armed with
pistols, we set off for the trip back to Laterina. We travelled by passenger train,
which seemed luxurious. When we boarded the train no Italians were allowed to

use the seats anywhere near us; the place was bristling with guns, and it made me feel very much a desperado.

Eventually we reached Laterina station, which was about nine miles walk from the camp. The first time I had arrived at the station, from Benghazi in August 1942 as part of a trainload of prisoners, it had been the middle of the night and raining heavily. This was when we had spent those hours standing in a wet field surrounded by sentries, waiting for daylight. Now, in August 1943, a year later, it was mid-afternoon, the sun was shining and it was pleasantly cool as Danny and I set off with our three *Carabinieri* for Laterina camp, loaded with our belongings like a couple of displaced persons.

Chapter 4

The Tunnel

On entering the camp at Laterina we were escorted to a small, newly erected compound near the main gate consisting of a barbed wire fence round a marquee tent. There were four or five fellows sitting in the marquee, and it proved to be the accommodation for returned escapees. When we were left alone, these chaps told us that the *Carabinieri* would arrive at dusk to shackle our legs for the night. This was a daunting thought, but we were told not to worry, just to put on as many pairs of socks as we had. Thanks to my mother's personal parcels I had a good supply, so I wore four pairs.

Sure enough, the *Carabinieri* arrived at dusk armed with lots of light shackles, rather like bicycle chains. Our ankles were bound together and a padlock applied. Mercifully, it was not done too tightly. As soon as the *Carabinieri* left I followed the example of the old hands and slid off my socks, whereupon the chains became loose enough for me to slide over my ankles. We then lay down to a sound sleep and woke early enough the following morning to slide the chains back on over one or two pairs of socks.

That morning, Danny and I were summoned before a court martial. The officer in charge had been the pre-war manager of an Italian bank in London who spoke excellent English and proved quite a reasonable, fatherly sort of fellow. We pleaded guilty to escaping and were duly sentenced to thirty days' detention, ten days rigorous and twenty days easy. It seemed ironic to be sentenced to detention when already in a prison camp. I suppose it was the nearest the Italians could get to solitary confinement.

The thirty-day sentence was to be spent in the escapee compound, the rigorous element being the shackling of our ankles for the first ten nights. On leaving the compound we would be housed in the designated escapee section of Hut 9. As returning escapees, we had to parade at the main gate for roll call every two hours throughout the day, and in Hut 9 the *Carabinieri* would visit us every two hours through the night for a head count. These two-hourly roll calls were to prove extremely inconvenient.

*

I was about to be introduced to a most exciting exploit – an escape tunnel. During the first day, three of the chaps in our little compound spoke to Danny and me separately. We were each asked if we would like another chance of escaping. Danny declined, but without hesitation I accepted. It seemed another swipe at the fact of having been taken prisoner. It was then explained to me that an escape tunnel was under construction in the camp. The organization was very strict, and membership of the escape party was restricted to twenty-five. If a member lost heart and dropped out for any reason, the vacancy was offered to the next returning escapee. There was a vacancy and, after a little consultation between the three, it was agreed that I passed muster and should join the party.

The three fellows who spoke with me were two South Africans and a Rhodesian, the leaders of the tunnel party, who had been held in a PoW camp in southern Italy at the time of the first Allied landings in the south. The whole complement of the camp had been transferred north, and during the journey they had managed to break free but had been recaptured almost at once. This classified them as returned escapees, and they had thus been put into the escapee compound at Laterina.

The design and construction of the tunnel had originally been planned by two New Zealanders who were miners, but they did not join the party. At the time of my joining, work had been in progress for three weeks. I do not remember the names of any of the other members of the party, except for a Liverpool chap called Peter. The basic plan was to dig from the end of one of the huts to several yards beyond the perimeter wire of the camp to a point at which a safe exit could be made.

Apart from some amenity buildings, the camp comprised twelve huts, parallel to each other and end-on to the perimeter wire of the camp, as illustrated in Sketch 2. Huts 1 to 11 were living quarters, and Hut 12 contained a storeroom, barber's shop and various facilities. Hut 13 was under construction. The choice of which hut was most suitable for the starting point of the tunnel had exercised much thought.

Parallel to the ends of the huts and about halfway to the trip wire a storm trench had been dug to run off excess rainwater. At the higher end of the ground, the Hut 12 end, the trench was a few inches deep, whereas at the lower end it was much deeper. It was calculated that opposite Hut 6 the trench was sufficiently shallow for the tunnel to pass safely beneath it. The storm trench drained into the River Arno, which flowed past just outside the barbed wire near Hut 1. A major hazard to the tunnel was the line of field latrines. It was essential that a route between two of those should be found. Hut 6 also satisfied that requirement, so that was the chosen route.

Every hut had an ablutions and toilet section situated at one end near the barbed wire. The projected toilet facilities inside the huts comprised a line of five Asian-type toilets, just a hole in the floor, built along the inside wall of the gable end of each hut. Beneath the toilets was a concrete-lined cistern about a yard wide and more than a yard deep. At one side of the hut it stretched a little beyond the width

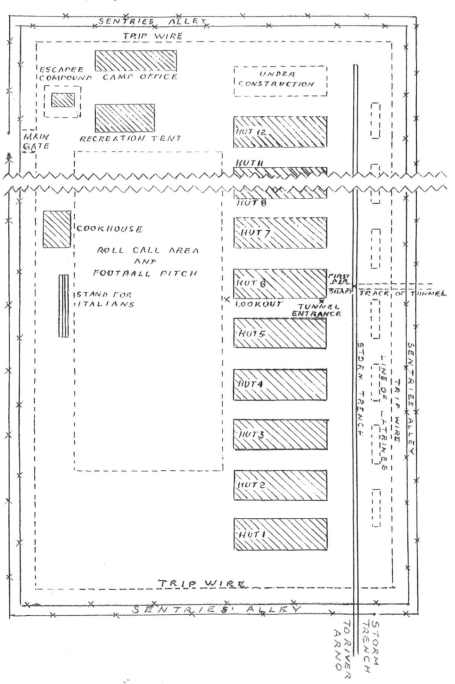

LATERINA CAMP

of the hut. In the small section of the cistern extending beyond the side wall of the hut there was a manhole giving access to the cistern. Each hut had a similar cistern, and the cisterns were all connected to each other by a series of wide calibre tubular concrete pipes.

Inside the huts the ablution benches had a constant functioning water supply, but the toilet system had no water. There was no prospect of a water supply being installed, hence the toilets remained unused, so the tunnel had been planned to start from one of the toilet cisterns directly towards and beneath the perimeter wire. Not many yards past the barbed wire there was a drop in the ground level of about two feet. We knew this because shepherds walked their flocks of sheep alongside the barbed wire each afternoon. The sheep close to the wire were in full view, but those beyond the drop in ground level only showed the top of their heads. So just past that drop was our target distance. The length of the tunnel would be a little more than 30yds.

In digging an escape tunnel, disposal of the spoil would normally be the major problem. In our case, however, we were blessed because we realized that we had been looking at the solution for the twelve months that the camp had been occupied. The line of latrines was constantly being extended, with the earth from each new one being carted by wheelbarrow to be tipped into a used latrine until that one was filled in. So the barrowing of earth was a daily sight to which the sentries paid no attention, and our wheelbarrow could operate in tandem with the legitimate ones.

To keep work on the tunnel running smoothly it was divided into two watches, Port and Starboard, with the two changing over every two hours of the day. A couple of fellows in each watch had separate jobs, such as producing the timber for shoring up the tunnel. At this time an Italian building contractor was building Hut 13, using PoW labour. The scaffolding comprised 10ft or 11ft slender lengths of tree trunk for the poles and long planks for the horizontals. Construction was going on all round the hut, so there were constantly large quantities of timber in use. This gave our two men plenty of opportunity to steal a plank here and a pole there, so they were able to meet our needs. Prison life sharpened everybody's wits, and when purloining something our thieves reached Artful Dodger standard. A saw and a hammer had also been stolen from a workman. A workman who lost anything in this way would be afraid to own up and admit that a tool was in the hands of the prisoners. The unfortunate man just had to produce another. Once any timber was ours, it could be stored in the cistern and sawn into the required lengths.

The main workers in each watch were three men taking turns digging at the tunnel face and pushing the earth back between their legs. Four hauliers took turns crawling forward to the diggers, piling the earth on to an empty sack and then crawling backwards, hauling the sack back to the cistern, as illustrated in Sketch 3.

The haulier then scooped the earth into a bucket. A man was in the cistern to hoist the bucket up. He centred the bucket beneath the manhole and another man heaved it up to ground level and tipped the earth into a wheelbarrow. It was then wheeled away to be tipped into a latrine. During a two-hour shift, the three diggers each did two twenty-minute stints at the face and the four hauliers each did two half-hour stints. I was one of the hauliers.

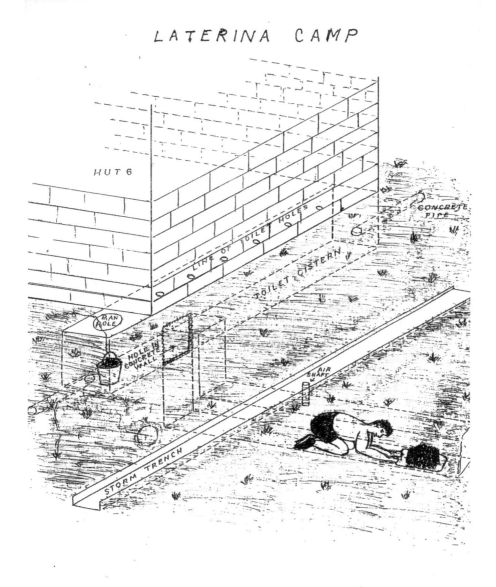

LATERINA CAMP

The first operation had been to break through the concrete wall of the toilet cistern. This must have been a great symbolic moment, and I wished I had been present. Once through the wall, work kept on at that level for about a yard. The break in the wall was about a yard wide, which would just about equate to the tunnel width. From that area digging went down about 5ft to form the floor of the tunnel. That ensured that we would pass well clear of the storm trench bottom and the tunnel could continue on forward from that point.

As the tunnel face advanced, roof supports were put in place. These consisted of a length of planking tight against the roof, supported at each end by a length of sturdy scaffold pole. They were sufficiently close to each other for the whole job to be a really solid construction. The horizontals were at a height that was reasonably easy to crawl under and the supports wide enough apart to allow a fairly hefty chap to crawl between.

A man was always stationed at the main gate of the compound to raise the alarm if any Italian entered the compound. Whenever this happened, he signalled to another man stationed at the near corner of Hut 6 who would then run the length of the hut to warn the team. The manhole cover was placed in position in a moment and the wheelbarrow placed alongside a latrine where it would not arouse suspicion.

There was one thing that made the tunnel much safer from the threat of detection. While I had been away at Borgo San Lorenzo, a party of prisoners from camps in southern Italy had arrived at Laterina. There was no room for them in the huts, so two lines of tents had been pitched parallel to the storm trench to accommodate them. Fortunately, these blocked the sentries' line of sight to the activity at the manhole, where the action of filling the barrows was taking place. If that had been visible to the sentries, there is no way the work could have remained undetected.

*

One day a crisis arose, when we learned that the camp authorities had given up the idea of using the toilets at the end of each hut and the system of field latrines and were therefore constructing a new building for showers and toilets. The showers had previously consisted of overhead pipes in the open air, and a shower in chilly weather had been a daunting experience. Running water was also a great improvement for the toilets, although they were of the Asian type. It was good to have indoor showers, although the water was still cold. However, the fact that there were to be no more field latrines meant there was nowhere for us to tip our spoil.

The twenty-five strong tunnel party held an emergency meeting. The outcome was an ingenious idea, provided we could convince the Italians. The football pitch at the opposite end of the huts from that at which we were constructing the tunnel was the site of our daily morning roll call, when the 250 occupants of each hut formed a long column in front of their hut. The ground was bare earth, and especially after any rain, thousands of pairs of army boots pounding it every day had turned it into a very bumpy and uneven state.

We therefore agreed to offer to level the football pitch, as a pretext for getting rid of our tunnel spoil. We approached the camp authorities, dangling as a carrot the suggestion that it would improve the football out of all recognition if we levelled the pitch. To our surprise, they applauded the suggestion and even offered to give us the tools for the job. Immediately we went to work with wheelbarrows criss-crossing the pitch every day. Soil was dumped all over it, raked in and trodden down. It was never going to be a permanent job, but it levelled the ground and also served our purpose admirably. So we were once again able to dispose of the soil, and work on the tunnel could continue.

*

At the time I joined the party, construction of the tunnel was well underway. After three weeks' work it was nearly half way to the wire and had passed beneath the storm trench, but the diggers and hauliers were suffering equally from the poor working conditions. With so little air in the tunnel, they were each struggling to complete their stint. So it was decided to bore a ventilation shaft from the roof of the tunnel into the bottom of the storm trench. This was accomplished by a chap sitting on the edge of the trench and repeatedly thumping heavily on the trench bottom above the course of the tunnel while another chap lying on his back below located the thudding sound and poked away with a spike to drive the shaft upwards. It was a great success, the shaft being finished to a professional standard when a metalworker made a lining for it from Red Cross parcel biscuit tins. To complete the camouflage of the shaft, the circular end of a biscuit tin lid was cut off and left alongside the hole. At any moment of danger the lid could be slipped on top of the hole. No prowling sentry or inspecting officer would demean himself to get down in the trench and pick up such a thing.

Fortunately, the weather throughout the exercise was fine, and there was no fear of rainwater draining into the airshaft. Down inside the tunnel the shaft also gave a comforting glimmer of light. It had already helped enormously with the air supply, but then came a further improvement. A skilled metalworker built a large fan, again using metal from Red Cross parcel tins. It had large blades and was driven by a heavy rubber band. The winding mechanism was hand operated. When it blasted air along the tunnel it made a huge difference to our conditions. With over 2,000 men in the compound, we could call on the services of a wide variety of craftsmen.

The team then approached RSM Cockcroft, the camp leader, with a request that a small daily ration of food should be issued to the team to supplement the meagre camp rations. This met with a firm refusal. When a further request was made for a small amount of olive oil for the lamps in the tunnel, an equally firm refusal was issued. So it was necessary to obtain these items by bartering with the sentries or people who came to the wire, using cigarettes or food parcel items not suitable for escape rations. The sentries were always ready to assist in passing bartered stuff across the wire.

Thus no assistance was forthcoming from the British authorities in camp, who considered the tunnel a source of potential embarrassment to themselves should it be discovered. However, the body of prisoners in the compound was all too aware of our efforts and gave us every encouragement. We certainly had no fear of betrayal by any of them, and our own authorities remained the one drawback.

A strange and rather disturbing situation arose as a result of this, more like some episode of Mafia gangsterism than normal life. One chap in the camp, Mick Coleman, was from my regiment and we had been together throughout the war. Mick was as rough a Liverpudlian as one could come across but he had always proved a loyal and reliable friend and ally when the going was tough. The attitude of the camp staff towards the tunnel group was known around the camp, and when whispers went round about the refusal of extra rations and olive oil, Mick approached me.

The gist of his message was that he knew of our difficulties and if there was anybody we felt should be taught a lesson he had the men to arrange it. He made it plain that he did not mean just a punch on the jaw in the night. He was talking about hospitalizing people. It was rather daunting to have this power thrust upon me, and I felt like some Mafioso boss able to say, 'OK, let him have it', and see a man carted off to hospital. I just told Mick not to be too hasty and to let us see what happened. I never mentioned it to the team, and the matter ended there.

The mechanics of excavating a tunnel are fairly straightforward, but a description of them does not give any sense of the feelings and commitment of the team. At first the work had not been too arduous. Everybody was fired with enthusiasm for starting the project. For the first yards of the tunnel it was a relatively easy task to move the earth the short distance from the tunnel face, but when I joined the team three weeks into the project, it was many yards long.

It soon became apparent just what a mammoth task faced us. As work progressed and the tunnel lengthened, the air was once again becoming less breathable, making the already difficult conditions even more arduous. The olive oil lamps we used gave us a flickering light but only at the expense of the smoke they produced. The lack of air at the tunnel face limited the face workers to very short spells before they had to come out for air. The hauliers, including myself, were able to stay down a little longer, but the work was gruelling. Every part of our bodies ached. Our necks and backs ached with the crawling movement along the tunnel floor, first forwards then much worse coming back dragging a load of earth. Our arms ached, while our knees became not only painful but were lacerated by being scraped along the tunnel floor.

As we could not turn round in the tunnel, there could only be one face worker and one haulier down below at any one time. Everybody sweated constantly; even those sitting down in the cistern were permanently bathed in perspiration. The only clothing we could tolerate was boots and a pair of shorts or underpants. When a shift ended we made straight for the showers, which offered great relief despite being cold.

Four of the team, including myself, were returned escapees, so were hampered by the two-hourly roll calls at the main gate throughout the day. The two-hour shifts were organized to coincide with the roll calls, but they imposed an additional burden in the rush to get rid of the perspiration and grime in time to be at the gate looking as calm and unruffled as everyone else in the camp. The *Carabinieri* never seemed sufficiently interested to raise questions about the occasional wild appearance of one or two fellows.

As the tunnel lengthened, life became ever more difficult. We were now so far past the ventilation shaft that we were again having serious breathing problems. The fan helped as far along as the ventilation shaft, but it was not having a great effect beyond that point. Additionally, the work for the hauliers was harder than ever because of the longer distance to drag the earth. However, our spirits never flagged, because as the tunnel face approached the target distance the excitement rose. So there was no dropping off in the rate of progress.

The digging had now been going on for about six weeks, and we knew from our measurements that we were already beyond the sentries' corridor. There were not many yards to go before the drop in ground level would be reached. We would then have reached our safe exit point and all of us in the tunnel team could finally make our escape. It was nerve-tingling to feel that the end was now in sight and we were only days from completion of the tunnel.

At this point we got together on the plan for putting the escape into action. The camp would be discreetly informed when a decision had been made on the best night for the escape. On that day all would-be escapers would have to be inside Hut 6 at a given time before dark, by which time all movement outside the huts was for-bidden. Each member of the team would be allowed to take one haversack or other item, which had to be of a size and weight the team considered negotiable through the tunnel. The first people through would be the tunnel party, one after the other at short intervals. Then after an agreed break to let the team get out of the area, the tunnel would be thrown open to all comers, or goers! The person in charge of Hut

1, a Regimental Sergeant Major from the East Yorks Regiment, had volunteered to come into Hut 6 and act as controller of the evacuation of any other would-be escapers after the team had gone. But first we had to finish those last few yards.

*

Then came the fateful day of 8 September 1943. Work at the tunnel face was continuing but had become almost intolerable, and it was decided that we must have another air shaft before we could continue. This meant a repeat of the construction procedure of the first shaft, with one man down in the tunnel to dig upwards, another at ground level to do the thudding to guide him and a third at the manhole as liaison man to pass any messages between the other two. I was at the top, Peter, the other Liverpool chap, was liaison and the Rhodesian was on his back in the tunnel.

I have not previously mentioned that in between the storm trench and the trip wire a row of vegetable patches had been developed. They were not particularly successful but they had produced some edible food. Now I was sitting in the middle of one of the patches armed with a large stone. I was under the nose of the sentries, as near as I dared to the trip wire, and rhythmically battering the ground as hard as I was able. Strange as such behaviour must have seemed to the sentries, it was just the sort of frustration-avoiding pastime that prisoners practised endlessly and which the sentries looked upon as prison camp eccentricities. This shaft was more difficult than the previous one because we were aiming up towards ground level and not just the bottom of the storm trench. Peter was kept busy encouraging the Rhodesian to prod ever harder at the shaft and imploring me to help the Rhodesian by bashing ever harder on the ground.

It was early evening and the short twilight was imminent. The valley in which the camp had been built was not very wide. On the north side of the camp the Italian quarters were alongside us, and a few hundred yards behind them a hill rose sharply up to the town of Laterina. The town stretched along the length of the crest, behind a massive retaining wall. The main approach road to the town ran along the high side of the wall, and this road was the site of the traditional Sunday evening *passeggiata*, the young people of the town promenading back and forth in little groups, dressed in their smartest clothes, with the younger girls accompanied by *Mamma* acting as chaperone.

As I sat in the marrow patch thumping the ground, I could clearly see all these goings-on. The *passeggiata* was normally a very quiet affair, so no sound carried down to the camp. It was a normal evening, and I was lost in my hammering, when a sense of something happening developed. At first it was just a murmuring, but then the noise level rapidly increased. I realized that not only were people making lots of noise, but there was also a lot of frenzied movement among them.

Peter and I did not know what was happening but, in fast failing light, we carried on with our task. This state of affairs did not last long because the uproar suddenly came much nearer as the sentries in the Italian quarters joined in the chorus. Rifle shots were then added to the din. We could not make out what the shouts were but we were not to be kept in the dark for long, as the excitement spread to the sentries around the wire. They were going wild, throwing their rifles in the air and shouting endlessly, '*La guerra è finita, la guerra è finita!*' ('The war is over'). It was the bogus radio announcement of Borgo San Lorenzo all over again, but this time it was real for Italy.

Peter and I were dumbstruck. So committed were we to the completion of the tunnel that it was hard to comprehend that events might cheat us of our triumph. We both slumped for a while but then collected our composure. We realized that the Rhodesian was still lying on his back, sweating away, as he drove his spike into the earth above him. We both shirked the act of shouting along the tunnel, 'Come on out, the war's over.' This we finally did, and eventually an indignant, disbelieving and dishevelled digger emerged from the tunnel to ask us what sort of claptrap were we giving him.

The tunnel group gathered for an emergency meeting in our escapee compound. Soon confirmation came through that although the war was not completely over, it was fact that the Italians had signed an armistice. So they had, in effect, finished their war. At the emergency meeting we were swallowing hard to digest the news. Passions were so strong that reason was taking second place.

The general feeling was, 'If the miserable bastards want to finish their war they can jolly well finish it, but we're going through our tunnel.' The thought that prevailed was that after so much back-breaking work we looked like being thwarted in the last few days. As we lay down to sleep, the feeling was one of determination that we should carry on digging the next day. A night's sleep left us in a more rational frame of mind. After a last inspection and sad farewell to our tunnel, which was quite a masterpiece, we were able to accept our new circumstances with proper enthusiasm and elation. It was clear now that momentous events were upon us but, no matter what happened, the tunnel would play no further part in it.

*

That first day passed quietly, with the Italians promising a statement as soon as the position became clear. That evening the five British medical officers and padres each addressed the members of various huts. The messages they gave were unconvincing. British troops were said to have landed at Livorno, seventy miles away, and would be in the camp area in a matter of days. A PoW Commission would be with the forward troops. The Germans did not know the location of our camp, and it was in our own interests to lie low and not broadcast our presence by wandering around the countryside. This argument left us unconvinced, and I agreed with my Rhodesian and two South African tunnel companions that we would remain prepared to go at a moment's notice.

The second day was the same, although there was a tension which affected everybody. The majority seemed content to accept the 'lie low' proposal. There was a nerve-tingling sense of imminent release in the air. Then a fortunate but bizarre event occurred; lorry-loads of personal parcels from our families arrived. I was lucky enough to receive one, and my mother had once again come up trumps. There were top quality army shirts, khaki shorts, underclothes, socks and a good supply of chocolate bars. Now I felt ready for whatever lay ahead.

The third day also started quietly, without any indication of the events about to overtake us. While I had been away in Borgo San Lorenzo, a second compound had been completed alongside us which was occupied by a couple of thousand South African and French Foreign Legion troops. The latter were a desperate lot, something which became apparent during the afternoon. Showing as little concern as possible, hundreds of them had congregated along the side of their compound bordering on the river. At a signal, they crossed the trip wire and threw themselves bodily on the first wall of barbed wire. This gave way under the pressure and tilted over towards the rear curtain of wire, trapping the sentries in a little triangular area under the wires. They were petrified and took no action as an enormous wave of men ran up the tilted wire, jumped from its top and went wading across the nearby River Arno.

Soon after, they came into sight as they started to climb the hill in front of them. Soldiers and *Carabinieri* came rushing from the Italian quarters armed with rifles and started to fire at the many figures scuttling up the hill some hundreds of yards away. Occasional rounds were sizzling across our compound. As we could not tell where they were coming from, it was wise to keep out of the way. A great many men must have been successful, but we later saw a lot of dejected looking fellows being hauled back to their compound.

Anything could happen now, and I agreed with my tunnel companions that we should be prepared to act on whatever did. The sentries were in a nervous state, and we decided to test them. We had a pair of wire cutters and we gathered at the trip wire near the machine gun tower at the corner of the compound by the river. A sentry was at that point and, when we told him we intended to cut the wire, he became frightened and begged us not to do so. We crossed the trip wire together, cut a head-high exit in the first wall of wire and entered the sentries' corridor. The sentry, still very frightened, took no action at first but then fired a single round in the air. The crew in the machine gun tower immediately above us hesitated and did nothing.

That shot must have been an agreed signal, because some minutes later a small, portly Italian Army officer arrived along the corridor between the wires, puffing for breath and dripping with perspiration. He spoke excitedly in halting English, asking why we were doing such foolish things and saying that he hoped his son, a PoW in India, was waiting patiently for the war to finish and not behaving like us. He left without giving any indication that anything would be done about the wire. We left it like that for the time being, but there was now only one curtain of wire between us and freedom. We slept that night knowing that events must come to a head imminently.

*

The next morning, 12 September 1943, which was a Sunday, dawned as brightly as ever. We knew this could be our day and our hopes were high. Even the weather seemed to be on our side, with the sun bright and warm in a cloudless sky. Again we were being exhorted by the British officers not to leave the camp, but patience was running short in a number of people. Groups were gathering at the point at which we had cut the wire and at the main gate, and any Italians entering the compound were being hassled.

In the confusion, word came through that the Italians had set up telephone contact with a lookout on a bridge over the River Arno just short of the main road, about nine miles from the camp. The plan was that if German troops left the main road and crossed the bridge, heading for the camp, the lookout would inform the camp and our compound would be thrown open at once. This did not seem a good deal, as we would only have about twenty minutes' start on the Germans. The afternoon was drawing on when Italian soldiers arrived in two large lorries and parked them near the main gate. We could see clearly that they were loaded with rations for the camp, so food appeared to be no problem.

Towards evening the Italian sentries on duty finally broke. To a man, on some given signal, they cast aside their rifles, climbed the outer curtain of barbed wire and went scampering across the field towards a nearby wood. This brought an outbreak of Italian officers firing pistols into the air. Our camp leader, RSM Cockcroft, felt that things were now getting totally out of hand and ordered everybody to the parade ground immediately.

RSM Cockcroft mounted a table to address us, and when he began to speak we could not believe our ears. The gist was that the Italians had panicked, the camp was perfectly safe, ten days' rations had just arrived and he was going to see that the camp remained intact. He forbade anybody to leave. The situation then degenerated into *opera buffa*, comic opera, as we watched about a dozen Italians run from their quarters to the wagon park and clamber all over the lorries loaded with rations. The motors spluttered into life and, with the Italians cheering and waving their hats, we watched lorries trundle to the camp entrance and disappear along the road, our rations no doubt headed for the black market that same day.

The RSM was not put out of his stride and announced that he intended to maintain discipline until the recently landed British troops arrived. He was not to know that they would not make it for another nine months. He called for the compound police, mostly ex-Redcaps (Military Police) and announced that each one of them with a team of volunteers would set up a sentry watch to stop people wandering out of the camp. Surprisingly, there was no shortage of volunteers. The rifles abandoned by the fleeing sentries were lying all over the place and were quickly issued to the new teams of guards who set off to take up positions around the wire. It was hard to believe that the compound was now to be guarded by sentries who were our fellow prisoners.

I discussed these developments with my Rhodesian and South African tunnel mates, who had become good friends. We knew it was time to move or we might never get away. In the escapee compound I emptied a palliasse of its straw and loaded all my kit into it. I was the only one of the four who had any kit at all. I had my newly arrived personal parcel of chocolate and clothes and an almost intact Red Cross food parcel, as well as the kit I always carried. Then the four of us made for the point near Hut 1 where we had already cut the inner curtain of wire.

Alongside one of the huts we passed a line of men stretched on the ground or leaning against the wall. They bade us various sarcastic farewells. Then we were passing the end of Hut 6, where we gave a nostalgic thought to our tunnel lying beneath us. When we reached the breach in the wire, a camp police fellow was just arriving there with a team of volunteer sentries to man the machine gun tower. They rather shamefacedly tried to convince us we should not leave and seemed to regret having taken the job on. We ignored them, apart from offering a few expletives, walked through the gap in the inner curtain of wire and began to scale the outer curtain. I do not know why we did not have the wire cutters, but we did not lose any time.

Clambering down the outside of the wire meant freedom once again. Escaping from Borgo San Lorenzo a month earlier, jumping from the wall had brought on an intense excitement. This time, strangely, it was not excitement but rather a feeling of sheer exuberance. It was still daylight on a calm warm evening, and this time I was accompanied by three companions with whom I had shared difficulties and whom I knew I could trust.

We picked up my kit and, as we set off, the pseudo-sentries still asked us to go back inside. We gave them short shrift. We asked what on earth they were doing guarding their own comrades and told them that if they had any sense they would be off their marks before the Germans arrived. If not, they would probably find themselves in Germany before they knew it. They ignored our advice and began to climb the ladder of the tower.

There was a farmhouse in view about 100yds way across the field, and we saw a group of prisoners leave the farm and set off back to the camp. They had gone straight out after the Italian sentries. Once in the farm, they had slaughtered a pig, which some of them were now carrying back in triumph. Those not carrying the pig were swigging away at flasks of wine. We turned our back on the lot of them. We did not know where the rest of our tunnel companions were or what they were up to. It struck us that nobody else had thought of making good their escape. If Germans did approach the camp, they would be caught like sitting ducks.

We then moved towards the river. It was the dry season, so the water was not too deep. As we stepped from the bank, all four of us were overcome with a sense of delirious jubilation. We pranced across the river, waving our arms and singing at the top of our voices. When we climbed the far bank it seemed like the Garden of Eden. We joined a track with the river to our right and a vineyard to our left. The grapes were lusciously ripe. Progress was slow as we moved from one row of vines to the next, stuffing ourselves with fruit.

We had no thought of caution. After some time, when a peasant came walking along the track towards us, we greeted him like an old friend. He raised no objection to our behaviour and asked us if the grapes were good. The way we were eating them he had no need to ask, but for good measure we told him the word 'good' was far too modest a description. After all, it was our first fruit in a year or more. As we carried on we passed occasional fig trees, the branches heavy with ripe fruit. I had never seen the like of them before nor had I imagined how good they could taste when picked, fully ripe, from the tree.

We ate that fruit until we could eat no more, then sat and relaxed for a little while. We thought of the tunnel and laughed at the six weeks of sweat and back-breaking work which had come to nothing, when all we had had to do was climb over 7ft or 8ft of barbed wire. At least the tunnel had given us something to think about and kept us free from the fear of insanity, which was always a worry in prison camp life. When we were ready we took to the track again, and our pace was unhurried and carefree.

Although we could not see anything across the river, we could hear a lot of vehicles. Heavy traffic on such a minor road was most unusual, and we guessed that the Germans were moving in to take the camp and solemnly shook hands at having made our move. We later had confirmation that a column of German armoured cars had encircled the camp almost immediately after we left.

Back on the track, we soon found ourselves veering slightly from the river, and the ground began to rise a little. The vineyards were now behind us and we were walking through pleasant open woodland of mostly young birch trees. We had not gone very far before we heard a few vehicles somewhere in front of us. This concentrated our minds, and we advanced more cautiously from that point. It was just as well, because it was not long before we heard voices.

As dusk was now approaching, we decided our best plan would be to move immediately off the track into the woods and find somewhere to lie down for the night. We soon found a suitable spot, a small clearing not far from the track but well out of sight. We were in an elated mood as we dined on a little of my Red Cross parcel food and water from our bottles. It had been an exhausting day, full of emotion, excitement and jubilation all mixed together, with nothing on the negative side. So when we finally settled down for the night in our little clearing we were in a contented frame of mind, and sleep came soon. I do not think I stirred all night.

When I woke it was early but already light. The air was still and smelt beautifully sweet. For some time I lay looking at the sky through the tracery of the treetop canopy above me. When I turned my head I was presented with a rare and amazing sight. The other three were still asleep, and we were lying a few yards from each other. On the ground in the centre of our group three beautiful cock pheasants were pecking away at the ground.

The pheasants were oblivious to our presence, just moving about among us. One came pecking at my overcoat only inches from my hand. For a moment the thought of how important food was in our present predicament crossed my mind. Inevitably the temptation flooded in to make one quick grab, and he would be ready for the pot. The thought died as it was born. It was an eyeball-to-eyeball situation and, moreover, down on the ground at his level. He was wild and I was free. I felt I was now as hunted as he was and I could not harm him. So I lay still, and soon the three birds pecked their way out of the clearing and disappeared. It was as though they had come to congratulate us on our freedom!

Breakfast was another meal from my Red Cross food, and when we had eaten we were ready for what the day had to offer. This morning Laterina was behind me and, for the moment at least, I was my own master. As we set off through the woods I had a feeling that, with a bit of luck and determination, our future could be exciting.

Chapter 5

Freedom

Having made the break from Laterina, we felt ready to face whatever might lie in store for us. As we knew that German troops had arrived in the area of the camp the previous evening, we felt it would be too dangerous to approach the nearby River Arno to wash ourselves. So we cleaned ourselves up as best we could and prepared to set off on our first free day. Our woodland glade had been a pleasant first taste of that freedom.

Before describing the journey on which we were about to embark I should say something about the Rhodesian and the two South African fellows with whom I had thrown in my lot. The Rhodesian had gone to England early in the war, enlisting as a pilot in the Royal Air Force. Serving with a fighter squadron in the Mediterranean theatre, he had been shot down, had ditched in the sea and had been rescued from the water by an Italian warship. The South Africans had both belonged to an infantry unit, part of one of the two South African divisions in Libya, and like myself, had been captured at Tobruk.

Now I was on the road with them in our attempt to rejoin Allied lines. I probably never heard their surnames and now find that I do not remember their first names, so they simply remain forever to me as my one Rhodesian and two South African companions.

We gathered our bits and pieces, all of which did in fact belong to me. I was fairly well clothed, having my desert clothing, a greatcoat, battledress and a fair number of shirts and underclothes, since in the previous forty-eight hours I had been blessed by the arrival of a Red Cross food parcel and also the personal parcel from my family, which included an invaluable supply of chocolate.

One of the South Africans, a tall well-built fellow with a rather distinguished air about him, was dressed in an almost threadbare shirt and had no jacket. Amongst the clothing in my personal parcel was a very good quality, large-sized pair of pyjamas. In the fashion of the day they were vividly striped: red, white, blue and black, in varying widths of stripe. My offer to replace his threadbare shirt with the pyjama jacket was accepted with enthusiasm, and although the effect was rather startling, the improvement in both his appearance and his morale showed at once.

Having got the biggest problem behind us, that of managing to put ourselves on the right side of the barbed wire, our minds were buzzing on what the next steps should be, and we found ourselves in turmoil. The army had always insisted it was a PoW's duty to attempt to escape, but there had never been a manual of 'What to Do Next'. A variety of improbable thoughts come flooding in at such a time, and these mingled with a realistic appreciation of how uncertain our predicament was, leaving us in a state of much confusion. Up to this point, the whole purpose of our days had been concentrated on how to escape from captivity. For me it had started as the germ of an idea in Tobruk fifteen months earlier, and as the months passed my determination had grown. The failure of my attempt from Borgo San Lorenzo had been a blow to my morale, but the immediate offer of a place in the tunnel party at Laterina had lifted my spirits sky high again.

Then the long gruelling days working on the tunnel, exhausting though they were, were a great boost to our morale. This had helped us all enormously, but getting to the other side of the barbed wire had become our horizon to the exclusion of all else. Foolish though it may now appear, we had scarcely thought about what lay beyond the wire. Now, having made the break, the world before us seemed a totally unknown factor that we were just taking from minute to minute. What to do now? In the aftermath of the Armistice one thing we were sure of was that Italy, and in particular any Italian authorities, would be in a state of chaos; for the moment, all official order would have collapsed.

So as we set off, our minds turned to possible objectives. Until a short time before our escape the only land objective open to us had been Switzerland, but this had changed with the Allied landings at Salerno and Anzio, south of Rome. Even that was some hundreds of miles south, so getting there still posed a considerable obstacle. The weather prospects were so much better heading south rather than going north towards the Alps that any thoughts of Switzerland were soon discarded. We had heard rumours of a further Allied landing about to be attempted at Livorno, on the coast only seventy miles west of us, but we had learned not to put much faith in such rumours.

As the morning went on the Rhodesian fighter pilot, almost apologetically, put out a suggestion. He thought that all routine order on Italian airfields would have collapsed and that if we could find an airfield it might well be virtually unguarded. If this proved to be the case, and we found a plane ready to be flown, he was sure he could fly it to Malta. This called for a measure of faith which was hard to swallow, but desperate circumstances call for desperate measures, and we agreed that if such circumstances presented themselves we should consider them.

The proposal gave the pyjama-jacketed South African the idea that he could put another shot in our locker. He claimed that in pre-war days he had held a commission in the South African navy and that he was experienced in marine navigation. So if we got to the coast and were able to steal a seaworthy boat, he was confident he could sail it to Malta. This was a much less daunting prospect than flying a plane and it was accepted more readily. The only justification for such harebrained schemes was that our position was quite precarious; when circumstances are suffi-ciently bad, no suggestion seems impossible.

Neither I nor the second South African had any comparable skills to offer. So, bearing in mind those two unlikely possibilities, in the meantime we set our sights on heading towards the Anzio bridgehead. However, in the hope that there might be another Allied landing at Livorno or somewhere along the coast, we decided to move west before turning south near the coast. This would also give us the oppor-tunity to weigh up whether or not the escape-by-boat scheme was available to us. These thoughts occupied our minds as we tramped through the woods at the start of our odyssey.

We were finding the sensation of freedom an exhilarating one, as our walk ini-tially took us through the woods, on the edge of which we had slept the previous night. Our chat was light-hearted and there was a spring in our step. It was not long before we came to cultivated land on gently sloping hills. We were fresh from a barbed-wire compound, and the prospect in front of us was now truly idyllic. We could not have been blessed with a more picturesque countryside in which to start our adventure.

It was mid-September 1943, and the weather was warm, with a cloudless blue sky. We were walking past seemingly endless vineyards, the vines heavy with ripe grapes. There were black grapes and white grapes, both equally luscious, so we gorged ourselves on gargantuan quantities of them. The grapes were destined to become that well known Tuscan product, Chianti, bottled at that time in the straw-covered flasks so long connected with the wine, but today, sadly, virtually disappeared. We were not to know that wine grapes were not at all like table grapes. That did not trouble us at the time, because nothing could have given us more pleasure than the little black grapes that we ate.

There were other crops to be seen. Tobacco fields became more common, and there was maize which was close to ripening. We saw occasional small patches of beans, tomatoes and turnips. There were fig and walnut trees near the road, and the figs were particularly good. So there was plenty of opportunity to nibble as we progressed.

Almost all the houses had a few jet-black cypress trees alongside. They just seemed to be part of the local landscape and they produced a particularly pleas-ant picture of the whole countryside. All the houses were colour-washed in pastel colours, generally brownish or pinkish, with red pantile roofs. We were seeing this in fine warm weather. The whole effect was wonderful and showed Tuscany at its best. We saw no cattle, sheep or goats, but there were many pure white oxen, usually in pairs, lumbering along pulling carts on the road or pulling a plough across one of the slopes in the hills. The weather remained warm and the roads very dusty, so we took regular breaks by the roadside to enjoy bunches of grapes.

People whom we met immediately recognized us as escaped prisoners and, when we passed a house we were often greeted with '*Venite in casa, un bicchierino*' ('Come in and take a little glass of wine'). This sort of welcome was an enormous morale-booster and gave rise to the hope that maybe our mission could prove successful.

*

On one occasion we found ourselves starting on a straight stretch of road at the end of which we could see a village. As we got nearer, we saw a few people standing in the middle of the road. More were gathering, and by the time we got close there was quite a crowd of villagers. Approaching the group we were a little apprehensive about what sort of reception we would get. Our worries were unwarranted, however, as they had guessed we were from Laterina and were simply curious about us. One fellow seemed to be the leading figure in the place. He welcomed us and congratulated us on achieving our freedom. There was a chorus of friendly welcomes from the villagers. They then slowly moved from the road into the village *piazza*, the square alongside, taking us with them. As we shuffled along in the crowd we became separated from each other, and the people around me were encouraging me to enter one of the houses. Being swept along, I was in no position to decline and I soon found myself in the stone-flagged kitchen of a house. It had the largest raised stone fireplace I had ever seen. People crowded in after me and the place was soon packed to the doorway.

I was asked if I was hungry, and a huge home-made, cartwheel-shaped loaf was produced. It was freshly baked and had a superb taste. More was to come, in the form of home-cured ham. Both for the bread and the ham the standard method for cutting a slice appeared to be for a man to hold the loaf against his chest and hack a wedge off with a large penknife. It turned out that every man carried such a knife. I was handed a wedge of bread and ham. The flavour was strong and beautiful. I could scarcely believe I was eating such food after my time at Laterina. I learned that the dry-cured ham was *prosciutto* as I was encouraged with the words '*Mangia su, senza complimenti*' ('Eat up, don't be shy').

Everybody in the room was talking at once and questions were being fired at me: 'What is your name?' 'Is it true you eat five meals a day in England?' and 'Do you live in a palace?' Once my name was established I became known as Franco, and calls of 'Franco' were echoing around the room. My still elementary Italian was being sorely tested. I had been given a couple of glasses of wine and was then offered a glass of *vinsanto*, the lovely Tuscan dessert wine. This was extremely pleasant but, not having drunk wine until a day or so before, my head was beginning to spin. Everybody was enjoying themselves, but I knew I must get into the fresh air so I just pushed my way to the door.

A doorway across the piazza was crammed with people and proved to be where one of my companions was. I had been worried about all three, as none of them spoke any Italian. When I got in I found that he was in a worse state than I was. I pushed him outside and we eventually discovered which house was entertaining the other two. They were equally unsteady. At least they had eaten well and, as for the wine, I think the spinning heads were caused not so much by the quantity imbibed as by the fact that we had never drunk wine before that occasion.

The last to emerge from the house was the pyjama-jacketed South African. He towered above the Italians, so we could see him in his colourful jacket. Then when he managed to push through the crowd and we saw him from head to foot, we could scarcely believe our eyes. He had done a trouser swap with a villager. His battledress trousers, which must have seemed like gold to the villager, had gone, and he was sporting a pair of thin white cotton trousers patterned with a very fine green stripe. These, together with the striped pyjama jacket, created such an improbable effect that we could scarcely stifle our laughs.

The people of the countryside had obviously thrown off the shackles of Fascism and were only too eager to be friendly. It had been a really enthusiastic welcome and show of kindness. The villagers wanted us to stay longer and celebrate with them. However, my head was a little clearer than the other three, and I felt sure we should leave while we were still standing. So we expressed our gratitude but insisted we must keep travelling. Then a bottle of wine was produced for us, and we waved farewell as we set off along the road.

We walked for a long time. Occasionally we met people, in ones or twos, on foot or sometimes riding bicycles. We were invited into a few houses but we found that whenever we entered a house it was virtually impossible to leave without taking a glass of wine. The wines were usually made by the family with grapes from their own vineyard and varied greatly in quality. Some of them were really fierce, but fortunately the glasses were always small and we always left after the first glass. At one house we were invited to take a bite of food and were introduced to a simple but delicious peasant dish, *minestra*, a clear broth with bread. It was a dish I was to enjoy very much over the months to come. Simple though it was, the flavour was quite beautiful. On the road, one thing which forcibly struck us was that we never saw a car or other powered vehicle of any kind. The only thing we encountered was an occasional cart, always pulled by two majestic white oxen.

There seemed to be no streams or lakes where we could gain access to water, so when we were invited into a house we sometimes asked if we could wash. Each time the family would immediately produce buckets of water and soap, which generally was of very poor quality and produced scarcely any lather, but every time we left much refreshed. As evening came on we looked for somewhere to spend the night. As the wood in which we had passed the first night had given us such a good rest, we chose another clump of woodland. We had water in our water bottles for an occasional drink and we dined well on some fruit and tomatoes from the fields, together with a little of my Red Cross food.

As we lay down and made ourselves comfortable, we contemplated what an incredible day it had been. I had spent the previous thirteen months in a field surrounded by barbed wire, and before that had lived in slit trenches in the Libyan desert for nine months without a break. Now, lying in a wood, it was difficult to credit that we had walked freely, been welcomed by people, enjoyed a sort of party in a village and been able to eat whenever we felt like eating. It was difficult to relate the tensions and anxieties of month after seemingly endless month spent behind barbed wire to the joyous and carefree feelings we were now enjoying. Once more the world seemed to be a pleasant place and, no matter what the morrow held, we felt we were going to be all right. These were my thoughts as I drifted into sleep.

*

We woke early the next morning, and I still had a sense of wellbeing that made me feel everything was going right for us. This time there were no pheasants to greet me, but there was a freshness in the air and a bright sun was filtering through the canopy of the trees out of a clear blue sky. We could look forward to breakfast, as my rations were lasting well, and we were never far from food to nibble from the fields.

It was not long before we spotted a house a little way from the road, and we were soon being made welcome there. When we asked for water to clean ourselves up we were handed brass water carriers and led to the nearby spring from which the family drew all their water. We were soon splashing about, and once we had sluiced down we shaved, all four using my razor with the same blade which did not augur well for my meagre stock of them. The exercise was a great morale-booster and we felt thoroughly refreshed. Before leaving the spring, we replenished our water bottles. On leaving the house, we accepted the family's offer of bread with a slice of salami and some bunches of grapes. They gave us a bottle of their wine, wished us good luck on our journey, and we set off in excellent spirits.

We had not been long on the road before I received an unpleasant surprise. Without any warning, my nose began to bleed. At first I tried to pass it off and just ignored it. However, the flow was persistent, and just brushing my hand across my nose soon had my arm in a very messy state. I had no great stock of handkerchiefs to use as a pad and soon I had to call a halt. I lay flat on the ground while my companions relaxed and waited for me. They were patient and considerate, but this was a problem nobody had anticipated. After a time the flow stopped. I had enough water to clean myself up and we set off again. I could not think of any reason for the problem. If I had been totally inactive for a long period in the camp, as so many fellows had been, it might have been understandable that suddenly spending some days walking all day would upset my blood pressure. On the contrary, however, I had spent three weeks slogging hard, dragging earth along a tunnel. Whatever the reason, there was nothing I could do about it except hope that I had had one minor hiccup and that the problem was now over.

*

So once again we set off. Before long the countryside became more open and we were walking along a track part way up a gently sloping hill with an unimpeded view of the fields below us. Along the track we came upon a solitary, very mature fig tree. We had previously tasted figs but the crop on this tree seemed stupendous. Every fig was enormous and seemed to be at optimum ripeness on that day. They were so good we settled down on the ground and prepared for a feast. On many of them the green skin and the inner white skin had burst open, showing the bright purple flesh within. My only experience of figs had been the dried fruit we had eaten at home on occasions like Christmas, but this tree produced an altogether new appreciation of the fruit. We soon all had sticky fingers and faces. For a while we just lay on the ground enjoying the sun and savouring our feast.

Then a young chap came walking along the track towards us. As he got nearer we were all struck by how scrupulously clean he looked. Standing there in bright sunlight, his white open-necked shirt immaculate, his face seemed to have been scrubbed and his dark hair well trimmed with not a hair out of place. It struck us all that we could not remember having seen such a clean person, and it was hard to imagine that we could ever reach that state again. As he looked down at us lying on the ground surrounded by fig skins he was obviously intrigued and he stopped to chat. We did not hesitate to say we had escaped from Laterina, which he thought was very exciting, and he wanted to know if we had any plans. We told him we knew that Allied troops had landed in the Anzio area and we hoped to get down there and cross the Allied lines. He went on to tell us that he was in Tuscany for a few days visiting family but that he came from near Rome, where his father was a railway stationmaster.

He was due to go back to Rome later that day and he offered to escort us on the train, assuring us that this would be secure. A safe house could easily be found for us in Rome. This sounded inviting, but there had been no mention of tickets or payment. It did not need much consultation to decide that to put so much criti-cal trust in a complete stranger, a boy younger than ourselves, was something we should not consider. He was quite crestfallen, clearly feeling cheated of some real excitement, but having said no we parted on good terms.

Our next contact with an Italian was more colourful, in keeping with the spirit of our cavalier progress through the countryside. It came as we reached the end of a track and joined a lane. Arriving at this junction at the same time was a pony and cart. The pony had been going at a gentle trot, but when the driver saw us he reined in and greeted us. He was a slight, wiry fellow with black curly hair, an enormous moustache and dark flashing eyes. He knew immediately that we were escaped prisoners and asked where we were heading. I told him we were not sure but that we had intended to turn left on the road. That was the direction he was heading, and he asked if we wished to join him. He looked an interesting character, and there was room for the four of us to sit on the back of his cart, so we threw our lot in with him.

Once we were aboard he let his pony go at its own pace to make up for the extra weight, so the going was easy. One thing we had not expected was transport and, as the cart moved along, life seemed to be getting better by the minute. We had been saving our bottle of wine for the evening, but now we were so comfortable it seemed the right moment for a swig. Corks were not used on home-bottled wines. Instead the liquid was sealed with a thin film of olive oil in the neck, and then a tightly folded chestnut leaf was pushed in to act as a cork. With the chestnut leaf pulled out, a flick of the wrist ejected the small amount of olive oil, and the bottle was ready to be passed around. Our swigs were deep, and soon the wine was just a lovely memory and our contentment even greater. I sat near our driver and chatted with him. The small amount of conversation I had been able to get in during these couple of days had already helped my Italian, and I was improving by leaps and bounds. I asked him what he did and to my surprise he told me he was a *contra-bandista*. This turned out to mean a small-time tinker dealing in contraband goods.

A number of commodities in Italy were sold under government monopoly and were strictly rationed. These included items like salt, sugar and cigarettes. It was these things in which he was dealing in the villages and isolated farmhouses that he visited. In return he offered carbide for lamps and also plug tobacco, amongst other things. None of the villages or outlying farmhouses had electricity or gas and every family was dependent on carbide lamps. These gave a small incandescent flame, which was pitifully weak for a large high-ceilinged room once darkness fell. The carbide was difficult to get and the people were dependent on our *contraband-ista* for supplies if they wanted a reasonable number of lamps.

The tobacco was an odd matter because the people did have a small ration of cigarettes. None of the women smoked, and most men found the two available brands of cigarettes, *Nazionale* and *Esportazione*, too disgusting, so they tried to get hold of plug tobacco which was not generally available. This was really fierce stuff. The plugs were fairly long and about finger-thick. A small piece could be cut off either for chewing or crushing and rolling as a cigarette. One taste was enough to put us off for life. Our driver friend told us that the plugs had been boiled in wine, and in fact there was a slightly moist and greasy feel about them rather than the almost dry feel of normal tobacco. It would have been fun to see him doing business, but this day he was on his way home.

So we were just ambling along minor roads, without any worries. After a fair number of miles we realized we were travelling north and that we had better change tack. He was an interesting, jolly fellow but as soon as we saw a road more suitable to a westerly march, we thanked him and waved goodbye.

*

Not long after we left the *contrabandista* my nose began once again to bleed profusely. I could not carry on walking because while I was upright I had to lean forward to avoid blood splashing down my clothing. This was quite difficult while I was carrying a fair amount of kit. There was no alternative but to lie down again and wait. I felt most depressed and I was concerned that there was no way I could find out what was causing the trouble. Once again my companions were very patient and urged me not to worry because the problem would very likely pass.

Once more on the march, the roads seemed strangely empty. The only people we saw were busy in the fields or vineyards. We were now moving into the low hills on the western side of the Arno valley. There was a little more woodland but the countryside was still as attractive as ever and the weather continued to be perfect. Food was not a problem. My Red Cross parcel food was holding out because we rationed it carefully and relied on the plentiful fruits of the field and the benevolence of the country people.

We had passed one or two hamlets, but when we eventually came to a small town we began to see a few people and also the first signs of Fascist propaganda. In prominent positions on some of the houses there were Fascist slogans stencilled in large black letters. These were exhortations such as '*Credere, Obbedire, Combattere*' ('Believe, Obey, Fight') and '*Il Duce Ha Sempre Ragione*' ('The Duce Is Always Right'). We learned that the locals were long since disillusioned with such ideas and no longer paid any attention to the slogans.

As we entered the town a man approached us, knowing that we were escaped prisoners. He told us that there was a gentleman in the town who would like to meet us. We were intrigued and decided we would go along to see what the man wanted. Then we learned that the fellow knew there were prisoners about but he had not met any and wanted to see the first ones who passed. The house to which we were taken was a large, imposing building. Once inside, the contrast between the bright sunlight outside and the subdued light inside was startling. Although the shutters of the venetian blinds were closed, they were of a sophisticated sort with four hinged louvred panels in each window, allowing the amount of light admitted and the air intake to be controlled very precisely.

The entrance hall was substantial, with a floor of polished marble, and the furniture and ornaments were all beautiful antiques. After a few moments we were ushered into a large study, where an elderly gentleman was seated at a big desk. He rose and came to greet us. I acted as spokesman, introducing him to the others. It was obvious he was one of the more important people of the town. We sat down, and a servant served us coffee. It transpired that he had called us in so we could tell him of the circumstances that had brought us to his town and to explain our hopes and intentions.

I explained the build-up in camp prior to the Armistice and our subsequent escape. I spoke of aiming to reach the Allied lines but did not refer to boats or planes. He seemed genuinely interested in our welfare. He warned us that even though we did not see Germans or Fascist militia, they were about, and that there were people who would betray us. When it came time to go he wished us good fortune and we thanked him for his hospitality. When he led us to the door the servant approached carrying a generous supply of bread, cheese and salami and a bottle of wine. As we left we waved a grateful farewell and looked forward to an enjoyable meal that evening. Leaving the town we realized we had not filled our water bottles, so we called at a house, where the family were only too pleased to supply water, and we spent more time talking to them.

*

After a while we were tiring and we knew we must rest. We were well out of the town and the road had risen quite a bit. On the right was the long boundary wall of an estate, the entrance to which was a very imposing set of wrought iron gates half way along the wall. Inside were groups of cypresses and some walnut trees. Although the villa was not in sight, the scene looked just like the label on a wine bottle. On the other side of the road was a large tract of sparsely grassed land with a few scattered clumps of trees. We decided to rest and picked a spot opposite the estate gates. Putting our kit down, we stretched out on the ground and made ourselves comfortable.

We then realized that a group of four or five young men had been tailing along behind us. Now, as we settled down, they approached and stood quite near. It was somewhat ominous the way they were silently looking down at us. The wine my three companions had drunk was affecting them and they were drifting into sleep. I was desperately shaking them, telling them that they must stay awake. This went on for some time until the youths suddenly turned and walked away. I had the feeling that if I had fallen asleep, we would have lost all our kit. This was the only occasion during my long spell of freedom that I felt under any threat from Italians.

*

The halts for my nose-bleeding trouble had taken quite a bit of time. Evening was approaching and we began to think of finding somewhere to sleep. The weather prospects seemed good and we had no qualms about another night in the open. So we settled in a pleasant spot on the edge of woodland, with a stream nearby. That evening we were able to feast in great style thanks to the generosity of our bene-factor, even to the extent of sharing a bottle of wine. The wine tasted just as good from our tin prison camp mugs as it would have from any lead crystal wineglass. Following the meal we washed in the stream and prepared for the night. I was tired and ready for sleep but worried as to whether I was going to be all right.

The next morning I woke to another lovely dawn. I had slept soundly through the night so I was hopeful that my nose bleeding had been a passing problem and that all would be well. After sprucing ourselves up and having a bite to eat we decided to sit down and weigh up exactly what our position was and whether or not there was any better plan of action we could think of. The result was a dismal assessment of our plight. We did not know exactly where we were, we had no map of any description and we had only the vaguest of ideas about where we wanted to go. To all intents and purposes we were lost, and we were acutely aware that it was still some hundreds of miles to friendly forces. There was no alternative, however, to our slow but steady progress, so we started the day carrying on as before. We ambled along the roads, stopping to pick food in the fields as our fancy took us and to talk with people on the road or in fields whenever the opportunity arose. The end result was that we were making slow progress.

We realized that we had been lured into a false sense of security which our posi-tion did not warrant. The friendliness of the people we met and the benevolence of the weather had led us to put all worries aside. I felt well but I was still concerned about the nose bleeding of the previous day. We had seen no signs of Germans or Fascists since we left the camp although we knew that Italy must be crawling with them. These thoughts projected a rather different picture, for enemy troops constituted a real menace. It was now mid-September. The fine weather could not last forever and we did not know whether the locals would continue to show us the same generosity and goodwill. Having come to these depressing conclusions, we realized that there was not much alternative for us but to carry on as we had been doing.

There seemed no point worrying about all this, and we took to the road again with a philosophical acceptance of things. We were free, the sun was shining and we were not hungry, so we just got on with it. It was not long before our optimism, especially mine, received a sharp jolt, when my nose began to bleed again. This meant another delay whilst I tried to staunch the flow. The episode passed off without any protest from my companions, but after another hour or so of progress I fell victim to yet another attack. I was now decidedly worried about my health.

I knew that I could not continue losing blood so repeatedly without recourse to treatment. I also realized that no matter how patient and understanding my companions were, they would not be able to accept such inconvenience indefinitely.

About this time we had left the road and were heading along an ox-track which climbed steeply toward a saddle between two slightly higher hills. Perched at the highest point of the one on the left were the ruins of an ancient castle, which towered over a few houses. It looked a splendid sight, with the irregular creamy-white stone of the castle surrounded by tall black cypress trees, gleaming in the warm sunlight and framed by the intense blue of the sky.

Vineyards covered the entire hillside and our track cut a path through the middle of them. As we were about to start the ascent we came across a peasant working on his vines. He straightened up and greeted us with a wave. Recognizing us immediately as escaped prisoners, he asked if we were hungry. In spite of our protests he insisted that he was going up to the village to get us some food. He wanted one man to accompany him, so the Rhodesian set off up towards the village with him. We three others were left behind, and this gave me the chance to lie down and relax. After some time the two came into sight descending the hill, our companion loaded with food and a flask of wine.

We weighed up the hill confronting us and decided that rather than struggle up it with our added load of food we would settle down to lunch with our peasant friend and eat the food he had given us. We sat in the shade of a walnut tree on the edge of a vineyard. Despite the heat, we were comfortable and thoroughly enjoyed our picnic. It was noticeable that we were becoming used to the wine a little more now. The peasant told us that the name of the village was Cennina. This is the first village name which stuck in my mind. We thanked him for his kindness and wished him and the people of Cennina well. Then we started on the climb up towards the ridge ahead of us.

The climb was a real struggle in the heat of the day and there was much relief as we saw there was a level road crossing our path just below the summit. When we reached the road we sat on the grassy edge and rested. I was relieved that my nose had not bled after all the exertion. A man was sitting on a large stone at the roadside quite near us. He was a small fellow of about fifty with a wizened face, knobbly like some of the characters in Michelangelo's Sistine Chapel ceiling in the Vatican. His mouth was set in a toothless grin and above his trousers he was wearing a strange off-white roughly knitted vest. I was soon to learn that this was the home-made clothing of the peasants. The wool was from the few sheep every family owned, hand-spun by the girls and women of the family and then knitted, still in an unbleached state.

*

When we walked over to him he introduced himself as Ginestrino Becucci. He assumed we were prisoners and asked us if we would accompany him home, going on to say that most farms in the surrounding area had had escaped prisoners passing through and his family were chivvying him because he had brought none home. We asked him where his home was and he told us it was not far along the road, so we agreed to accompany him. As we walked along our ego took a mighty blow when he told us that what he really wanted was to take some black men home, but as he had not seen any, we would do. The second compound in Laterina camp had held a lot of black South African troops, so when the breakout came there were lots of black men dispersed around the countryside. The local people had never seen a black man before.

The trek along the road went on, rising all the time, with no sign of Ginestrino's home. We were tired and becoming impatient. He exhorted us to keep on because it was not far to go, but then he turned off the road on to a track that climbed gently and disappeared over a crest. We were on the point of refusing to go any further when he pointed to the top of a haystack ahead of us and announced that that was where he lived.

Sure enough, we reached the haystack in a few minutes, and a short distance behind it was a farmhouse. The name of the farm was Colli. When we arrived we were able to see that the family lived on the upper of the two floors and that the ground floor consisted of storerooms and stalls for the animals. Ginestrino had been telling us that he worked the land with his two oxen and that he had a few pigs and sheep. Access to the upper floor was by an outside set of stone steps alongside the front of the building.

The farmhouse was solidly built of weathered stone, with a pantiled roof. It looked as firm as a rock. At a rear corner of the house was the customary clump of towering black cypress trees. We were entering the Chianti hills and were higher up than at any other time in our walk. The ground surrounding the house was part of a rocky outcrop and was uneven and rather untidy. A short distance in front of the steps was an enormous manure heap.

From the front of the house a track led along a flat stretch of ground about 50yds wide to a rise a couple of hundred yards ahead. It formed a flat ridge, with the ground on each side falling away sharply into wooded hillsides. As the trees were quite tall, there was no panorama at all. This, together with the crest just beyond the end of the track ahead, meant that the farm was locked into its own enclosed patch of hilltop. At the edges of the track there were small areas of vineyard, rows of tomato plants and a vegetable patch. On each side of the ridge the sloping woodland was foraging ground for the pigs and sheep in their search for acorns, woodland mushrooms and truffles.

As we arrived there was no sign of Ginestrino's family, but as soon as he called people began to appear. The news that prisoners had arrived set them all buzzing, some hurrying down the steps and others appearing from ground floor storerooms. His wife, Rosa, was a tiny lady, a typical peasant farmer's wife. She was dressed in a black shawl and a long black skirt, with her head tightly bound in a black scarf. Her face was a mass of wrinkles and her voice was shrill. She was very shy, but she welcomed us warmly and her smile seemed to soften all the wrinkles. Then we met their seven children. The two eldest were girls: the aptly named Primetta (first born) of twenty-one and her sister Iolanda of eighteen. The younger children were all boys: Eduardo, Roberto, Enrico, Ricardo and Fortunato, from fourteen to six years old. My three companions had not been in the company of girls for many months, and, in my case it was almost two years, so there was quite a buzz amongst us.

Primetta had her mother's sharp, pointed features. Iolanda, her younger sister, was an attractive girl with long dark hair and a trim figure, which had not yet been marred by the rigours of life on a peasant farm. Her glory lay in her pretty face, her lovely eyes and her smile. I thought Byron might have had someone like her in mind when he wrote of Italian women in his poem 'Beppo', which summed Iolanda up to a tee!

> I like the women too, forgive my folly,
> From the rich peasant cheek of ruddy bronze,
> And large black eyes that flash on you a volley
> Of rays that say a thousand things at once.

They were all excited at meeting us. They asked our names and told us theirs and we were quickly being treated like members of the family. We were called to a spot near the corner of the house where there was a low wall on which we could sit. The wall was built around three vertical sides of a deep stone-lined pit. The fourth side of the pit was open and the ground became a long stone slope. The pit contained muddy water that was probably quite deep. We learned that it was the water supply for the animals. As there was no other source, the animals depended entirely upon it. The only supply to the pit was rainwater, so in time of drought the animals were in trouble. Poles made from chestnut saplings grown on the nearby wooded slopes had been formed into a pergola covering the pit. This pergola supported a vine heavy with countless bunches of the most luscious looking grapes. We were invited to taste them and they were the most flavoursome, sweet fruit imaginable.

I told Ginestrino of my nose-bleeding problem and he immediately said that we must stay at the house until I recovered. We did not know what accommodation was available, but the thought of sleeping in a proper house was beyond our wildest dreams. I had not done so since my embarkation leave three years earlier. Ginestrino and his wife went up to the house, leaving us with the seven youngsters. My three companions were beginning to pick up snatches of Italian and were able to make a stab at some conversation. This made them less dependent on me. For myself, my mother's little Hugo's dictionary was proving invaluable, and my vocabulary grew with every conversation.

The youngsters were all interested in the four strangers who had landed at their home and they were full of questions. It was strange that the questions were so similar to those I had been asked at our first village halt, and there seemed no end to them. Then the two girls began to sing. They both had very pleasant voices and went through quite a routine. Some of their songs were the slow, rhythmic melodies of the day and others were old Italian folk songs. Together, they all melted into magic moments.

It could hardly have been a more entrancing setting, sitting underneath the pergola alongside the farmhouse, superb ripe grapes above our heads and the sweet melodies of Italian songs on the cool late afternoon air. We sat watching a beautiful sunset, followed by a short twilight, and then the darkening sky began to twinkle with a myriad stars. It was difficult to concentrate our minds on war and the fact that we were hundreds of miles from friendly forces. It was easier just to accept the good things of today and think about tomorrow when it came.

So the singing and talking went on, but then the inevitable happened. They wanted us to sing a song in English. This brought forth four mumbled protestations of being unable to put any notes together at all. I was picked on and put under special pressure but I have always been unable to sing. I said I would have to take a great deal more wine before I could think of even trying. My refusal caused disappointment, but the reason was totally honest. Then we were called up to the house.

*

At the top of the steps we entered a very large kitchen, which was also the dining room. The floor was stone-flagged and along one wall was an enormous raised stone fireplace about 7ft by 5ft, and 15ins high, such that it formed a platform on which they built the fire to cook their meals. The fire consisted of a large heap of brushwood which was set alight and then reduced to a mass of embers. A small amount of embers was scraped away from the fire and an iron trivet would be placed over them, then a shallow earthenware dish was placed on the trivet for the meal to be left to cook very slowly. Above the fireplace a stone canopy projected from the wall. Below this a cauldron was hanging which could easily be swung over or away from the fire. A fire of smouldering embers was gently glowing.

The room was sparsely furnished. Near the fireplace was a long table of very heavy wood, with benches along each side. On the left wall was a cupboard-cum-chest of drawers, and against the wall facing me was a large chest, which proved to be storage for pasta and bread-making ingredients and implements. A couple of wooden chairs near the fireplace completed the furniture.

On the wall alongside the door were some brackets holding a couple of ancient looking shotguns and bags for cartridges. Some items of clothing hung alongside. An open door gave on to a storeroom and pantry. The other doors, which were closed, presumably led to bedrooms. Now that darkness had closed in, the room was poorly lit, with the only light coming from a couple of carbide lamps. These threw an intense incandescent light around the area of the lamp, but the rest of the room remained gloomy. This was my first introduction to Colli, but I was to get to know it so well as my home that it is imprinted on my memory.

Rosa, the wife, had been busy preparing a meal, and soon we sat down at the table. A large flask of wine appeared and everybody's glass was passed to Ginestrino for a liberal helping. He had produced this wine from his own grapes and, as it had been a good year, he was very proud of it. We complimented him on the quality and were soon calling for a second glass.

The meal started off with the dish we had been given by a family on our first day of freedom after leaving Laterina camp, '*minestra con fagioli*' (with beans), a sort of clear soup with bread and a few haricot beans. A couple of slices of bread were first placed in the bottom of a bowl and the liquid was then poured in, consisting of chicken, pigeon or rabbit stock, which was all the villagers had available, together with a few haricot beans, a little pasta of a very small type and a variety of herbs which added delightful flavours.

Then followed a dish of potatoes and what seemed to be spinach. The potatoes were nicely fried in a way quite different from normal chips. The spinach turned out to be turnip tops. Then we had thick rounds of toasted Tuscan bread liberally covered with tomatoes, olive oil and a sprinkling of salt. This was *bruschetta*, now a popular dish well known in England. It was a simple meal, but to the four of us it felt like a banquet. The family were obviously very poor peasants, but their willingness to share their food with four strangers was remarkable. Later a large bowl of walnuts appeared which we enjoyed, together with further refills of wine. It was a wonderful introduction to what a Tuscan peasant farmer's wife could produce with such simple ingredients.

Throughout the meal Ginestrino had kept us liberally supplied with wine, and the chatter was lively all round the table. The farm was fairly remote and it may well have been the first time the family had ever entertained guests, but they were enjoying themselves immensely. Ginestrino was mocking the Fascists, the *Carabinieri* and the Pope. He cackled uproariously at his own jokes. We four were all a little tipsy and the meal had developed into a really merry party. The girls began to entertain us with songs again and the request for an English song inevitably cropped up once more. We were still as insistent as before that none of us could put two notes together.

Then came a startling development. I hardly noticed Iolanda leaving her seat, but soon she was standing behind me and put her hands over my eyes. This surprised me. Then with her arms around my shoulders, she leaned down and whispered, 'Franco, sing an English song and then you can come to me tonight.' The suddenness and unexpectedness of this had the effect of making me choke on my wine, then dwell for a moment on the pleasures in store, while I rapidly scanned through my repertoire of Army songs. But such thoughts ceased abruptly when I thought of Ginestrino and the shotguns near the door. I glanced up to the head of the table and saw that, although he did not seem to have any precipitous action in mind, he had stopped telling jokes.

Meanwhile, my three companions were hacking me on the shins under the table and urging me to sing. 'Sing, you idiot, sing! Sing anything! Sing God Save the King!' The thought came that I had been invited to make this house my home until I was quite recovered from nose bleeds. So the prospect of being thrown out or worse was sufficient to convince me I should not sing. With a lingering touch of sadness, I assured Iolanda that I could not possibly sing until I had had much more wine. This we all proceeded to have, and when everybody finally left the table, all thought of Iolanda had disappeared. All I wanted to do was to fall into a bed and sleep.

*

There must have been some rearrangement of family sleeping accommodation, because we were led to a room with two beds which must normally have been for the family. There was no bathroom or toilet in the house, so we first had to go down the steps outside to relieve ourselves. Ginestrino and some of the boys accompanied us. We must have looked a strange bunch, all standing around in the moonlight. As there were no facilities for washing we had to put that aside until morning. Then we returned to our bedroom where I, being the only one with pyjamas, prepared myself properly, while the others took off their top clothes and we all collapsed into our beds, sleeping soundly till morning.

The following morning we woke early to the sounds of the family bustling around the house and of the animals below. So we dressed and went in search of washing facilities. We found a large zinc basin in one of the storerooms and filled it with water from the animals' drinking pit. With oxen, sheep and pigs all drinking from it, it did not do to think too much about the composition of the water. But that being the only supply, we just got on with it.

Once spruced up, it was time for breakfast. This proved to be a most informal affair, with everybody being served a bowl of coffee, and a heap of bread and a pile of grapes being placed upon the table. These grapes were from the vineyard and not the luscious table grapes from the pergola. The coffee was the same as we had been served in the prison camp. It was not made from coffee beans but was an ersatz preparation seemingly made from chestnuts, as that was all that was available to most Italians. The family dunked the bread in their coffee and, after a couple of rounds, just supped the coffee from their bowl, grabbed a few bunches of grapes and set off about their daily round. One thing we noticed was that although it was now well into September, the children were all present and there seemed to be no thought of school.

Soon we were alone at the table, so we too made our way down the steps. It was strange not to start walking as soon as we were up and dressed. Faced with a static day ahead we were at a loss as to what we should do with ourselves. Curiosity decided that we should explore the various features of the farmstead, so we started on the ground floor. There were quite a few doors and the first one we tried proved to be the pigsty. The stall was empty of pigs but the manure littering the floor made it evident what the place was used for. We learned that the responsibility for the pigs lay with the six-year-old Fortunato, who was already out in the woods with them and would stay out for most of the day. The pigs were given no food at the farm but relied on their daily visits to the woods. There were many scrub oak trees in the woods, small puny specimens, but they supplied sufficient acorns to feed the pigs. The sheep stall was in a similar state to that of the pigs. The sheep also thrived on a diet of acorns, and another of the boys was already out in the woods looking after them.

The stall for the oxen seemed to be in a poor state, with a strong stench permeating the place. When it had last been cleaned new straw will have been spread, but now it was a mess. The two oxen were magnificent animals, huge and pure white, with enormous horns. When they were not at work they remained in their stall, their urine and dung soon fouled the straw and then they were left to stand in it. There were two iron rings embedded in the wall to which the oxen were tethered. A manger which was filled with chopped straw every day was attached to the wall in front of each animal. On this day Ginestrino was already out at work with them. We decided to take on the job of cleaning the stall while we were at the farm. The hens were dealt with much more easily. They were closed in their house at night but released in the morning. They pecked away at scraps on the ground all around the farm. They laid their eggs all over the place, but the family always knew where to look for them.

That left only the farm's storeroom to visit. It was a surprisingly large room, full of dust and cobwebs. The room held a wide range of manual implements. There were spades, adzes, sickles, forks and a host of tools we did not recognize. The largest of all these implements was an iron, hand-operated machine for chopping up the straw for the oxen. Hooks on the wall were provided for the oxen's yoke and the leather straps that went with it. Alongside that were household articles such as the wooden frames used for holding bed warmers. At that time I did not recognize what the latter were for, but as winter came on I learned to appreciate them. Another interesting item was an iron for pressing clothes which was heated by placing burning embers in the metal tray in its base. There was also a considerable supply of provisions, such as sacks of flour and haricot beans and large terracotta jars of olive oil. The flour was of two types, wheat for making bread and pasta, and maize for making *polenta*, a thick, yellow, porridge-like dish.

Most of the morning passed in this inspection. On going up to the kitchen we found the girls busy with a mound of flour, preparing dough to make pasta. If eggs were plentiful, a few eggs would be mixed in with the flour. This was done on a large flat wooden board. After much kneading the dough formed an enormous ball and the rolling out began. The rolling pin was amazingly long, both arms having to be outstretched to use it. Once the work started it was surprising to see how quickly the ball of dough became a very large wafer-thin circle. When it had reached a satisfactory thinness it was very carefully rolled. The roll was then cut into slices and each slice unrolled and laid on the board to dry. In a remarkably short time we were looking at an appetizing supply of fresh *tagliatelle*. We complimented the girls on their handiwork. They then produced smaller quantities of ingredients and invited us to try. We were given a helping hand to start, but our efforts produced much laughter and we soon gave up.

After a quick lunch the girls surprised us by saying they proposed to dye all our outer clothes. They considered that the khaki we were wearing made it far too obvious that we were Allied soldiers. They proposed to go to Ambra, a large village about five miles away, to buy the dye. This they did that afternoon and returned with green, brown and black dyes for the job. The track to Ambra was all downhill but the return journey represented a long, tiring, unbroken climb for the girls. The task of dyeing did not start until the following morning, when we were asked for all our khaki clothing. We were told that we could confine ourselves to our room if we wished but that there was no objection to our moving about in vest and pants. We kept to the room at first, but the South African's freedom to go about in his green and white trousers overcame any self-consciousness on our part, so we were soon walking around without a care. The cauldron hanging above the fire was used for the task of dyeing, and clothes were soon being dropped into the various dyes.

The girls decided that my battledress was too big a job, so they just did my desert shirt and shorts and the khaki shirts I had received in parcels from my mother. Oddly enough, in spite of its size, they decided they would do my army overcoat. That was the only item dyed black. All our shirts were dyed green and our shorts brown. When they were taken out of the water they were laid outside on the ground to dry in the sun. It looked a very impressive job. When we eventually got them back we were delighted with the result. There was a certain oddness about the outcome, but at least it got away from the British Army look. My black overcoat in particular was a great success, although its new colour was eventually to become a cause of much inconvenience to me.

This emphasized how far the family were prepared to go to assist us. We had walked into their house and, without any hesitation, been given a room and beds. We never fathomed how much inconvenience was caused to the family or how they rearranged themselves. We had joined the table at mealtimes and shared the family's already meagre food supplies, and now came this spontaneous decision to dye our clothing. Their goodwill and concern for our wellbeing seemed endless.

Chapter 6

I Leave My Companions

The next day I was feeling really good again. I was delighted with my new colourful outfit, and the clothes did not seem to have suffered any shrinkage from their treatment. Even more encouraging was the fact that my nose had not bled for several days. This led to thoughts of moving on, because we were all four keen on making progress. We discussed it and decided that we should stay for that day, then tell Ginestrino in the evening that we felt it imperative we should resume our journey the following morning.

So we decided to make ourselves as useful as we could for the rest of the time we were there. One thing we were able to help with was carrying water for the house. The emergency rainwater pit alongside the house was used by the animals so that was no good to the family. All water for their own use had to be carried from a spring on the hillside. This meant a considerable effort, as it was a 50yd walk across open ground to the wooded hillside, then the same distance downhill through the trees to a spring. The path was steep and quite worn through daily usage, and the return journey required a formidable effort. At the spring a small pond had formed and it was filled with beautifully clear water. The water carriers were made of heavy brass, to a pleasing and practical design which was probably traditional. Carrying water in two of these was hard work, even when the weather was dry, but the steep path must have been most difficult in wet conditions. This was our first manual labour for some time and it was surprisingly taxing, but it was not too long before we had sufficient water at the house for all the washing, cooking and drinking for some days.

We had already decided to clean out the animals' stalls. This seemed to have been neglected for a long time and we felt that the animals, especially the oxen, would appreciate it. After swilling out the floor of their stall we laid a deep layer of straw all over the floor. It looked like a new place. We also used the straw chopping machine to provide food for the mangers. The animals could eat that but the straw laid on the floor was so quickly fouled that it was useless for anything else. The large manure heap outside the house which contained all the waste from the animals' stalls was meant to be contained inside a low wall. Over time it had spilled so much beyond the limits of the wall that it now reached quite near the steps of the house. It not only looked bad but it smelt pretty awful, so we set about containing it inside its original wall. The finished job, although it did not remove the smell, certainly improved the look of the place.

This routine of farm life that I was introduced to at Colli was quite new to me, but I was to learn much more of it at Colli and other farms during the coming months. Each of the different animals served its particular purpose on the farm. The pigs and rabbits were a source of food for the family, and there was cheese from the sheep's milk. The poultry produced a regular supply of eggs and an occasional chicken for the table. The oxen performed the heavy work of the farm, both ploughing and pulling the ox-cart every day.

So we spent the whole day throwing ourselves into any jobs we could find. By the end of it we felt we had contributed a fair effort towards improving the place. We decided to explain our departure plans to Ginestrino at dinner. As it happened, he invited us to come and sit around the water pit with its vine-laden pergola. He produced some wine and invited us to take a bunch of grapes each. We were once again treated to some lovely Italian singing. Fortunately, this time we were not pressed to contribute ourselves. Everybody was chatting away and it was a happy enjoyable evening. It was just as idyllic a setting as it had been some evenings earlier, but this occasion was even more cordial because by then we all knew each other so much better.

*

When we felt the moment was right to announce our decision to resume our progress, it was left to me to introduce the subject. The company with us consisted of Ginestrino and the children, Rosa being up in the kitchen preparing dinner. They had obviously not been contemplating our departure, and their immediate reaction was one of total shock. Then came floods of protest from everybody. The two girls began to weep and Fortunato ran into the house to his mother. We realized how much our stay meant to them. We had been accepted as part of the family. It was an emotional moment when this was suddenly brought home to us, and we had to swallow hard ourselves. Soon it was time to go up to dinner. When we entered the kitchen, we found that Rosa was also in tears.

By the time dinner started the mood had calmed and we were able to explain that we had no alternative but to keep going as hard as possible to try to reach the Allied lines. They accepted this, and gradually the talk around the table became light-hearted again. Rosa had prepared two rabbits for dinner and they were the basis of a scrumptious meal. Ginestrino played his part by being extremely liberal with the Chianti. There were some half-hearted attempts to persuade us to stay longer, but our departure now seemed to be accepted by everyone. So again there was a lot of happy chat to accompany the excellent food and liberal supply of wine. The children did not drink the wine neat, instead taking it watered down. They called it 'aquarello' ('little water'). I found it a better daytime thirst-quencher than wine on its own.

When the meal was finished Ginestrino thought everybody should give toasts to us and to the family. *Vinsanto* was produced, and this time everybody joined in. They said how much they had enjoyed our stay and they wished us well for our journey. We then took the opportunity to express our gratitude for their having offered us their home, shared their food and done so many other things, including dyeing our clothes. The chatting through the meal had gone on for a long time, but it was still not particularly late. However, darkness came early, and early to bed was custom for the family. So we took ourselves to our room with a little carbide lamp and were soon sleeping like tops, as we had done every night.

Staying at Colli, in just a few days we had seen life as it may well have been lived for hundreds of years. They were isolated from the world and were almost entirely dependent on their own primitive efforts. They produced almost everything they ate and made a lot of their clothing. They made occasional trips to the village of Ambra, but most of the family would go long periods without seeing another soul. Although most of the children were of school age, there was no sign of any schooling. Sometime later, there was an awkward occasion when I learned, much to their embarrassment and my own, that no one in the family could read.

When we presented ourselves the following morning, the family were already busy about their tasks. Ginestrino was away with his oxen and some of the boys out with their animals, but young Fortunato had not gone with the pigs. Rosa, Primetta and Iolanda were busy about the house. After breakfast I asked for a basin to take down to one of the stalls to wash and shave. I had done this every morning, first of all going down to the spring to carry the water. This particular morning Iolanda asked me what I used to shave myself. I showed her my safety razor, shaving brush and a stick of shaving soap. To my surprise, she asked if she could shave me. My three companions thought this a great idea, and their roars of approval meant that I had no chance to refuse Iolanda this time.

The operation took place in the kitchen, with the spectators crowding eagerly round us. I showed Iolanda how to first wet my face with the brush before applying the shaving soap. Then, as she began to use the brush and the lather appeared, there were gasps of surprise from the family. The only soap available to them was in the form of hard cakes that produced hardly any lather. Iolanda was all over the place with the brush and as the snow-white mass began to obliterate my face it was all summed up by little Fortunato saying, '*Ma guarda, che saponaccia*' ('Look, what an enormous lather'). They had never seen anything like it. I was lucky that my razor was a safety type, as I would have been concerned if she had been wielding an open cut-throat. When the operation was over, my face was wiped and I had survived with only one or two minor nicks. I was relieved with the result, and Iolanda was congratulated all round.

By the time we had all cleaned ourselves up and I had packed my bits and pieces it was near lunchtime, so we agreed that we should stay for a bite to eat. Ginestrino and the rest of the family had come back to the farm in anticipation of our departure. It was very emotional and demonstrated how they had all grown very fond of us and were desperately sorry that we were leaving. We were realizing just how good it had been to share in the family atmosphere. It brought home to me how much I had missed life with my own family for the last four years, after being mobilized in September 1939 and spending twelve months in camps in England, followed by two years' active service and then fifteen months in captivity. So we were not really looking forward to filling our water bottles and striking out again into the wide blue yonder.

During the meal Ginestrino left the table and went outside. A moment later he called me to join him. I wondered what could be in store. When I joined him at the top of the steps he put an arm around me and said he wanted to give me some advice. He went on to sum up our progress as foolish and likely to end in disaster. He predicted that although we had been fortunate up to now we were bound to run into trouble sooner or later. The other three chaps were all much bigger than I was, and he felt that it would be the small chap who would take the brunt of any trouble. I was very touched but did not agree that I was more at risk than the others. Then he came to the point and asked me would I let the other three carry on and I could stay on with his family. This took me by surprise. I gave it some thought but soon realized I did not have any choice but to carry on in the hope of reaching real freedom.

I told him how deeply I appreciated his suggestion but that progress was imperative and I must leave with the others. I thanked him for the hospitality the family had shown and for the chance to recover from my nose-bleeding problem, that now seemed to be resolved. He was sorry but accepted this, and we rejoined the family. The meal finished and we prepared to move off. At this point the family became quite emotional. Rosa, who had not seemed to stop working since our arrival, was tearful, and it was not long before Primetta and Iolanda were alongside her in an equally tearful state. The boys were less sentimental and just wanted to embrace us in farewell. Ginestrino was not tearful but was clearly much affected and hugged me long and hard. Then, looking resplendent in our newly coloured clothes, we set off.

As we walked along the straight stretch of Ginestrino's land in front of the farm we periodically looked back and waved to the family, who remained in front of the farm steps. Eventually we reached the short rise at the end of the track and on the crest we took our last look back. The farm was still clear but we were now too far away to pick out any features of the family. My heart was heavy as we moved on and, just for that moment, I did not have much enthusiasm for whatever might lie ahead.

*

We soon found that we were now entering an entirely different type of countryside. When we had met Ginestrino and walked with him towards his farm, the ground had risen a lot. Now we found that just a couple of hundred yards from the farm we were on the summit and that his farm was a little higher than most of the surrounding hills. Before us was a lovely panorama of wooded hilltops. There was not much difference in the height of any of them. A couple of hilltop villages could be seen some miles ahead but there was no sign of any other dwellings. We guessed that if we headed down to one of the valleys, we would be able to thread our way through them in a general westerly direction.

Soon we spotted a track leading downwards through the woods. The track descended sharply and we soon emerged into the sunlight in a pleasant valley. There was not much sign of any agriculture, except for one or two patches of maize. Our view of the valley stretched for some way and we could now see that our estimate of its direction had been wrong. It stretched not westwards but towards the south. This did not upset us too much as it was just as important to progress southwards as it was to head west towards the coast.

A river ran gently along the valley and our path followed it. We passed a number of smaller lateral valleys coming down from the hills on our right to join our major valley. Each of these brought down a small tributary to join our river, but it still seemed quite a minor stream. The late afternoon was still warm and it was so pleasant in the valley that we decided to make our camp there. The edge of the steep wooded slope on our left came down to within a few yards of the far side of the stream, and our side was covered with lush, soft and bone-dry grass. It looked a comfortable bed space and we decided it should be our camp area for the night. We were assured of all the water we wanted and would be able to wash and clean ourselves.

There were a few small trees dotted along our bank of the stream, so we decided we would sleep around one of them. I suggested we should discuss our food position. We were still carrying some of my Red Cross parcel food and I questioned whether it was worth doing so any longer. It had dwindled to a quite small amount and no longer formed any practical emergency supply. We had consistently found that the local people were willing to give us bread, salami, cheese and a bottle of wine, so we would not have gone hungry even if I had not had my Red Cross food. The outcome was that we decided to have a good meal that evening and finish the rest of the stock for breakfast before setting off for the day. Ginestrino had given us a loaf and some cheese and we munched that while sitting on the grass discussing our menus. A short distance ahead of us we saw that there was a very large bank of brambles, and inspection showed it to be full of the largest, most succulent blackberries. Needless to say, we sampled them on the spot. Later we made a small fire, heated tins of soup and bacon and dined really well on those and other titbits.

The evening was idyllic, calm and warm with the gentlest of breezes. The sky slowly darkened through an ever changing range of shades and, as it did so, a myriad stars grew brighter. We chatted until we were all ready for sleep and then we prepared to bed down. As it was still warm I thought I would fold my overcoat for a pillow instead of draping it over me, even if I decided to change during the night. I said goodnight and put my head on the overcoat. At that moment the bottom seemed to fall out of my world. I realized my nose was bleeding copiously. All thoughts of sleep disappeared and I set about stopping the flow. Eventually I lay down again, this time with a heavy heart, and I knew there and then that I was not going to set off with my companions in the morning. In spite of my disappointment I drifted into a deep sleep.

*

As I woke I could hear voices and thought my companions were up and about or at least talking to each other. Then I realized the voices were speaking Italian. This realization brought me fully awake in an instant. It was not yet dawn but a faint pre-dawn light was creeping into the sky. I first focussed on the leaves of the tree under which I was sleeping and which were silhouetted against the faint glow in the sky. Then I turned my glance a little and was sickened to see the dark figure of a man standing near me and looking down at me, with a gun crooked under his arm so it was pointing down at me.

A couple of the man's companions were standing some yards away and I thought I could see that they too were armed. My escape from the camp at Borgo San Lorenzo had lasted about a week, and now I could see myself being marched back through the gates of Laterina camp after the same miserably short period. It then struck me that, with a gun at my head, the gates of Laterina were probably the best I could hope for. This was all flashing through my mind in seconds, and then he spoke, asking me in Italian who I was. I could think of no credible alternative on the spur of the moment to admitting that I was an English prisoner escaped from Laterina, so I did that.

He called over to his companions to tell them this and then, looking down at me, asked why we were sleeping on a river bank instead of going to a farm. This anticlimax was almost too much. I had lain there thinking that at best I faced returning to captivity or at worst that I might be shot. I did not answer his question but plucked up courage and asked him who he was. I did not know whether to laugh or cry when he told me they were from a village on the hill immediately above us and were out for a morning's rabbit shooting. The gun pointing at my head, and which in the faint light of dawn I had taken to be a rifle, turned out to be a shotgun.

The conversation was waking my companions now and they were obviously as alarmed as I had been, but I allayed their fears at once. The hunters then said they must be off. They advised us to find a farm, where we would certainly be given sleeping space, rather than sleeping rough. They wished us luck and disappeared along the track. It had been an uncomfortable experience, and I put my head on my pillow again and waited for daylight.

Once daylight arrived we roused ourselves and got ready for the day ahead. Washing was no problem as the stream was at our feet. There was no sign of my problem, but I confirmed to the others that I was going no further for the time being. I had decided that I would find my way back to Colli and take up Ginestrino's offer. I also confirmed that we would polish off the remainder of my Red Cross food for breakfast. After that it would be a case of beg, borrow or steal, although the local people were looking after us so well that we had never faced any great problems.

Before we started on the food supplies we walked along to the blackberry bushes and once again gorged on them. While we were standing in a line along the bushes just eating the berries we had an unexpected encounter with another former inmate from Laterina camp. He was a chap named Harris, who had been one of the most tiresome and boring men of the 2,000 men in the camp. He was known to all by the nick-name 'Meatroll'. This came about because one of the items in many of the Red Cross parcels was a tin of meat roll made by Harris, a Wiltshire company specializing in meat products. With food being one of the most frequent topics of conversation in the camp, these items were constantly being discussed, and so the title seemed a natural for Harris.

When Harris approached, we greeted him and asked how he was faring. He told us that he had been on the go since escaping from his working party and had walked a considerable distance. He went on to say that he was heading for a place that everyone had been recommending and which must now be very close. He said the place was called 'Bosco' and asked if we had any idea how far he still had to go. At this I had to work hard to suppress a smile, as the word *bosco* simply means 'woodland'. So the people had merely been telling him to stay in the woods for safety. We also told him he was heading back towards Laterina. He was not at all perturbed by this and wished us good luck as he went plodding along the track waving goodbye. We never saw him again, and I wonder how he fared.

It was now time to go, and I stuck to my decision to leave the party and go no further with them. I was very worried about my health and, with no doctor to advise me, felt I had no choice. A bond had grown between the four of us as we had shared the sweat and toil in the tunnel for three weeks and then travelled together since leaving Laterina, and I was filled with emotion as I wished them good luck. This time the farewell carried a much deeper feeling, which came out of shared experiences and perils. I watched them go round the bend past the blackberry bushes and, with a final wave, they disappeared out of sight. I never learned what happened to them.

*

I felt so very alone and hoped I would soon be able to find my way back to Colli. My best course seemed to be to get out of the valley, so I waded across the stream to the start of the wood to begin climbing. I walked back along the edge of the trees and came across a path which seemed to head up into the wood. This tempted me, and I started to climb. At first the going was quite easy and I made reasonable progress as I pushed my way up the hill. Then it gradually became more difficult and I found my path had run out. I had made a lot of progress, however, and thought I might even be near the top. Rather than go all the way back down, I decided to carry on in the hope that I would succeed in reaching the top or strike another path. The trees had now become thick woodland. There were many small scrub oaks and a large number of sweet chestnut saplings. I learned later that they would be harvested at about ten years old and used as props to support the vines. It was a pity a lot of them had not been harvested just prior to my brush with them.

Progress through the wood was extremely difficult and the climb was beginning to tell on me. It was very hard going pushing between the trees with my army haversack over my shoulder and my overcoat hooked around the haversack. Inside the wood it was very hot, and perspiration was dripping from me as if from a tap. A couple of times I just flopped down to rest and take a swig from my water bottle. It was frustrating that although the trees were not very tall I was not able to see where my position was in relation to the top of the hill. I had been going so long that I knew I must be nearer the top than the bottom, and there was now no choice now but to keep heading on upwards.

Then suddenly all changed when I came across a track leading upwards. I sat down for a while to recover my strength and get my breath back. The track was on a gentle slope, not at all as steep as the climb I had tackled, and I thought how foolish I had been to start on such a flimsy path. This new track was wide enough for an ox-cart and the ground was firm. So when I was ready, I set off up it. Soon afterwards I heard children's voices ahead and stopped to consider the position. I had no intention of going back to the valley and wild horses would not have dragged me back into the wood, so the only way was along the track.

I set off again, going cautiously, and soon came across a group of four or five girls who were standing around a spring at the side of the track. With them was an elderly white-haired man. They had come to draw water from the spring, so I guessed I must be somewhere near a village. They fell silent as I approached

and eyed me with curiosity. I must have looked a strange sight after my struggle through the wood and I was shy and embarrassed about speaking to them.
So I kept on walking slowly and, as I passed, I muttered '*Buon giorno*'. The man
answered my greeting, but I felt their eyes burning into me. Soon I came to a minor
track on the left and, as I knew Colli lay somewhere in that direction, I headed that
way. The trees began to thin out and soon, to my relief, I came to flat open ground.

There was a wire fence bounding the wood and I leaned gratefully against a
fence post for a while. Then I froze. From a clump of trees some way beyond the
fence a man was walking towards me. He was wearing a black cap, a black shirt and
black trousers. My heart sank as I thought of the struggle up that hill only to have
the bad luck to walk into a Blackshirt, one of Mussolini's Fascists, at the top. I was
too tired to think of running anywhere and I let him approach me. As he reached
me he asked, 'È inglese Lei?' ('Are you English?'). I admitted I was.

His next words came as a total surprise. It was almost too much of a shock for
me when he asked if I was looking for a bed for the night. I told him I did not know
where I was sleeping and he invited me to come with him. He introduced himself
as Lello. So I climbed the fence and we set off. I could see that we were very near a
village to the right. I learned that evening that this village was Montebenichi. I was
pleased when Lello and I headed to the left and were travelling in the direction in
which I guessed Colli lay, which could not be too far away. Lello told me he had a
friend, Vittorio Sbardellati, whose home was not far ahead and who would be able
to look after me.

We were walking on a track that stretched along the top of a wide ridge. After
about fifteen minutes, a house came into view. It was a farm, Poggialto ('High
Hill'), set in truly attractive countryside. The wooded ground to the south fell
away sharply, giving way to an attractive view of rows of wooded hills fading into
the distance to the south. Occasional hills had a village perched on high and gleaming in the late afternoon sun. The ground climbed a little higher as we approached
the house. It proved to be a semi-detached farmhouse with a family living in the
left-hand half and Lello's friend, Vittorio, occupying the right.

As we arrived, Lello called up to the house and Vittorio emerged. He was a slim,
wiry fellow, a little older than myself. Lello explained that he had brought me along
to see if Vittorio could offer me a bed. This took Vittorio by surprise and he was
obviously frightened. Although he thought it was much too dangerous to have me
sleeping in the house, he was happy to feed me and find me a place to sleep outside.
He knew that if any Germans on a prisoner hunt found me in the house he would
probably be shot. This contrasted somewhat with Ginestrino's total disregard for
danger, but his fear was entirely understandable and I felt I could not blame him.

Soon afterwards Lello left, but I thought how very fortunate meeting him had
proved to be. Vittorio took me inside and left me to wash and clean myself up

whilst he prepared some food. I was hungry and ready to enjoy whatever was produced. I was not disappointed. Vittorio prepared a mixture of fried potatoes and
fried tomatoes, both vegetables well cooked in olive oil, sprinkled with salt and
fresh herbs, the pan having first been rubbed with garlic. The result was quite
mouth-watering and I relished it enormously.

When I had finished, Vittorio said he would show me where I could sleep. Some
little way in front of the farm the ground dipped into a terraced vineyard. On the
first terrace down, a stone lean-to construction had been built against the retaining
wall and seemed to be a wood store. It was about 8ft by 5ft and projected upwards
to a pantile roof some feet above ground level. On one side of it there was an access
space that measured not much more than 5ft long by 2ft high. Inside, brushwood
had been stored. As it was my only offer, I decided to try it. After some contor-
tions, although I filled the whole space, I was inside and could lie comfortably.
Even though it was day, no light could enter and it was very dark. It seemed like
getting into a coffin, but the brushwood was dry, soft and yielding and I knew it
would be comfortable. So I crawled out and told Vittorio it would do fine.

Vittorio told me he was walking into the village to hear the news from
Radio London and asked me if I wanted to join him. The village proved to be
Montebenichi, about a mile away. We set off on a beautiful still evening, with dusk
falling as we approached the village. It was my first visit to a Tuscan hilltop village,
and I found it quite stunning. As we reached the start of the village, the lower
piazza, we turned into a narrow curving road, which after 100yds brought us to
the upper piazza. Night was now falling. There were no streetlights, but even so I
could see how attractive a central piazza in such a village could be. I wished I could
have seen it in daylight. At the start of the piazza the village wine shop was on our
right, and we went in. It was a small place and formed the evening meeting place
for the men of the village. It seemed as though most of them must be crammed
inside it.

Standing alongside the bar a number of men were engaged in animated conversation and sipping wine, whilst on the floor of the shop men were seated, four at a
table, playing cards. I learned that the game was called *Briscola*. It appeared to be
a simple form of whist, at which cheating took place as a matter of course. It was
played with great gusto, cards being smacked down on the table with resounding
bangs. When a game was won there was much excitement and the shopkeeper,
Signor Barucci, made his way to the table carrying a large sweet jar. This held
sugared almonds, of which he dished out a small number to all four players, the triumphant winners chortling delightedly while the losers paid a couple of centavos.

Most people in the shop were puffing away at the fiercely strong *Nazionale* and
Esportazione cigarettes, which I have mentioned before. The heavy fog of tobacco
smoke filled the room and made my eyes smart. Vittorio had passed the word that

I was an escaped prisoner and everybody was friendly. Whenever anybody saw me without a glass of wine one was at once passed to me, and I was also given small packets of biscuits. It was the first time in a very long time that I had been in such convivial company and I was thoroughly enjoying it. This went on until somebody called out that it was news time.

The radio was not in the village shop so everybody at once began to move out. I was just carried along with the crowd. Once outside, we all headed across the narrow lane and through a doorway in a long wall. After passing through a small anteroom I found myself in a huge barn-like space, quite empty apart from a table with a radio on it. I learned that such a place was present in all villages and was known as the *Dopolavoro*, literally 'The Afterwork', equivalent to the English working men's club. It seemed to be a relic of Fascist days but appeared now to serve no purpose other than to give the villagers the opportunity to do some clandestine listening to the news from Radio London. Listening to what was officially considered enemy propaganda was a punishable offence, but none of the villagers seemed unduly concerned about that.

The radio in the *Dopolavoro* was the only one permitted in the village and hence it was the place where all the men congregated to hear the London broadcast. The only other place in which it was possible to listen to a radio was in a priest's house. In Montebenichi the church was half a mile down the road into the valley.

Once inside the *Dopolavoro* I was ushered to the radio, and soon everyone was pressing in around me. The set was switched on just before the broadcast was about to start. The lead-in to the programme was a repeated Morse code letter V, three dots and a dash, 'BomBomBomBooom', sending out the message V for Victory. This brought a surge of excitement to the Italians and they began to chant, parrot fashion, 'Breeteesh Brrroadcasting Corrporassion'. They lapsed into silence when a resonant announcement came: '*Qui Londra. Parla Mario Verdi*' ('This is London. Mario Verdi speaking'). The news which followed proved to be an hourly cycle of four fifteen-minute broadcasts in Italian, English, French and German.

The Italian broadcast was listened to by the assembly. Immediately it was over they all turned to me insisting that I listen carefully to the English text and then pass on the information to them. They reckoned their Italian version was just propaganda but now that they had the chance to learn the English version they would get a true picture. Needless to say, there was not a scrap of difference between the two. They were surprised to hear from me that the broadcasts seemed to be identical, but they took my word for it.

I was enjoying the hubbub all around me and being the centre of attention of such a crowd, but suddenly I was filled with a sense of alarm and foreboding. I was hemmed in and unable to move. I began to worry about whether I could trust these people. How did I know that a message had not already been sent to the Fascists or

Germans that there was a prisoner in the village and that I would once again feel the uncomfortable prod of rifles in my stomach? As these thoughts filled my mind there was a momentary break in the crush and an attractive young girl pushed through, holding a saucer of peanuts. She smiled and offered me the peanuts, saying, '*Per te, Franco*'('For you, Franco'). This simple act of friendship somehow reassured me that I was among friends and that I need have no fear of betrayal. The girl was Giuliana Giovannini, later to become a lifelong friend.

Once the news was over there was a period of discussion of what they had heard, and then there was a drift towards the door and everybody made off to their home in the village or to one of the outlying farms. Vittorio and I set off up the hill. With the warm autumn weather still holding, it was a very pleasant walk to his farm. Earlier in the day, when I had said goodbye to my companions, I had been worried about how I would fare alone. Now I felt much more at ease and relaxed about my future prospects.

On reaching the farm Vittorio invited me up to wash and clean my teeth, so I spent a little time up there. Then came the time to say goodnight. Vittorio offered me a pillow and I went down the steps contemplating my strange bed. I levered myself through the opening and stretched out. The brushwood made a comfortable mattress and, with the pillow for my head, thinking I had slept on much worse beds than this, I was soon fast sleep.

Chapter 7

Pietraviva

The following morning I woke early and wasted no time in scrambling out of the wood store. At the farm Vittorio was already busying himself about the house but immediately prepared a breakfast of bread, grapes and a bowl of coffee. It followed the pattern of breakfast at Colli, dunking the bread in the coffee. I asked Vittorio if he could take me back to Colli, the home of Ginestrino. He told me it was only a couple of miles away and that he could do that. However, he had an alternative suggestion. He took me just a short distance from the farm to the edge of the hillside, from where the view to the south was quite stunning. Below us lay the Ambra valley and beyond a succession of low hills, mostly wooded, with sunlit villages gleaming on some of the hilltops and the distant horizon lost in a morning haze. The object of Vittorio's interest was not towards the horizon, however, but right below us in the Ambra valley.

This being Sunday, Vittorio was visiting his girlfriend, Lina, at a farm in the valley. He told me that near the farm there were six escaped prisoners living in a vineyard. He invited me to go down with him and meet them, and I immediately agreed. So we set off, passing through Montebenichi and turning down into the valley. Our walk turned out to be just over two miles, using steep cross-country tracks, but Vittorio told me it would be more than six miles using the road. So after passing the vineyards surrounding the village we left the road and took a path leading downhill through dense, low-growing shrubs. We passed a farm, Montesoni, where we were invited in for a glass of wine. As we carried on, eventually the ground levelled out at the valley bottom and we were again passing through vineyards.

Soon Vittorio indicated that we were almost there. Ahead of us I saw a very small shack on the edge of a vineyard beside the track. It would normally have been used by workers in the vineyard to take a break from the sun. It was just about 4ft high and 6ft square, hardly worthy even of the name of shack, and consisted of a frame of very thin chestnut saplings, the walls being made from a thin curtain of reed. The end we were approaching was open. Inside I could see three fellows lying alongside each other and occupying the whole floor. They were fast asleep, and I asked where the other three were. They proved to be lying in the shadow on the ground behind the shack, just as fast asleep as the three inside.

We waited for a while and soon one of them stirred. I learned his name was Roy Page and that he had served with the Tank Corps. We were to become very good friends, spending the rest of the war together and returning to England together nearly two years later. On finding they had company, he roused his companions. All six were suffering from hangovers from the previous evening, when they had been invited to dinner at the mill in the nearby village, Pietraviva. The miller's wife had served a very good meal and the miller had been particularly liberal with the wine. He was a staunch Anglophile, since he had been rescued by a British warship after his warship had been sunk in the Mediterranean during the First World War. He hated the Germans and was always semi-intoxicated, claiming he was going to stay that way until the Allied forces liberated the area.

Vittorio told the six that I was a friend who was seeking company, and I introduced myself and asked what was the prospect of my joining their group. Vittorio then left to meet his girlfriend. The group were now awake and went into a huddle. To my surprise, I realized that they were cautious and suspected that I might be a German plant. They had all come from a party of fifty prisoners in a working camp at the Villa La Selva, two miles down the hill from Montebenichi. They had not met any prisoners travelling from outside the area and they did not trust me.

However, they had originally come from Laterina camp themselves, and I was able to convince them that I really was an escapee from there. Even so, I found that I was still not in the clear, because they then went into a huddle to decide whether or not seven fellows in the same group would be an unwieldy number. What eventually decided them in my favour was that it was obvious I spoke much better Italian than any of them, so they thought my presence would be useful.

It was now about lunchtime and, being Sunday, nobody was working in the fields or vineyards. We had a clear view from the vineyard for about half a mile, and a strange sight began to manifest itself. Small family groups began appearing, coming from isolated farmhouses and from the village of Pietraviva, which was about half a mile away. The group of six had been living at this little shack since they had broken out of their working party. The whole countryside knew this, and people had been bringing them food whenever they could. Weekend visits to the shack were becoming family outings, and it was strange to see a number of groups converging on the shack at the same time.

The whole afternoon was devoted to receiving visitors and accepting the food they brought. There was soon much more food than we could eat in many days, but nobody seemed to mind this. A few families brought billycans of fresh warm pasta to be eaten there and then. Besides that there was bread, *pecorino* cheese, salami and sausages, as well as grapes, figs and peaches. Wine was plentiful also, all made by the families bringing it and all nominally Chianti. The standard varied wildly because some of the peasants had been less fortunate than others in the quality of their vintage the previous year. Nevertheless, it was all given with good heart and we were sure that we could cope with a plentiful supply of wine. All these gifts were piled around the shack because we had no storage space at all.

One thing which the afternoon accomplished was to convince the group that I was worth my place with them. The chat was continuous and, because my Italian was now approaching a reasonable fluency, a lot of it centred on me. One small incident demonstrated the value of the Hugo's pocket dictionary I had received from my mother. In answer to a question an Italian had replied '*Punto*'. I did not know the word and when I asked the meaning it was made obvious that it meant 'none at all'. I pulled my dictionary from my pocket to look the word up, but the Italian dismissed it, saying, 'It won't be there, it's just a little dialect word.' I carried on, found that the word was included, and one of the meanings given was 'none at all'. They gave the dictionary full marks for this, and they considered me a promising student of Italian.

As evening came on we sat chatting, swapping stories of what had happened since they left Laterina some months before me. Their working party at Villa La Selva, half way up the hill to Montebenichi, had been engaged in developing a new vineyard. They had been able to break out of camp when the sentries absconded on hearing of the Armistice. They said that one of the prisoners, named 'Titch' Wells, of the Essex Regiment, had become friendly with the daughter of the peasant farmer attached to the villa and had stayed on in the farmhouse. Titch and I had become friends while we were at Laterina, until he left for the work camp some months previously.

I told them of my time at Borgo San Lorenzo and my unsuccessful attempt at escape, followed by my return to Laterina and the tunnel job, my second escape and the travels which had landed me that day at their shack. This satisfied everybody. So there was no further suspicion of me and I was welcomed into the group. As the evening drew on we lapsed into nostalgia and reminiscing, fortified with a plentiful supply of wine. Settling down to sleep that night seemed strange. I had slept under various unusual conditions since leaving Laterina, but this night seemed the strangest of all.

The shack was capable of holding three in some discomfort, and the rest had the choice of stretching out on the track or lying between the rows of vines in the vineyard. I took my turn lying between the vines. There were no nearby trees to lie under so the ceiling was starlit. This did not seem to worry anybody, so I fell in with them, and deep sleep came easily. It was strange to wake in the morning, covered by my greatcoat, and be able to reach up for a bunch of grapes.

The fine weather seemed unending, and we awoke early to a bright sun shining from a clear blue sky. The washing point was a couple of hundred yards away, up the hill immediately to our north. A tiny brook tumbled down the hillside and at one point it fell a couple of feet over rocks and formed a small pool before running a short distance across the valley to the nearby River Ambra. It was ideal for our ablutions, and we went up in ones or twos for our wash and swill down. The pool was a lovely spot which offered complete privacy. The low banks of the brook and the hillside were covered with low-growing brushwood plants, including heather and potentilla.

In those early days of freedom I still had Red Cross parcel soap so I could always enjoy a wash down. One strange thing about this little pool was that it was the first place I ever saw fresh water crabs. They looked exactly the same as their seashore cousins, were quite small and posed no problem at all. They were always in evidence on our arrival but disappeared as soon as feet started to splash about in the pool.

At lunchtime a few of us decided to walk down to the farm, Poggigiobbi, which was on the roadside half a mile down our vineyard track, at the point where the track met the main road through the valley. It was built on a small knoll and surrounded by large broadleaf trees, not the usual cypresses. Like so many others, the farm building was semi-detached. Up one flight of steps lived a chap named Felice. He had been well named, *felice* meaning 'happy', because he was always cheerful, with a broad smile across his face and a twinkle in his eye.

The other half was the home of the Meliciani family, in whose vineyard we were sleeping. There were three brothers, Anselmo and Guiseppe, known as Beppe, a third whose name I cannot remember, and two sisters, Gina and Maria. The other chaps knew them well so they invited us up the steps and I was introduced. We were immediately given a glass of wine and invited to share lunch with them. Anselmo showed me around the farm, where I saw once again an array of very primitive but nonetheless serviceable farm implements. He was very proud of his two oxen, and there was the usual stock of pigs, sheep and rabbits. The barn was a large stone building, as solid as the house. One wall of the barn was festooned with corncobs from which the husks had been removed. Hundreds of them were suspended on a system of cords and were quite closely strung so that, as they ripened, the wall glowed like a golden curtain.

*

I found I was not settling in with the group and was beginning to regret that I had not asked Vittorio to guide me back to the farm at Colli. It was a rather dull life sitting around the shack idly talking and waiting for people to bring us food. These feelings were shared by two of the others, who announced they were going to set off south in the hope of reaching the Allied lines. I weighed them up but decided they were not companions I would want to share such a journey with. I had now suffered two let-downs, one prior to an escape and the other the day after escaping.

I did not want to suffer another, so I was wary about choosing companions and did not suggest that I might join them. We all wished them well, and they set off. We heard no more of them, but I hope they made it.

The following day two girls arrived from Montebenichi carrying a variety of foods and some flasks of wine to present to us. They had not come by road but by the tortuous track down the long steep hillside which Vittorio and I had used, and then up and over a smaller hill past the farm at Montesoni, carrying their burden more than two miles. They were Onelia Pieraccini and Corrada Landi, both eighteen years old, and they had heard about the group of prisoners near Pietraviva. They chatted with us for a while and before returning home said that they would appreciate having the flasks back when they were empty, as they were hard to replace. This was one of the most sincere and moving examples of assistance I had met, because carrying that weight so far on a difficult track needed a great effort.

A day or so later word came from the mill at Pietraviva that if any of us wanted to go for dinner we were welcome, so we accepted. The group already knew that it was the miller's instructions that, for fear of us being seen by Germans or Fascists, we should never arrive at the mill in daylight. So it was dusk when we got there. It was my first meeting with the miller and, sure enough, his voice was slurred as I had been told it would be. We were soon informed that the meal was ready, and I was introduced to his wife and family. Their daughter was Serafina, and she had a friend, Argentina. There was also a young boy called Arcangelo. The other fellows told me that they had successfully taught him to sing 'You Are My Sunshine' in English.

We enjoyed the evening very much, not least because the miller lived up to his reputation of being liberal with the wine. He led the way, but he saw that our glasses were regularly charged. Arcangelo then gave his rendition of 'You Are My Sunshine', which came over clearly and without much hesitation. As it ended, we all joined in with an enthusiastic encore.

When it came time to leave none of us were very steady on our feet. We had a little more than a mile to go, first along the road to the farm at Poggigiobbi and then along the track to our little shack. When I woke the following morning I had a hangover. I was one of the three sleeping inside the shack and I could recall nothing of having arrived back the night before. As I got up I saw that I had only one sock on and I wondered where the other could be. In the tiny shack there were not many places to look and I soon realized that I had lost one. I did not worry because I had a number of other pairs.

However, worse was to come, because when I went to put my boots on they, like my sock, were nowhere to be found. This was serious. It was a bleak prospect to think of a future without my good, friendly, solid Army boots. I was more dejected than I could remember, wondering if I would ever find them again. Then things became even more bizarre. I thought I might as well get rid of the single sock I was wearing, but in taking it off I found that the missing one was underneath and that I was wearing both socks on the same foot. This set me off wondering what on earth I had been up to the night before.

I had little heart for breakfast and sat glumly outside the shack. Towards the end of the morning we saw an ox-cart trundling up the track towards us, with Gina and Maria, the girls from the Poggigiobbi farm, walking behind. As they drew along-side us they burst out laughing and triumphantly held up a pair of Army boots. Nothing could have given me more relief than seeing them being waved at us, and I walked over in my bare feet and accepted them gratefully. I asked where they had found them and this turned out to be half way up the flight of stone steps to their farmhouse. So I must have left the road at Poggigiobbi, called at their farmhouse and gone up the steps, where for some reason I had taken my boots off and then walked along the track to our shack in the family's vineyard. I have never been good at walking barefoot, but I must have managed it for those few hundred yards the previous evening.

Chapter 8

My Introduction to Montebenichi

The incident of the boots confirmed my feeling that I did not want to throw my lot in permanently with the group at the shack in the Meliciani vineyard. A morning or so later I decided to take the now empty wine flasks up to Montebenichi. I asked if anybody wanted to walk up there with me. Only one fellow, Frank Biddis, who I think was from the Green Howards regiment, said that he fancied a walk. He had now been on the loose for about six weeks, but in spite of having much contact with Italians he had not picked up a single word of the language. Moreover, he showed no sign of wanting to. He was not the companion I would have chosen for the visit. Nevertheless, we picked up the empty flasks and set off. We decided not to use the road, which was a much longer route, but to try to find the track on which Vittorio had brought me down and which the two girls had used in bringing us the food and wine.

Once on the crest we soon spotted the Montesoni farm, with the much higher hill crowned by Montebenichi in the background. It seemed uncanny the way the country people always knew when somebody was approaching their home. Sure enough, as we approached the farm, the family were at the door and we were invited to take the inevitable glass of wine. They remembered me, and this time the call was '*Franco, un bicchierino*' ('Franco, a little glass'). The wine proved to be of good quality and we enjoyed our short stay.

Soon after, we crossed a narrow valley and began to climb. Considering how wild and remote the place was, the path was surprisingly well worn and we had no difficulty finding the way. As we approached the village we carried on through the terraces of vineyards and olive groves. It had been a strenuous ascent and we were quite out of breath when we climbed on to a track sloping up alongside the village. At that point we reached the lower piazza of the village. A high retaining wall ran along one edge of the piazza, forming the southern limit of the village. At the far side of the piazza the track became a tarmac road, still flanking the retaining wall and leading down towards the main road that ran along the valley of the River Ambra, known locally as the Valdambra.

The western side of the square comprised only one building, a towering, castellated fortress. A plaque on its wall recorded it as the Palazzo Stendardi, generally known as *Il Castello* (the Castle), one-time home of Gregorio Stendardi, known as Goro of Montebenichi, a mercenary Captain of Arms. In spite of the wall plaque, the piazza is known by the villagers as Piazza Capitano Goro.

The north side of the piazza was dominated by the enormous bastion of the houses of the upper village. The only breaks in this towering mass were a number of small windows belonging to houses that faced on to the upper piazza. A short flight of steps led to a tiny chapel built alongside the base of the bastion. The east side of the piazza held the gable end of the home of Valentino Giovannini, the father of Giuliana, the girl who had welcomed me in the *Dopolavoro* when I had been concerned about my safety. The Giovannini house was the large building at the end of the long, curving conglomerate of houses which faced on to Piazza Capitano Goro. Built in the sixteenth century, the house had belonged to the Medici family. It is not known whether it was ever used by the Medici, but it is believed that it was a hunting lodge kept by them for use by their friends and guests.

From the north-west corner of the piazza a narrow lane led uphill to village homes. From the north-east corner a lane with houses on the right hand side curved round for 100yds to the fan-shaped upper piazza, known as the Piazza Gorizia. The straight side formed the magnificent and beautiful façade of a tall, centuries-old castellated building from the Renaissance period. Known as *Il Castelletto* (the little castle), it was occupied by the *fattore*, the estate manager of the local wine producer and merchant. That family lived on the Villa Giusterna estate, a quarter of a mile outside the village. The *Castelletto* had been sacked in battle a couple of times but had been restored to its former glory in about 1900.

Facing the *Castelletto* was a continuous arc of three-storey houses in which many families lived. Flights of stone steps with wrought iron railings led up to the front doors, with a little balcony outside each front door. Colourful displays of flowers decorated the steps and balconies. In one corner of the piazza there was a most attractive well, formed by a circular wall supporting two columns with a lych-gate type roof on top and a hoisting device for the bucket. Bathed in both warm, bright sunlight and deep shadow, the scene was a spectacular display of *chiaroscuro*.

*

As we entered the village, Frank Biddis and I made our way to the upper piazza, passing the *Dopolavoro*, the working men's club, on my left and the wine shop on my right. I remembered them from my first visit with Vittorio. On that occasion, quite late in the evening, I had not been able to appreciate the beauty of the piazza in front of me, but this time I was able to take in all its superb features. What added the final touch was that now there were a number of villagers dotted about the piazza. Women were standing talking or busying themselves outside their front doors, and we saw two or three men entering or leaving their homes.

By now I was confident meeting strangers and, after just a moment's hesitation, we approached the nearest women. Recognizing me from the evening in the village with Vittorio, a few of them came over and greeted me with '*Buon giorno, Franco, benvenuto*' ('welcome'). I knew then I was among good friends, as I had been when standing in a crowd listening to Radio London and Giuliana Giovannini had offered me some peanuts.

When the villagers saw the empty wine flasks in our hands they assumed that we had come for refills. However, I explained that we were returning them and that we were looking for two girls named Onelia and Corrada. It turned out that neither family lived in this upper piazza. One lady offered to act as guide to Onelia's home, which was the nearer and part of another great mass of dwellings. When Onelia was called and came to the front door, her face broke into a broad smile of pleasure on seeing us standing there holding her wine flasks. She invited us into the house and immediately sent someone to call Corrada.

We entered a very small room. The largest feature was the enormous stone fireplace, on which a heap of brushwood embers was glowing. A small table with a few chairs and a small glass-fronted display cabinet mounted on a wall filled much of the rest of the space. The cabinet was an ever-present item in the peasant houses, and tucked into the edge of the glass panels there were always faded photographs of family groups and deceased members of the family. Framed on the walls were certificates of military service, together with the campaign medals awarded to the person concerned. In this case it was Onelia's father, who had served in the First World War.

Another thing common to the living room walls in all these homes was a light coloured patch on the smoke-darkened wall. Until the Armistice six weeks earlier, this patch had held a portrait of Mussolini. Its presence had previously been *de rigueur* in all homes, and its absence would have been taken as indicative of anti-Fascist sentiments. As soon as Mussolini fell from power, the portraits had been consigned to the fire.

Onelia introduced us to her parents and we were immediately offered a glass of *vinsanto*. Her father was the village blacksmith, a short, stooped, man of very stocky build. Like so many Italian men in the villages, he seemed to wear his trilby hat all the time, both in and out of doors. Her mother reminded me of Rosa, Ginestrino's wife. Signora Pieraccini was short and hunched. She was dressed entirely in black, with a black scarf wrapped tightly around her head. Her face was a mass of wrinkles and her voice a loud cackle which always seemed to have a humorous note to it. Onelia's father seldom spoke and when he did, it was usually just a series of incomprehensible grunts. Her mother, however, kept up an incessant flow of questions and wanted to know all about us. I never learned her name and always addressed her as '*Signora*'.

Corrada soon arrived and was delighted to see us. In fact, I think the two girls were as pleased to have their wine flasks back as they were to see us.

In villages in wartime Italy such things must have been at a premium. We were immediately installed at the table and offered some *minestra* from a dish which was sitting above the embers on the large raised fireplace. We accepted and were served a glass of wine and some bread with the *minestra*, which was seasoned as nicely as that at the Colli farmhouse. Onelia's young brother, Giancarlo, then came in to be introduced to us. He was just five, a very late addition to the family, and was a most pleasant youngster. We learned that an elder brother, Enrico, was with the Italian army and had been posted missing on the Russian front. There was also a sister, Maura, who had suffered from meningitis and needed constant care.

Corrada was keen to introduce us to her family, so as soon as we had eaten we left together with the two girls for Corrada's home. The house was in the lower part of the village and adjoined the end of the Palazzo Stendardi, but it had none of the faded splendour of that building. There were two doors alongside each other, one being the family entrance and the other a stall for the family's two oxen. Inside the house a flight of stairs led to the living quarters. When we entered we found ourselves in a truly enormous room. Not only was the floor space large, but the ceiling seemed incredibly high, as though there was a floor missing above us. There was the usual high stone fireplace and a table with a long bench on either side. A variety of chests and cupboards lined the walls of the room. Once again, there was the usual military certificate with a photograph and medals, and a light patch on the wall marking Mussolini's absence.

Two tiny windows let in such a small amount of daylight that the carbide lamps were in constant use; even then, only the area of the fireplace and table received any illumination at all, the rest of the room remaining in gloom. I found these scenes reminiscent of Dutch old master paintings.

The only family members at home when we arrived were Corrada's parents. A fire was glowing against the wall at the back of the raised fireplace. The couple were sitting perched on stools, one either side of the fire. The fireplace seemed even bigger than most we had seen, with comfortable room for a stool on either side. Corrada's parents seemed the oldest, most wrinkled couple I had ever seen in my life. Her father was leaning forward, propped up by a stick, wearing an old suit. There seemed to be nothing inside the suit except skin and bones. As was the local fashion, he was wearing his hat. His wife sat sphinx-like on the other side of the fire. She was in the usual long black dress and tight black headscarf. They seemed to be in a world of their own and neither said a word. When we were introduced to them no word was passed but there seemed to be a sign of acknowledgement in the old chap's eyes as he raised his head. I did not in any way feel offended by their silence and was grateful that he raised no objection to our being guests in his home.

Corrada had two older brothers. The first, Corrado, arrived soon after us. He was a slight, wiry character, a little older than us, with curly black hair and a constant smile on his face. He was very friendly and I took to him at once. His elder brother, Guido, with his wife Lisa, arrived soon afterwards. Guido was a very different chap, short like Corrado but very stocky, with his straight black hair plastered down. He was a more serious fellow but equally friendly. Lisa, although still young, was dressed all in black in the fashion of the older women.

It became obvious that Onelia's and Corrada's families were not impressed with my companion, Frank Biddis, who had remained silent since our arrival in the village. On leaving the camp at Laterina I soon discovered that the Italians did not mind how badly you spoke their language as long as you had a go. Even sign language was considered an acceptable attempt. They had no time, however, for anyone who remained silent and made no attempt to communicate. Frank Biddis fell into that category, and the villagers soon lost interest in him. As we were both named Frank, initially there was a problem, but the Italian language is well versed in sorting out such problems. I was the smaller of the two so took the diminutive form of the name, Franchino (Little Frank), whilst my companion became Francone (Big Frank).

After chatting around the table for a time, Corrada asked us if we would like to see around the village. The day was now cooling and we said we would like that very much. Although a small village, it was full of interest. Almost every house seemed centuries old; a few were detached but the majority were in two or three ancient massive rambling complexes of a very attractive and pleasing style. As we passed around the edge of the village, the views in all directions were spectacular. The most impressive was to the south, where in clear weather, between rows of rolling hills, the towers of Siena cathedral and the Torre di Mangia could be clearly seen, about thirteen miles away as the crow flies.

In one or two corners of the village, in the shade of trees, women were now sitting in little groups at tables outside their homes. They were passing the time chatting whilst they engaged in knitting or embroidery. Young girls were setting off armed with brass water carriers. They carried a short wooden yoke across one shoulder with the carriers suspended, one at the front and one at the back. Watching girls returning with the loaded carriers, we saw that this was no light task. I recognized some of them as those who I had seen near a spring when I passed near Montebenichi while struggling up the hill some days earlier. I asked why the water had to be drawn from a spring below the village when there was a well in the upper piazza. It turned out that the well water was no longer drinkable.

While we were walking around, a number of people recognized me from my previous visit and welcomed me very warmly. Signor Barucci of the wine shop saw me and invited us in. This time the shop was almost empty, with just a couple of men taking an aperitif. It was inevitable that we should be asked to join in so we had a glass with them. We also visited one or two other homes, one belonging to the Francini family, the father and son being charcoal burners.

*

Frank Biddis and I were tired now and were thinking it was time we made tracks to rejoin our group down at the vineyard. However, Onelia and Corrada insisted that we could not possibly walk back to Pietraviva that evening. Dusk was coming on and they maintained that the only thing to do was to have dinner and then stay the night at Montebenichi. We thought this over and felt it was sensible. At least we would have a roof above us instead of lying down between rows of vines. We would in any case have had to take the much longer route by road, because we could not risk losing our way in the dark on the steep, narrow tracks we had used that morning. Walking was the only way we could travel, because nobody in the village had a motor vehicle of any type whatever.

When we asked where we could sleep, the girls said that they already had that worked out. Corrada's family owned a small stone shack only a couple of hundred yards from the village and we could sleep there. It was too dangerous for the villagers to risk our being caught sleeping in a home in the village, and it was courageous of them even to offer us this shack. There was always the danger of somebody acting as a spy and alerting Germans to the presence of escaped prisoners, and this would most likely have led to villagers losing their lives.

We walked down to the shack to see what it was like and, having inspected it, thought it promised a comfortable night's sleep. It was an unusual building. From the direction we approached it, the shack appeared to be a single-storey stone building with a pantile roof. However, the ground dropped away so steeply that at the rear the building was two storeys high. There was no door, and entry was through an aperture in the front wall, about a yard square, a couple of feet above the ground. There was a purpose-made piece of timber that could be placed against the aperture to act as a door. The floor inside was covered with a good depth of straw, and that formed our bed. In the wall opposite the entrance aperture there was a tiny window about 1ft square. Like the entrance, this window was an open aperture without glass, but it served the purpose of letting in a faint glimmer of light when the entrance was blocked.

Below this small window there was a door on the lower storey. This part of the building served as a hen house, with the hens having freedom to come and go. This set-up offered Frank and me the prospect of cockerels crowing at all sorts of unsociable hours. Such thoughts did not dismay us, however, and we readily took up the girls' offer. That settled, Corrada told us we were having dinner with her family and we made our way back into the village.

Onelia went off home, and in the Landi house the whole family were present, so we were eight at table. The parents ate in silence but the rest of the family were all interested in us so there was plenty of chat during the meal and time passed pleasantly. I was learning much of the etiquette of the village. This time I was chided for leaving chicken bones on my plate instead of dropping them to the floor for the dog.

Then towards the end of the meal Corrada broached the subject of our future, with a suggestion that took us by surprise. I had told Corrada and Onelia of how, together with three companions, I had been trying to make my way south but that I had repeatedly suffered severe nose-bleeds and I had been forced to drop out of the venture. Corrada and Onelia told us that they had talked the matter over and discussed it with some other villagers. They were proposing that until the Allied troops arrived Frank and I should stay in the Landi family shack and that Onelia and Corrada would arrange our food supply.

We took this up immediately as an excellent suggestion. We had a promise of a place to sleep and a regular supply of food, so we put our trust in the villagers of Montebenichi. We had met with nothing but friendliness from everybody in the village. Most importantly, it gave me the opportunity to break away from the lifestyle of the group at the Meliciani vineyard, which was exactly what I had been looking for. Just one or two reliable companions seemed the optimum number, and the prospect of being based here in Montebenichi, where everyone had been so very welcoming, was infinitely more attractive to me. Frank Biddis was not the companion with whom I would have chosen to share such a venture, but by that stage there was little I could do to change things.

We told Corrada we were very grateful and would like to put ourselves in the hands of the villagers. She was delighted and said that all would be made final the next morning. As soon as the meal finished, the two brothers walked down to the barn with us and saw us comfortably installed. I did not have my pyjamas and neither of us had our toilet gear, so we just had to leave thoughts of washing until the next day. The straw proved a comfortable mattress and we had a good night's rest. The hens down below wakened us early, but their cackling and crowing seemed a comforting, friendly noise rather than a nuisance. We did not know whether we should go into the village, but before long Corrada and Onelia appeared. They had brought a little food and showed us the list of families who would be looking after our food for the next few days. As soon as we had breakfasted we told them we would go down to Pietraviva to collect our belongings and would return to the shack soon.

So we set off down the track, with which I was now becoming quite familiar. On reaching the little shack in the vineyard we told the remaining three fellows of the previous day's developments and our decision to return to Montebenichi.

They were surprised at the news but wished us well. It convinced them that they must look for a more permanent and secure arrangement for themselves. They had some wine and, after we had drunk a toast to each other, we picked up our kit and set off up the hill. At the little pool in the brook we stopped and had a thorough swill down to clean ourselves up.

When we arrived at the shack the settling-in procedure was just a little edgy as we were not quite sure what to do. There was nobody there, and we had been warned not to visit the village in daylight. So we sat on the ground outside the shack. It was not long before we were rewarded with the sight of a couple of people starting down the track from the village. They introduced themselves as Girolamo and Ida Pieraccini, cousins of Onelia. They turned out to be a lovely couple, who had a very likeable five-year-old boy, Giorgio, a cousin of Giancarlo. They were first on the list of families to feed us. In the afternoon a number of people came down from the village to meet us, and we were made to feel that we were amongst good friends whom we could trust.

What I had thought would be a one night stop-over in Montebenichi now looked like turning into a longer period of shelter in the village until the Allied troops arrived. My nasal bleeding had not bothered me since the time when I left my three original companions. However, I was concerned that if I started on another long trek there could be a repeat. I had been very fortunate to find this current offer of shelter. To embark on another long trip into the unknown might prove to be catastrophic. Almost everyone I had met since leaving Laterina believed that within a month or so we would be freed by Allied troops, so I decided that for the time being I should stay in Montebenichi and its neighbouring villages, looked after and sheltered by the villagers.

Chapter 9

Village Life

Frank Biddis and I soon settled in at the Landi family's shack, which was to be our home. I was relaxed now that I had somewhere to stay, Onelia's and Corrada's food plan was working well and we had been told which families would be supplying us for the next week. So the future looked rosy. The meals were usually warm pasta with a little wine for our lunch and something like bread and cheese, salami and a little fruit, either grapes or figs, to eat in the evening. The village was a poor and primitive community, and it was humbling to think that people who had such meagre resources would take on the task purely out of the goodness of their hearts.

There were no normal shopping facilities at all in the village. The only store was the village wine shop, and there one could buy a few minor items like soap, matches, razor blades and shoe polish. I never had any money, but the villagers kept me supplied with these things. There were no butchers, grocers, greengrocers or bakers. In all those commodities the villagers had to be totally self-sufficient. The only alternative was to travel to Ambra, the larger village about five miles away, but nobody in the village owned a vehicle of any sort.

Every family kept a few pigs, chickens, rabbits and pigeons, and most families also had three or four sheep. The sheep were not raised for food but for the wool that they provided at an annual shearing and which was used for a great part of the family's clothing. The women and girls had to spin the wool and knit all the socks and underwear as well as the woolly hats to be worn in winter. The one food that the sheep did provide was milk, which was made into cheese. This cheese, *pecorino*, was formed in small circular blocks. It was always aged for many months and was consequently quite hard, but the flavour was excellent.

Some families had access to a plot of land outside the village and were able to produce a small crop of wheat or maize. When harvested this could be taken to be ground at the mill at Pietraviva. The wheat flour supplied all their needs for bread and pasta, and the maize flour produced *polenta*. I found the thick porridge-like *polenta* rather lacking in flavour. Families without any land just had to buy their flour. Beans, turnips, and pumpkins were amongst the other vegetables that they grew. Even the leaves of turnips were cooked, like spinach.

Most families owned a small area of vineyard and were able to produce enough wine to supply their needs for the year. The communal wine-press for the village was built into the base of the castle, and families took turns at putting their grapes through the press. As soon as the juice started to flow, a saucerful was taken and tested for sugar content. As the result became known there was either great joy or dejection from the waiting family, because this indicated the quality of their wine for the coming year. Those unfortunate families who had a poor vintage knew they faced a year of drinking rather unpalatable vinegar-like wine that had no sale value either.

Another crop to which some families had access was chestnuts. Montebenichi lies at the end of a road some four miles up from the valley floor, at the highest point of the hill on which it stands. Beyond the village an ox-track led along the ridge of a hill into the countryside. Various tracks branched off this main route and led down through wooded hillsides to remote farmhouses. In the woods along-side the tracks many mature sweet chestnut trees grew in groups of two or three. Chestnuts were a valuable crop and each family owned two or three trees. Harvest time was late October, and families helped each other out with the harvest. A num-ber of large white sheets were spread on the ground around the tree trunk. Then ladders were placed to allow the men and boys, armed with long lengths of bam-boo-like cane, to climb into the foliage high in the tree, where they flailed the branches around them. The ripe chestnuts were easily dislodged and fell into the sheets, whereupon they were gathered up.

A lot of the land on the hillsides had been developed as olive groves, which produced a considerable crop. This harvest took place in December, and again the families helped each other out. The system of gathering the fruit was the same as that used for chestnuts, although with olives the task was much easier as the trees were so much smaller.

The only form of transport in the village was ox-carts. These were all very old and appeared to be everlasting. Made of wood and iron, they were very heavy and cumbersome but, being squat and low-sided, could carry a considerable load. A central shaft accommodated two white oxen, one on each side. The oxen were often tortured by the myriad flies that constantly buzzed about their eyes. A device to keep these swarms away from the animals' faces and eyes was a length of cord attached to each side of the harness headband. Attached along each length of cord were nine or ten pieces of bright red leather. As the animal swung its head from side to side the waving leather strips kept the flies from settling. The animals were a magnificent sight as they ploughed the fields, the farmer following, managing his very primitive plough. The pure white of the animals was enhanced by the waving of the vivid red fly swats.

A task which occupied many families on dark winter evenings was the weaving of a whole range of baskets and trugs. These included large, very shallow, oval bas-kets used for spreading out grapes, tomatoes, figs or similar fruit to dry in the sun.

They were made from osiers, the thin twigs sprouting from willow trees. Baskets of all shapes and sizes were made for general use or for the various harvests. Working at them in the dim light of carbide lamps was a particularly arduous task.

Another country craft in the village was charcoal burning, done by Franco Francini and his son, Tonino. I used to spend days in the woods helping Franco and Tonino build the kiln and, days later, exposing the glistening charcoal. Franco's wife was a plump and pleasant lady. There were also two daughters, Iolanda of about eighteen and Tosca, who was about sixteen and undoubtedly the prettiest girl in the village.

Another woodland task carried out periodically was brushwood clearing. Teams of three or four men passed through all the woodland in the countryside cutting the brush. Once cut it was tied into sheaves and built into haystack shapes, and the teams then moved on elsewhere. This was a vital item for the kitchen. Masses of it were ignited on the large raised fireplaces, and the heaps of glowing embers it produced were one of the secrets of Tuscan cooking.

The village church, Santa Maria in Altaserra, the former name of Montebenichi, lay half a mile out of the village down the road towards the Ambra valley. It was a very old church, the site being mentioned in the early eighth century, and its jurisdiction in the Middle Ages stretched over a large number of surrounding villages. A travertine sarcophagus of the third century was discovered on the site and is displayed in a local museum.

The church played an important part in village life. Almost all the villagers attended Mass regularly on Sundays. Early every Sunday morning the church bells called people to prayer, and a stream of villagers was to be seen walking down to the church, all dressed in their Sunday best. The church bells themselves played quite a big part in village life, and the clear air seemed to carry their peal far and wide around the countryside. Devoted though most people were, they were still able to poke fun at the church.

On one occasion when the church bell rang for the Angelus at midday in San Vincente, a neighbouring village across the valley, I remarked to a villager, 'Twelve o'clock already.'

The reply was, 'No, Franco, it's just to tell the priest his lunch is ready.'

One thing which caused discontent among the families living in the outlying farms around the village was the crop-sharing system, known as the *mezzadria*. The owner of a farmhouse and land was an absentee landlord, who paid all the taxes and looked after the upkeep of the buildings. The tenant farmer and his family lived on the farm, working the land and tending the crops throughout the year. At harvest time, the landowner and the farmer took equal parts of the various crops. To avoid dishonesty, the timing of the start of the *vendemmia*, the grape harvest, was governed by local government decree. Large posters were displayed in all villages to announce the decree giving the date before which grapes should not be gathered. Farmers who might have been tempted to cheat the landlord and remove part of the crop from the vines early tended to comply. They either respected the decree or were frightened of the consequences of ignoring it.

In spite of the many difficulties that made for a hard life, the villagers seemed to accept their lot with grace and just got on with things. Their main dislike was of the Fascist authorities, who had maintained the harsh way of life that the peasants endured. Following the Armistice of September 1943, most Fascists seemed to have tried to disguise their former connections with the party. Generally, people seemed to avoid discussion about the Fascist Party, with just occasional brief references which made clear their dislike.

Whilst being sheltered by the villagers of Montebenichi and the neighbouring villages of the Ambra valley, or Valdambra, it struck me just what a different world I had entered. It was as if Montebenichi, sitting perched on its hilltop, was quite unaware that the passing of time had left it behind. I was to find that this was reflected in most villages of the Valdambra. Life did not seem to have changed from what it must have been like several centuries earlier. It was a poor and primitive community. There was no electricity or gas supply, so there was no refrigeration, and the only form of lighting was oil lamps or incandescent carbide lamps. Nor was there any piped water or flush toilets. The water from the picturesque well in the upper piazza was no longer drinkable, and all water for washing, drinking and cooking had to be carried from springs on the wooded slopes surrounding the village.

By no means all the villagers were agricultural workers. The leading personality in the village was Valentino Giovannini, who owned much land and lived in the house that had at one time belonged to the Medici family. Valentino's brother, Cesare, living in a large detached house that had been in the family for centuries, was equally well off but was handicapped by having suffered from meningitis in his infancy. A man named Piccardi and his family lived in the Castelletto, with its magnificent and attractive castellated facade of the Renaissance period. Piccardi was the *fattore*, the estate manager for the local wine producer, who lived a little way outside the village.

Others included Signor Barucci, who managed the village wine shop, Onelia's father, Signor Pieraccini, the village blacksmith, Dante Carnasciale, who looked after the roads, Lello Capanelli, the builder, Tomaso, who was the carpenter, and Franco Francini and his son Tonino, who produced charcoal in the local woods. There were yet more I do not remember, but all in all it all made for a self-sufficient community where people looked after each other.

*

Frank Biddis and I received a message from Valentino Giovannini that he wanted to see us. Valentino, a tall, very commanding figure, was very friendly when we entered his home. We exchanged greetings and he introduced his family. We met his wife, Guiseppina, a calm matronly lady who for many years had been the village school mistress. Giuliana, aged sixteen, was there and also her younger sister, Maria Pia, aged fourteen.

The room which we entered was extremely large. It had a stone-flagged floor and six doors leading from it, each one framed in sculpted stonework. I think the stone used was grey travertine. There was a mahogany wardrobe with intricate relief carvings of fruits and foliage down both sides and a Medici heraldic shield at the head of each corner. There were also two finely crafted, slender-stemmed brass oil lamps from the Medici days, complete with all their hanging attachments. On another wall was a plaque bearing Valentino's three hunting guns, and above it was mounted the huge head of a wild boar. Valentino was a keen hunter and had two dogs, a setter called Kiss and a black hound named Jack.

Along the centre of the room was a table large enough to accommodate all the family and a good number of guests. Other items included a traditional wooden chest for storing all the equipment used in the preparation of pasta, bread and *polenta*. In many homes today these chests are treasured items that have been in the family for generations.

The most prominent feature of the room was the fireplace. It was large and fitted with the usual array of equipment: trivets, cauldron, bellows, a multitude of fire irons and the ratchet-geared mechanism for swinging the cauldron over or away from the fire. The glory of this fireplace lay in its canopy, sculpted in the same unpolished grey stone as the doorframes. Projecting from the wall significantly higher than head height, it curved down for about two feet. Half way along the front of the canopy, still in the same stonework, there was a huge heraldic shield depicting the six Medici balls. The whole thing appeared to be carved from one enormous block of stone, with not the faintest trace of a joint showing, although that may just have reflected the skill of the Renaissance craftsmen.

One of the doorways led out to a delightfully picturesque terrace, from which there was a stupendous view of the rows of wooded hills of Tuscany south of Chianti, stretching away, one after another, until they faded into a misty horizon. The terrace was bounded on two sides by a low wall, and at the junction of the walls a delicate wrought iron hoist could lower a bucket about 20ft to a well below. The source of water had long since disappeared, but the wrought iron hoist was still an attractive and decorative feature. Showing us around and explaining everything, Valentino was clearly proud of the history of the house and its ownership by the Medici family. In the room with Valentino it was as if I could feel the very essence of Tuscany around me.

Once the inspection was over, Valentino sat in his armchair and became rather more serious. He started by questioning us a little about ourselves. It was all done in a friendly manner, and then he led on to our presence in the village. He stressed that the entire village was pleased to offer us shelter and care, but said we must remember that our very presence put the lives of the villagers at risk. If we should be captured in the village, or working in the fields with villagers, retribution from the Germans would most likely be dire and lives would be lost. We must not be seen in the village in daylight or observed joining in work in the fields.

I gave a lot of thought to Valentino. There must undoubtedly have been a Fascist presence in Montebenichi, and with Valentino being the most authoritative and imposing person there, it was hard to imagine that he would not have been its commanding figure. I do not think any such commander could have been tolerant but, to be fair to Valentino, none of the villagers spoke badly of him. In fact, none of them ever made any reference to Fascists at all. On the other hand, throughout my stay, I never saw him mixing with other villagers. There was one genteel elderly lady named Rosa who, every time she met me and Frank, gave the warning, '*State attenti, ragazzi, a questi squadristi*' ('Be alert, boys, to these Fascists'). Those instances were the only references to Fascism that I can remember.

Valentino told us that on the day the prisoners had escaped from the working party at the Villa La Selva down the road, many of them had come up to Montebenichi straight away. He had spoken to three of them and offered to shelter and look after them, provided they would accept certain conditions. A shack had been built in a secluded spot unlikely to be found by the Germans, and he arranged for them to be fed every day. They had agreed to stay in the immediate vicinity of the shack and not wander around the countryside.

Valentino asked us to accompany him to visit the three the following day. We agreed, and together with Valentino, Giuliana and Maria Pia we set off down the hill on the north side of Montebenichi, the same hill that I had climbed after leaving my three original companions. This time Valentino used a path. Even though it was narrow, winding and tortuous it was passable, and we were soon down on the valley floor.

The shack had been built just inside an area of woodland, using chestnut saplings and brushwood. It looked comfortable and rainproof and contained three bunks. There was a small stream running nearby, thus ensuring a supply of fresh water. It was the same stream that I had slept alongside on the night the rabbit hunters had wakened me.

Valentino introduced me to the three prisoners. They were two brothers, Tom and Ken Bowers, and Norwen Davis, all from a Nottingham TA Anti-Aircraft Regiment. As we chatted, it became obvious to me why Valentino had asked me to visit their shack. He produced two pieces of paper from his pocket, one with a note written in Italian and the other blank, handed them to me and asked me to write a translation of the Italian. The note stated that he, Valentino, had undertaken to shelter the men and see to their welfare until Allied troops arrived. Valentino had arranged for the shack to be built and was now sending food to the men every day. I wrote out the translation and Valentino got the three to sign it.

As the most prominent man in Montebenichi, Valentino would have realized that the Allies or the partisans would on arrival be examining the record of any prominent Fascists, looking for evidence of atrocities. This signed note could be his passport to clemency at their hands. It must be emphasized, however, that I was only assuming that he had been a leading Fascist; none of the villagers had spoken badly of him.

The incident left me thinking about what I should do myself. The position of the three men down in the valley seemed to me to be akin to another form of imprisonment. I had Ginestrino Becucci back at Colli farmhouse to fall back on. He had pleaded with me to stay with his family, and I knew that I would always be welcome there. And there was the mill at Pietraviva, where the miller was a great Anglophile and where I had dined a couple of times. I also knew from my wanderings that most people in the countryside were well disposed to escaped prisoners. I was aware that there were four or five other villages in the Valdambra. This led me to think that if I stayed in circulation around these villages, nobody would know exactly where I was at any one moment.

*

First of all, though, I wanted to cement my position in Montebenichi, so I decided to stay in the Landi shack for a while. I soon got to know pretty well everyone in the village, and I found them all to be very friendly. There were no young men in the village, since they were all away with the Italian forces, or in hiding, or they had been rounded up like escaped prisoners and taken to Germany for forced labour. There were a few boys up to around fourteen years old, but many more girls than boys.

On occasions I spent the day in the woods with a boy of about fourteen, Enzo Capanelli, whose aim was to capture small songbirds to supplement the family's meat supply. When he found a place he liked we would clear the undergrowth from around the base of a tree and then make a hide nearby from fallen branches. He had a bundle of twigs soaked in sticky pine tar and wrapped in a rabbit skin, and with a small machete he made five or six slashes down one side of the chosen tree and repeated that on the other side. A gummed twig was then slipped into each slash.

We then took cover in the hide and Enzo produced a stuffed rabbit skin with two chickpeas stuck on it as eyes. This was tied to a stick and poked through the branches of the hide to suggest a perched owl, which small birds like to mob. The final piece of equipment was a small disc whistle, which Enzo could put inside his mouth and use to imitate birdsong. When an unfortunate bird was enticed in to settle on a pine-tarred twig it panicked, and once its wings touched the pine tar it fell to the ground. Enzo was then out like a shot and despatched it at once. Although this seems abhorrent now, it was not wanton hunting but provided the family with a meal when there might not have been anything else. It was certainly a lesson in survival skills and, ironically, an introduction to my post-war hobby of bird watching.

One of the regular jobs for the girls was to take the family's pigs or sheep into the woods to forage for acorns all day, just as Fortunato had done at Colli. The oak trees in the woods were a small scrub variety covered with lichen, but they produced quite a lot of acorns. This was a safe job for me and I often went out with Onelia or Corrada. While they were in the woods guarding the animals they would often spin wool. They used to take with them a huge bundle of raw wool and a distaff, rather like a large spinning top. When the distaff was suspended from a short length of wool that had been teased from the pile, it began to spin. Slowly, as it was teased from the bundle, the strand became ever longer and wound itself around the spinning distaff to finish eventually as a large ball of spun wool.

While Onelia or Corrada wandered in the woods, following the pigs or sheep, they would be listening out for the loud tinkling of the bell around an animal's neck which told them that it had found some *funghi*, woodland mushrooms, among the fallen leaves. They then had to get to the animal before it had sniffed out the mushrooms and eaten them. This was a pastime in the woods that almost everybody took part in during the autumn *funghi* season.

On one occasion when I was in the woods with Corrada, her sheep unearthed a few good mushrooms, so she was very pleased. The local woods seemed to produce every type of *funghi* possible, with the exception of our English field mushrooms. However, on this occasion, as we emerged from the woods on the way home we arrived at a patch of open grassland, and as we crossed the grass, to my surprise I saw a cluster of field mushrooms in front of me.

I knelt to collect them, saying to Corrada, 'These are the ones I was telling you about.'

When she saw them she shrieked, '*No, Franco, non si puoi mangiare. Morirai*' ('No, Franco, you can't eat them. You'll die').

She appealed to the other ladies to persuade me not to pick them. However, I did pick them and showed Corrada how I knew them by the perfume and also because the top skin could be peeled off. That evening, Frank and I were to eat with the Landi family, so I took the mushrooms along. Corrada flatly refused to cook them and so did her brothers, Corrado and Guido. Guido's wife Lisa volunteered, however, and Frank and I ate them with our dinner and enjoyed them, much to the concern of the family. Soon after, we left and walked the couple of hundred yards along the track to our shack, climbed through the opening and were soon lying comfortably chatting on the straw.

Some time later we heard approaching footsteps on the track, so we lay very silent. We had not heard of prisoner sweeps by night, but there was always the fear that somebody might have betrayed us. The shack lay some yards off the track, and when the footsteps were alongside us we heard the person turn and approach. Alarm bells were ringing, but then we heard a whispered 'Franco'. I moved over to the timber and opening it, found Corrado standing there in the dark.

I asked '*Cosa c'è?*' ('What's the matter?').

Both Biddis and I roared with laughter as we heard, 'The family sent me to see if you're still alive.'

We assured Corrado that we were in excellent form and, as he trudged back to the village, we felt we had won the battle on behalf of the field mushroom!

*

Within a couple of weeks of Valentino's advice to keep my head down, I found myself ignoring his warning. It was the start of the *vendemmia*, the grape harvest. One of the first vineyards being dealt with that day was immediately below the village, and five or six families were joining forces to pick the grapes. Many of the group were youngsters and they insisted that Frank and I should join them. Our protests were swept aside and we joined in. Everybody was really enthusiastic about the arrival of the season and worked away happily.

Every person was equipped with a pair of clippers and a large basket. The vines seemed to be loaded with endless bunches of grapes, and the click-click of the clippers never stopped, as bunch after bunch was dropped into baskets. As a basket was filled it was taken to an ox-cart carrying a number of much larger baskets, into which grapes were tipped. When that cart was fully loaded it was taken back to the winepress in the village and another cart took its place. Throughout the day there was a sense of achievement mixed with merriment. Everybody was thoroughly enjoying themselves. The weather was perfect, with a blue sky and a warm autumn sun. It was as though something had happened that let people just enjoy themselves and forget there was still a war going on.

We shared that feeling all morning, but there was still more to come. Tables and benches were brought out and laid out for a picnic lunch. Five or six tables were laid in a long line for the pickers, with others to hold the food and wine. Plates, glasses and cutlery were set out, and the pickers were then called. There was one person there not from the village, a girl in her late teens from a Florentine family whose father was the landlord of one of the outlying farms. A few members of her family, afraid of bombs on Florence, had come to Montebenichi and moved in with the peasant farmer. The girl spoke some English and talked with me a lot. She gave me an English Penguin book by Robert Graves. It had been a most enjoyable day for me and I felt good to have contributed a little towards the tasks undertaken by the villagers. However, I was worried about having gone against Valentino's warning, so I did not pick grapes in Montebenichi a second time, nor did I ever see the girl again.

One family, the Meliciani at Poggigiobbi farm in Pietraviva, did not use the village wine-press. Instead, they practised the time-honoured method of treading the grapes, in large, straight-sided barrels. Men and boys rolled their trousers high and hopped into the barrels. Then, knee deep in grapes, they trampled them until every drop of juice had been squeezed out. There was much hilarity whenever this was going on.

One of the most laborious jobs in the village fell to the women. This was the laundry, and it seemed to be done on an almost daily basis. The women had to walk down the road from the village for ten minutes carrying heavy baskets of washing. They then turned down a steeply sloping path through woodland. At one point a stream gushing down the hillside tumbled over an 8ft bank into a brick-lined pool, then overflowed across the track and plunged down the hillside. The pool was surrounded on three sides by a concrete wall about 6ins high, against which the women would kneel and pound the washing on the inward sloping coping stone of the wall, which was about 15ins wide. The place was known as La Castagnola. The only soap available was of poor quality, so they just hammered the clothes against the concrete. About ten women could wash at the same time, but there were always others waiting, and the spot was a centre for village gossip. Their return journey up the steep slope back to the village, carrying baskets of wet laundry, was a really formidable task indeed.

Every morning in our shack I was wakened early by the sound of passing ox-carts as the men of the village set off to their various plots of land. The one man sure to wake me was Guido Landi. The moment he left the village his voice could be heard venting his frustration repeatedly at the lumbering progress of his oxen. '*Do'vai? Brutta Bestia!*' ('Where are you going? Ugly Beast!') echoed around the countryside, and when he passed the shack his voice, together with the creaking and groaning of the ox-cart, was certain to waken the deepest sleeper.

Alongside the track near our shack was an emergency water supply sunk into the ground for the animals. With three sides being vertical stone walls and the fourth a sloping approach to the water for the animals, it was identical to the one I had seen at Colli but did not have a vine-laden pergola above it. Alongside was a row of low bushes. One day Corrada made a surprise offer to launder my clothes.

Frank, aged eighteen, in Territorial Army uniform, May 1939.

(*Above left*) Frank with Bill Pople in Cairo, November 1940.

(*Above right*) Ron Taylor, Bill Pople and Frank in Cairo, November 1940.

(*Below*) Frank's German identity tag, 1944–45.

(*Above left*) A post-war photograph of Frank's mother and father.

(*Above right*) Frank's sister, Betty, lost at sea, aged twelve, in September 1940.

Frank's father outside his grocery shop in Kirkdale, Liverpool – Frank's home, to which he dreamed of returning throughout his years of captivity.

(*Above*) Post-war Territorial Army exercises. Captain Paterson, Gun Position Officer, and Frank (his assistant) at his side, with the signaller, driver and two others.

(*Below left*) Roy Page, 2002.

(*Below right*) Don Wigley.

(*Above left*) Frank returning (with Roy) to Tuscany, seen here in San Gimignano in 1949.

(*Above right*) Roy Page playing a clarinet from the Montebenichi band at a village festival, 1949.

(*Below*) View of Montebenichi, where Frank and Roy were given a wonderfully warm welcome on their return in 1949. (*With the permission of Marco Gasparini*)

(*Above*) Revisiting the site of Laterina PoW Camp, showing the huts and the parade ground, used for roll-call and as a football field, 1949.

(*Below*) Frank at Laterina PoW Camp, by then an industrial estate, with the town of Laterina in the background, 2005.

(*Above*) Frank with Signora Roselli, Mayor of Laterina, on the occasion of the inauguration of a stone to commemorate the suffering in the wartime prison camp, 1999.

(*Below*) The plaque on the commemorative stone, 1999.

Il Comune di Laterina "al di là del filo spinato"

...a memoria di questo luogo,

dove si consumò il dolore

della prigionia e dell'esodo,

con l'auspicio che

si schiudano

orizzonti di libertà,

di pace,

di civile convivenza...

28 marzo 1999

(*Above*) Montebenichi showing in the lower right hand corner, the Landi family shack, where Frank was sheltered for some months, 2006.

(*Below*) Montebenichi, as seen from the air. (*With the permission of Marco Gasparini*)

(*Above left*) The grape harvest with the Meliciani family at Poggigiobbi, Pietraviva, 1949.

(*Above right*) Roadside memorial to Giuseppe Neri, shot by the Germans for re-soling the boots of an escaped PoW, 1949.

(*Below*) The Giovannini family: Valentino, Giuliana, Maria Pia and Giuseppina, 1949.

(*Above*) The Giovannini house, 1949.

(*Below*) The Giovannini house, now incorporating the restaurant 'Osteria l'Orciaia', 2003.

(*Above*) Frank retracing his wartime steps to Montesoni, an isolated farmhouse, 2005.

(*Below*) Marjorie and Maria, outside the shack belonging to the Landi family, where Frank had sheltered, taken in the 1980s.

(*Above*) Frank and Marjorie at Montebenichi on the 50th anniversary of Frank's first arrival in Montebenichi, 1993.

(*Below*) Frank with Enrico (brother to Onelia) and Piera Pieraccini in Montebenichi in 2003. Enrico was the village blacksmith who made the spit and uprights for the feast in 1970.

(*Above*) Maria Pia, Marjorie, Ewa, Simone, Gino, Frank, Peter (*Frank's* son) and Giuliana in the Osteria l'Orciaia in 2001.

(*Below*) The façade of the Castelletto as it is today. (*With the permission of Marco Gasparini*)

(*Above*) Frank with Giuliana and Maria Pia at the Osteria l'Orciaia, reminiscing over old photos, 2006.

(*Below*) Simone Biagi, Mike Unwin (Frank's grandson) and Gino Biagi in the kitchen at the Osteria l'Orciaia, after a lesson for Mike in Tuscan cuisine, 2016.

Frank and Marjorie outside the Osteria l'Orciaia, where they held their 50th wedding anniversary celebrations, 2003.

Frank and Betty at Buckingham Palace on the centenary of the Blind Veterans UK (formerly St Dunstans) in June 2015.

Frank on Remembrance Sunday, 2008.

This was most welcome, because I had had great difficulty kneeling on the sloping stones and had only been able to rinse them as I had no basin or soap. Corrada had no soap either but she found no problem kneeling at the water's edge and pounding the dirt out of the clothes. She then spread them on the bushes alongside and they were dried in a short time by the warm sunshine. This kind gesture brought about a great improvement in my life, and from then on Corrada came to ask for my laundry every three or four days.

My relationship with the girls of the village was quite a problem for me. Those of eighteen or nineteen had no boyfriends to pair off with, as the young men were all away. The only two young fellows available were myself and Frank, but the villagers were becoming ever cooler towards him, which left only me. It was a very difficult situation, because a number of them were really lovely girls.

The experience at Colli when Iolanda Becucci had made a startling proposal at the dinner table stood me in good stead as a warning of what might lie ahead. On that occasion, the fixed stare on the face of Ginestrino, her father, and the three shotguns hanging on a display rack behind my head, had imprinted on my mind that my wellbeing and possibly my life depended on not offending the people who were sheltering me. There was no monastery for me to take shelter in, but I made up my mind that while I was living under those conditions, I would lead a monk-like life.

Oddly enough, it was Iolanda again who made the next pass at me. It happened while I was staying at Colli for a few days with Ginestrino and his family. I left the farmhouse together with Iolanda, both of us carrying water containers, and headed for the nearby spring which was fifty or sixty yards down a steep and narrow leafy track through the trees. The small pool formed by the spring was in a tiny clearing in the trees.

Iolanda was in a very happy mood and we soon had the carriers filled. I picked up my two and turned to climb the path, when I heard behind me a softly voiced 'Franco'. When I turned I found that Iolanda was lying back on the sloping grass, looking absolutely beautiful. Eve can't have put on a better show in Eden, only the serpent and the apple were missing! Looking down at her it needed the willpower of a saint, not just that of a good monk, to say, '*Andiamo, Iolanda*' ('Let's go, Iolanda'). Happily, she just got up and came with me, and our friendship carried on as before.

After that experience I was able to avoid any entanglements with the girls. There were perhaps eight in all who were between about sixteen to nineteen, and almost all of them were really attractive. The hard life of a girl growing up in a peasant family in wartime Italy had not yet taken its toll on them. The exception was Corrada, who was short and tubby with rather frizzy hair, but she had the loveliest smile. Her eyes lit up when she grinned, and she seemed always to be full of laughter. Without doubt, she was the warmest-hearted of them all.

It was surprising that, other than Iolanda, the only girl who had made a pass at me was Onelia Pieraccini, the girl I was most attracted to. This made it particularly hard not to respond. Onelia teased me a bit when she was rejected but she accepted it, and again our close friendship continued. The small boys of the village had all seen through us, and any time I passed a bunch of them sitting around, they shot me suggestive little comments about Onelia. That was the least of my worries, and I just winked at them.

One day I was starting up the hill out of Montebenichi when I was joined by Onelia's mother. She was going to the woods with her three pigs to let them forage for acorns.

The conversation started normally, but suddenly she looked at me and said, '*Niente ricordi, Franco*' ('No souvenirs, Franco').

'*Che ricordi, Signora?*' I enquired innocently, and her hand just made a semi-circular movement in front of her stomach.

I thought, 'Don't worry, Mum, your daughter's safe' and went on to assure her of that, but it made me realize that there must have been a number of mothers in the village worried about their daughters. I had never thought of the need to tell them that I was just thinking of saving my own skin and that my intentions towards their daughters were entirely, if regretfully, well intentioned.

Chapter 10

A New Home, but Danger is Never Far Away

T hen the men of the village gave Frank and me a wonderful surprise, which illustrated the level of their concern both for our welfare and their own safety, as well as the lengths that they would go to in order to look after us. They said they had all thought the Landi shack where we were living was too dangerous, being so close to the village, and they asked me to go with them. We set off up the track out of the village, and at a point about half a mile away I was guided into the wood on the right of the path. About 50yds down the hillside we arrived at the edge of the wood on a small round plateau jutting out from the hill. The plateau had been cleared of any vegetation, except for one small pine tree, and there before our eyes stood a superb shack. It was A-frame in shape, made of slim chestnut saplings and covered with a thick layer of brushwood that the men assured me would be fully waterproof.

The site was south-facing, and from this elevated position the view was breathtakingly beautiful. The Ambra valley lay below us, with the village of Rapale glistening on the first crest beyond; then there was a succession of ridges of the rolling hills south of Chianti, each more indistinct than the last, until they finally were lost in the distant haze. Occasional villages topped the distant ridges and, in the far distance, the towering slopes of Monte Amiata supplied the backdrop to the scene. Even the door of the shack faced south, so the view from inside offered the same staggering panorama. Inside the hut were two comfortable bunks also made of chestnut and brushwood and fitted with sheets and a pillow. I could not believe my eyes and did not know how to thank the fellows who had built this perfect place.

I went back to the old shack, where I found Frank asleep, and we carried our kit up to our new home. He was as pleased as I had been and for once showed a spark of life. There was a small pool very close beside the track known by the villagers as the Horseshoe Spring. The track led for some hundreds of yards down into the valley to an isolated farm, Vencia, occupied by the Bindi family. So the track to our spring was seldom used, and it was ideal for us to take either a quick swill or a good strip wash. The new place meant a long uphill walk for those bringing food to us, but this seemed to make no difference to them.

Once installed in the shack, we were much more comfortable. We were well fed and after the healthy life we were living we were now extremely fit. Furthermore, the remote position of the new shack meant that it was unlikely to be found by any roaming Germans, so the villagers were much less at risk.

*

Both the Germans and the Fascists made occasional sweeps of the countryside for escaped prisoners in hiding, but the local people were usually one step ahead of them. The small town of Bucine held the *Carabinieri* station which policed the Ambra valley, and the *Brigadiere* at the station would be approached by Germans or Fascists and told that a number of his men would be needed for a prisoner sweep on a particular day. At the far end of the valley there was a castle called Montalto, which was the home of Princess Mina Carafa Palmieri. She was no lover of either Germans or Fascists, and parts of her castle had been requisitioned for high-ranking German officers.

The *Brigadiere*, once alerted to the sweep, immediately sent one of his men by bicycle the twelve miles or so to the castle to warn the Princess of the news. She in turn organized the families of the farms on her estate to visit the villages of the valley and see that all prisoners in the district disappeared the day before the sweep and did not return until the following day. Consequently, the sweeps were always abortive.

One way in which the Princess showed kindness towards the prisoners was with Red Cross food. Prior to the Armistice, the men of the working party at the Villa La Selva, where Roy had been imprisoned, had bartered with the local people, exchanging items from the parcels for things like rabbit or chicken. Following the Armistice, when escaped prisoners were scattered around the countryside, it was learned that a lot of the parcel items had found their way to Montalto Castle, the Princess's home. Subsequently, she rode on horseback to visit nearby places on her estate where prisoners were being sheltered and handed out items such as packets of tea and tins of bacon or salmon to the surprised men. In Montebenichi I did not benefit from this because the village was beyond the Princess's estate, about five miles' walk from the Castle. However, the Castle could be seen clearly, because the distance as the crow flies was only about three miles.

*

The men of Montebenichi were all enthusiastic hunters. Largely because of this hunting, game was not particularly plentiful. However, when they bagged a couple of pigeons or a rabbit there was a good dinner for the family that night. On occasions a man would strike lucky and shoot a hare or a pheasant. That warranted a gala dinner, and the prize was added to whatever had been on the menu for that evening. Fortunately for us, Frank and I were often invited to those dinners by the lucky family and so enjoyed these special treats.

The nearest farm to our shack was Pignano, a two-family, semi-detached building like Poggialto. In the left-hand half a couple lived with their two children, a boy and a girl about six years old. In the other half an elderly widow, Zara, lived alone. The track from the farm ran horizontally along the edge of the hillside about 100yds away from our shack and then curled into the woodland behind us to join the Montebenichi track. This gave us a view of the track near the farm for a distance of about fifty yards.

We often saw the two children walking along the track, loudly singing popular songs and leading the family's three pigs to forage for acorns in the wood. Their voices rang out so clearly, echoing around the valley below us. It was a beautiful sound. One song I learned from them was the Italian version of 'Lili Marlene'. On one occasion, when we met the children returning to their home for lunch, we learned that the secondary purpose of their morning stroll was to catch songbirds. On the outward journey they set traps at the trackside, and then they collected any catch on their return. When we met them they had caught two goldfinches.

*

I then decided to have a short spell exploring away from Montebenichi. I chose to start at Colli and see the Becucci family, so I told Onelia I was going and that I would let her know when I arrived back. I set off on my journey, passing Poggialto, the home of Vittorio who had introduced me to Montebenichi to hear the news bulletin on the radio. Then I had to find my way across a mile or two of mixed uncultivated land. After one or two errors in navigation, I found myself on the long narrow ridge of grass leading down towards the farm at Colli. The family were all at home and recognized me when I was still some distance away. On my arrival they gave me a great welcome. It was good to be with them, and we spent a very happy evening together.

The following day I volunteered to fetch some water. Climbing back up the track I spotted something white in the undergrowth. It proved to be a leaflet that had been dropped by plane. The left-hand side was in German and the right in Italian. The message was offering a reward of 200 lire for any information leading to the recapture of any Allied prisoner. The lira had an entirely different value in 1943 and this would have been a great amount to any peasant family. I put the leaflet in my pocket and carried on.

On arrival back at the house the family were all inside and I passed the leaflet first to Iolanda saying, 'Look what I've found, I've got a price on my head.'

She looked at it for some moments and then passed it sheepishly to her father. He took it and looked at it, equally embarrassed. At that point I realized that none of the family could read. I was then embarrassed myself and, apologising, I read it to them. I had known that there was no schooling, either for the young children of the village or the children at Colli. It came as a great surprise, however, to find that in a family of parents and seven children aged between six and twenty-one no one was able to read.

The fun had gone out of the leaflet. It left me thinking that the Germans were wasting their time distributing such things to an illiterate community. I wish now that I had kept it as a souvenir, but in those days life was for the day and not the future, and I will have just thrown it away.

Rosa told her husband that there was no meat for that evening, so Ginestrino said he would take his shotgun out and see what he could get. He was away for a couple of hours. When he arrived back and took his prize from the poacher's pocket in his jacket there was great hilarity, because his only bag was a squirrel. Nevertheless, it was skinned and cooked and added to the *minestra*, so we all had a morsel of squirrel that evening.

I was bemoaning the fact that I had heard no news of the Allied advance from the south for some time. The family suggested that I should make my way to Dudova, a village about a mile away, where they told me the priest had a radio he would let me listen to. Although I had heard of Dudova I had no idea where it was, but I decided to go there. The journey was all downhill and through woods all the way, because there was no track from Colli to Dudova. After dinner the family gave me directions and, with darkness falling, I set off. It was quite bewildering, but I just kept going downhill and it was not too long before I found a small village. It seemed quite deserted in the dark and I had to knock on a door and ask for the priest's house. When I found his home the housekeeper let me in.

The priest welcomed me, giving me the freedom of his radio. He was a plump, elderly man, seated at a large heavy wooden table wearing his priest's hat and busying himself with recharging used cartridge cases for his shotgun. He had a heap of cases and a mass of shotgun pellets, and he filled each case with pellets and stuffed them in with a piece of wadding. He continued to do this throughout my visit.

I knew the BBC wavelength from my visit to hear the news in Montebenichi with Vittorio. I listened to the news but it was disappointing, telling me that the Allies were having great difficulty making progress in the south of Italy. After the news a music programme began, but it was some kind of American jazz. One song I remember was 'Ole Man Mose Has Kicked the Bucket', but it was a frantic tune and just too much for the priest, so at that point I switched the radio off, thanked my host and left. Finding my way back to Colli in the pitch dark was more confusing than the trip down, but I just kept going uphill as direct as I could. After a while I recognized the Colli area and soon I was home.

*

As winter approached, a favourite pastime was sitting around the great fireplace with the Becucci family at Colli and roasting chestnuts from the new crop. As November arrived the weather turned nasty, with strong cold winds and persistent rain, and the warmth from the fire was a wonderful comfort. Chestnuts were plentiful, and evenings were spent enjoying them while laughing, joking and telling stories about each other's lives. The vessel used to roast them was a large, heavy, iron frying pan. It had many holes in the bottom, which were made in an arrowhead shape nearly half an inch long, the point being punched up into a vertical position. This roasted the chestnuts perfectly.

After staying a few days at Colli, I returned to the shack and Frank Biddis. I had not invited him as he did not warm easily to Italians and I did not want to impose more than necessary on the kindness of the family and their willingness to share their meagre resources.

Although we had met the children from Pignano, the nearest farm to our shack, we had never met their parents or their neighbour Zara, the elderly widow. One day Zara came to the shack with an invitation to a *Tutti Santi*, a dinner on All Saints night, which in England we call Hallowe'en. There we met four other prisoners from a village across the Ambra valley. It was very good to chat and hear how other fellows were managing such a vagabond life. The atmosphere was great in the farmhouse. The stone floor, the enormous built-up fireplace with its great heap of glowing embers and the carbide lamps all formed a perfect setting for traditional Tuscan farm life. The dinner proved to be a great success but held one surprise which came as a shock.

We were six prisoners at the table, Frank and I, and the other four with the Italian who had brought them. Conversation was flowing, swapping experiences, discussing the progress of Allied troops in the south and the lack of news about any prospect of early release. Zara was busy seeing things kept moving. The meal started with the usual salamis followed by pasta, with plentiful Chianti. It was all wonderfully delicious. The surprise came when the main dish was carried in. It consisted of three bowls, each containing a different type of bird, all roasted on a spit. The largest bowl contained birds which were obviously pigeons, another had birds the size of blackbirds or thrushes and the third one held smaller birds like finches.

This was a shock to both the system and our consciences. Nothing was said for some moments, and then we just eyed each other, but we all realized that we could not decline her offering. Zara was a very poor peasant lady and in wartime Italy she must have struggled for everything she had. It was just a fact of life that for the people of the countryside anything that they could catch was fair game, and this included small birds. Once we accepted that, we just got on with it, and they were very tasty and satisfying. One food item Zara showed me was a quantity of various types of *funghi*, woodland mushrooms, which she had collected and preserved. They were held in two or three large sweet jars and covered in olive oil. She told me she used some in almost every meal she cooked.

*

We then heard that in Rosennano, one of the two hilltop villages a little north of Montebenichi, a family had been caught sheltering a prisoner. This may have been the result of someone betraying the farmer. When the Germans troops arrived the soldier was not present and so was not captured. However, the head of the family was beaten almost to death and all the farm stock loaded on to lorries and driven away. Frank Biddis and I on one occasion came within an inch, or in reality 30yds, of a similar calamity.

An elderly, white-haired gentleman in Montebenichi had offered to repair my army boots, which were badly worn at the soles and heels. With all the constrictions of wartime, the Italians had no leather and had to wear wooden shoes known as *zoccoli*. I did not know what state my boots would come back in, but I gladly accepted the offer. The old chap told me the boots would be ready in two days. Meantime, I was given a pair of *zoccoli* to wear. They took some getting used to.

Two days later Frank and I took the steep and rough path that led up the hill to our old shack and entered the village at the corner of the gable of Giuliana Giovannini's house. As we turned the corner, Giuliana appeared from around the gable just 30yds away. Clearly alarmed, she hurried towards us, wagging her finger and putting it to her lips for silence. Once near us, she whispered one word: '*Tedeschi*' ('Germans').

We needed no more warning and turned on our heels. The track immediately behind us dropped some 7ft or 8ft on to a terraced hillside, and the first terrace down held a line of large chestnut trees. In a bound we were across the track, then we leapt down to the chestnut trees, carried on through the terraces of an olive grove into the safer cover of a patch of woodland and fell to the ground. We just lay panting for some time until we were sure nobody was on our track. Only then could we relax. Even the *zoccoli* had not impeded my flight.

When I eventually got my boots back I could see that the cobbler had made a superb job of them. Somebody had been sent down to the valley to barter with the Germans and get enough leather for the repair. Moreover, they no longer had the telltale feature of British Army boots, a horseshoe-shaped steel band around the underside of the heel. When walking in damp mud, this left behind a clear imprint of the horseshoe, and after the mud had dried it carried lasting evidence of the presence of British prisoners. The Italians hated the imprints.

The escape had been one of our luckier moments, all over in a matter of seconds. If Giuliana had been moments later, we would have walked around the corner to find ourselves just a couple of yards from two German military vehicles. Half a dozen German soldiers were there, and Giuliana's parents were at the front door being questioned about escaped prisoners. They were able to put the Germans off, but it must have been a frightening time for them. A short time later the Germans inspected the rest of the village and then left. Although at the time we did not know it, one of the vehicles had a recaptured prisoner aboard.

I later found out that the prisoner was Titch Wells of the Essex Regiment, whom I had been with for eight months in the concentration camp at Laterina, until he left for the work camp at the Villa La Selva. The Italian officer in charge of the camp had stayed on in his quarters when the prisoners had escaped at the time of the Armistice, and Titch Wells was the one prisoner who had not left. He had been sweet on the daughter of the peasant farmer attached to the villa, and when the all other prisoners left, he moved in with the farmer's family. After some months he fell ill and was confined to bed. It seemed that the Italian officer who had been in charge of the work camp had then decided to inform the Germans of Titch's presence at the farm.

Without warning, the German soldiers arrived at the farm with a car, a truck and two large lorries. The farmer was absent, but the Germans entered the farmhouse and demanded of his wife to know where the Englishman was. She denied that there was anybody there, but when a pistol was put to her head the terrified woman had to admit that Titch was in bed upstairs. He was immediately hauled out and placed in the truck. The car and the truck, with Titch aboard, then left for Montebenichi in search of more booty. By the grace of God they drew a blank. If Frank and I had happened to walk to Montebenichi by road, instead of using the rough uphill track, it is certain that the Germans would have picked us up.

Meanwhile, at the farm where Titch Wells had been found, the remaining Germans were busy loading the lorries with all the farm livestock and produce. They took everything: pigs, sheep, wheat flour, maize flour and everything else they could lay their hands on. It was fortunate for the farmer that he was not present. Had he been there, there is no knowing what would have happened to him. I never heard any more of Titch – I never knew his proper first name.

Sometime later, a cobbler from Pietraviva repaired the boots of one of the prisoners hiding in that village and was then betrayed by someone informing the Germans. When German troops caught him on the road just outside the village, they shot him. A roadside cross was later erected at the spot with the legend: '*Vittima di Guerra* (victim of war), *Giuseppe Neri, 1900–1944*'.

*

I was incredibly foolish on one occasion. I was with Vittorio Sbardellati at his home, Poggialto, where I had slept for my first night in Montebenichi. During the day he asked me if I would like to go to the cinema. I told him I would love to, and he promised to take me the following evening. The following day I was relaxing at the new shack, and the couple bringing the midday food were Girolamo and Ida Pieraccini, Onelia's aunt and uncle.

They must have been somewhere in their forties, Girolamo a tall athletic figure and Ida a still voluptuous woman. I was about to gain an insight into the Latin temperament. Once I had eaten my pasta, we stood chatting outside the shack. The space between the shack and the surrounding bushes was about 2yds wide. Suddenly Girolamo turned and, without warning, unbuttoned his fly and began urinating on the ground.

Surprised, I protested, '*Girolamo, che fai? Quest'è mia casa.*' ('Girolamo, what are you doing? This is my home').

Girolamo was a little shamefaced but said nothing.

However, Ida came staunchly to his defence: '*Franco, gli uomini fanno così. E Girolamo è uomo. E che uomo! Sai, Franco, la prima notte. Sette volte! Sette volte, Franco!*' ('Franco, men do that. And Girolamo is a man. And what a man! D'you know, Franco, the first night, seven times! Seven times, Franco!').

I nodded humbly to Girolamo and said no more.

The chat then resumed. They knew that sometimes families in the outlying farms invited me to dinner, so Ida just idly asked where I was going that evening. I waited a moment and then, tongue in cheek, told them I was going to the cinema. Girolamo scoffed, but Ida stared at me a while and then, quite excited, said '*Si va*' ('He's going'). They left soon after, and I was not sure whether or not they believed me.

That evening as dusk was falling I joined Vittorio at Poggialto and we set off for Ambra, the large village down in the valley. It was five miles away but downhill all the way, so it was not too long before we were approaching the village. I had not been near such a large place before, and there was an air of excitement about it. My clothing looked reasonably civilian. I was wearing an orange pullover with a zip neck and a collar, which an elderly lady, Rosa, had given me, but my gait was different to that of the locals and my hair was much blonder than theirs. I was just trusting that in the dark nobody would recognize me as an Englishman. As we got into the centre there were many more people about. Then came disappointment, when we reached the cinema and found the place in darkness. There was no show that night. I felt terribly flat.

We stood for a moment and then Vittorio said, '*Andiamo al bar*' ('Let's go to a bar').

He told me he would enter first and a minute or two later I should follow and join him at the bar. So I waited a short while then opened the door and entered. It was a narrow room with white painted walls and about eight tables. Vittorio was at the bar beyond the tables. There were around twenty men seated. In such a group there is always the din of incessant chatter.

The moment I put my head through the door everyone fell silent. It was obvious they all knew there was an Englishman amongst them. I walked as nonchalantly as I could up to Vittorio, who already had a glass of wine. He ordered one for me but at the same time indicated to me that we should drink up and leave. I quickly drank mine, and as we walked between the tables not a soul looked at us.

I was glad to be out in the evening air, but Vittorio was not finished yet. '*C'è uno più piccolo qui vicino. Proviamo lì*' ('There's a smaller bar just nearby. Let's try there').

Sure enough, there was a bar very near and we repeated the process. This time I found another white room, with only eight or nine men sitting at three tables. Again Vittorio was at the bar beyond them, a drink in his hand. A drink was produced for me, and I received another nod to drink up and leave. Not an eye turned towards us as we walked past the tables. I had not heard a word from the drinkers while we were in either bar. This time Vittorio had had enough and thought we should leave Ambra.

We were now faced with the five miles of uphill walking, not all of it along roads, so we were both very tired when we reached Poggialto, and I had to go on another half mile to reach my shack. Frank was asleep and it was not long before I was in my bunk and fast asleep too.

The next morning everybody in Montebenichi knew I had been to Ambra. They were all furious with me, and I think the first wave of feeling was that I should be banished from Montebenichi. Then, as it seemed that there were to be no repercussions, the mood softened and it was made very clear to me how reckless I had been and the terrible damage that might have ensued. I promised I would never act so foolishly again, and things slowly returned to normal.

It was not long after this that another major scare occurred. I cannot recall why, but for some reason Frank and I were lying up by day in a small hut across the track from the Landi family shack. We were just lying comfortably in the straw when the owner of the shack, Valeriani, burst in.

Out of breath, he closed the door and then blurted out, '*Franco, Tedeschi*'.

We were on our feet at once. The view from the door opened on to the track leading uphill out of Montebenichi. I opened the door an inch and saw two

German soldiers, rifles slung over their shoulders, walking down the track towards us. They would soon reach flat ground, where they would lose sight of our shack for a few moments.

Valeriani had already disappeared. It was too risky to stay in the shack so we had to get out. About 12yds to the left of the door there was a very thorny hedge growing along the edge of the hillside. Immediately behind the hedge the ground sloped downwards, covered in thick scrub woodland. We quickly agreed on a 'One, Two, Three, Go' action. On the word 'Go' we moved like lightning. I was first to the hedge. Crossing my arms in front of my face, I hurled myself at it. Frank was on my tail and in seconds we had made our way through the thorny hedge and were well into the woods.

By that time we were so fit and we knew the area so well that, given a few yards start in the woods, nobody would ever have caught us. We learned later that the two German soldiers had just walked along the road skirting the southern edge of the village and carried on down the road towards La Selva. We had no idea what they were up to, but they might well have been on a prisoner sweep. As our original shack and Valeriani's shack, in which we were at the time, were the first two buildings in the village, the Germans might just have decided to search both.

*

Just before Christmas I went down with a heavy cold which was developing into flu. The villagers brought me extra blankets and told me to stay in bed, where I remained over Christmas. After the Titch Wells affair, when he had been recaptured while ill in bed at the farm of the Villa La Selva, the villagers were afraid of taking me into the village, and all my meals were brought to the shack. Once again, Onelia and Corrada showed extraordinary thoughtfulness. They knew of a farm several miles away at which the farmer kept a few cows, and they walked there and brought me back a couple of pints of fresh milk. This was the only time I saw milk in Montebenichi.

After a couple of days a Dr Fantoni was brought up from Ambra to see me. He confirmed that it was a touch of flu and nothing worse. He had brought some medicine and told me to stay in bed a little longer. After a few days the medicine had done its job and I was feeling well again. If his visit had become known to the Germans, like the cobbler Giuseppe Neri who repaired a PoW's boots, he would have been shot on the spot. His visit exemplified the extraordinary courage of both the peasants and the professional classes.

My illness caused me to miss out on Christmas in the village. However, it was not long till Epiphany, which was observed just as much as Christmas. The church was busy celebrating mass through the day, and in the evening the children of the village did a round of the houses playing 'trick or treat'. Sadly, the treats could not comprise much more than a few sugared almonds from the wine shop. Nevertheless, a good time was had by all.

January 1944 turned out to be a good month. The ground was always frost-bound after very cold nights, but every morning a bright sun shone out of a clear blue sky and in an hour or two the ground had thawed. The daytime could be chilly, but Frank and I faced up to it by rising early and getting to our spring for a brisk wash to liven ourselves up. The villagers had commended us on how we kept ourselves clean, so we made sure to maintain our standards. Sometime earlier two Sardinians had settled in the woods near the village and the villagers found them to be scruffy and dirty. They had not been made welcome.

*

The villagers who kept pigs, either in a pen near their house or just outside the village, had two or three pigs killed every January. Rabbits, chickens, and pigeons would be killed as and when they were needed. The pigs were quite small animals, but every scrap of them was put to good use. One man, Lello, was the pig killer for the village. It was he who had met me, back in September on my first visit to Montebenichi after I had left my three companions, and he had introduced me to Vittorio Sbardellati.

Lello spent a day with each family to carry out his work, and the pigs were soon despatched. He stood astride the animal, his left arm around its neck, and swiftly plunged a sharp, narrow knife into its heart from beneath. The pig's throat was then cut and the blood was drained into a basin. I attended the first day's proceedings. Although it was a shocking thing to see for the first time, I had to admire the speed and efficiency with which Lello carried out the task.

At that point the family joined in to help. The two back legs were tied to hooks high on a wall and the carcass suspended there. A cut was made from tail to throat to open up the pig, and the innards were removed. The children then took over and trimmed all the snippets of lean meat projecting from the various cuts. These tiny pieces of meat, gently simmering in olive oil, wine, and garlic in a small earthenware dish placed on a trivet over a heap of embers, formed part of their dinner that evening. The carcass was now ready for Lello and the men of the family to prepare the various cuts which produced hams for curing, meat for sausages, chops, loin, salami, trotters, tripe and various other titbits. The head would be cooked and served up at the table. These items formed a major part of the family's meat supply for much of the year.

I was surprised to find that the blood was also used. It was left in a basin until it had congealed and become a mass of firm dark red jelly lying in a clear liquid. It could then be drained, sliced and fried, and was served at a meal. Initially I felt somewhat squeamish about it, but I put that aside and found that it was quite palatable. Some of the foodstuffs I mention in the story are strange and rather bizarre. However, seen in the context of a totally self-sufficient and somewhat primitive community, they all formed a necessary part of people's diet.

Whenever Lello carried out these tasks he was guest of honour at the family's dinner table that evening. Frank and I were extremely fortunate because we were invited to many of these dinners. Each one was a pork extravaganza.

Except for the cauldron holding the pasta, which would boil away furiously, as I had first seen at Colli, all cooking was done very slowly by placing earthenware dishes over embers and leaving them to simmer gently. To start a dish cooking, a small pile of embers was scraped away from the heap and an inch-high iron trivet was placed above the embers, with the earthenware dish on top of it. The earthenware cooking dishes would then be warmed up, with olive oil and garlic in them, before the meat or vegetables were added, together with a selection of herbs and wine. On these special festive occasions, as the cooking progressed, up to seven or eight earthenware dishes, ranging from saucer size to large dishes for the main courses, would be in use, each one simmering above its own pile of embers. I believe that it was this combination of slow cooking over embers, with the addition of garlic and various herbs, that created what I so loved about traditional Tuscan peasant cooking.

Once everybody was at the table and serving was about to begin there was a toast to Lello, and the evening was set for the enjoyment of a beautifully cooked dinner and an ample supply of Chianti from the family's small vineyard. The pig-killing season lasted nine or ten days and it was one of the best of the local festivals which I was able to attend.

A week later I was in Solata, a tiny village a few miles from Montebenichi, where I saw a different procedure for preparing a pig. A flat, open-sided cart was pulled into the village by two oxen and on it was lying an extremely large pig that had recently been killed. The skin of the small pigs in Montebenichi was almost hairless, but this large sow at Solata was covered in strong, spindly bristles. The family then placed the pig on the ground and brought out bundles of straw which they heaped over and around it. The straw was set alight and burned fiercely. When the fire subsided the pig was turned and straw heaped on its other side. A lot more straw was burned over the pig before two men, armed with long blades, began to scrape the skin. When the men had finished, the pig's skin was hairless and pink again and the carcass was ready for treatment.

*

I had a scare on one occasion when I was walking back from Colli to Montebenichi down a sloping field with a hedge on my right-hand side. As I reached the bottom of the field, the ground dropped about 3ft vertically down a bank on to a quite substantial track leading downwards towards Ambra. A thick hedge of low-growing bushes ran along the top of the bank, so I had to jump over them to get to the track. Immediately after I landed, I realized that fifty yards to my right two figures were approaching. They were in uniform, one obviously an officer and the other a private soldier. I did not recognize their uniform, which was a light grey-green colour. The officer was wearing a Tyrolean hat. Both were armed, the officer with a pistol at his waist and the soldier with a rifle across his shoulder. They were now so close I had no option but to carry on walking.

As we met I just said in passing, '*Buona sera*' ('Good afternoon').

I was very worried when they stopped me, but they showed no animosity and no weapons were drawn. They asked me who I was and I told them I was from a town on the River Arno a little to the north but that I was visiting friends in the area. I am quite sure that they were not deceived by this and, replying tongue in cheek, the officer said that he had taken my accent to be Venetian. With that they saluted me, returned my '*Buona sera*' and resumed their walk towards Ambra. I carried on, but my heart was beating wildly and I thought I was in dire trouble.

When I arrived at my shack I thought I had better go on to Montebenichi and explain to the villagers just what had happened. As I began to tell the tale they became very worried, but when I described the uniform they told me I had met two of the *Guardia Forestale*, the equivalent of our Forestry Commission officers. It was just very fortunate that I had bumped into two who were non-political and non-military. If they had been wearing any other uniform it would have been the end of my freedom and could have posed a serious threat to all the villagers who were sheltering me.

I heard a story that an Italian had approached two prisoners in Rapale, the village across the Ambra valley, claiming to be a member of a band of partisans. He said the band was led by a British Army officer and volunteers were wanted. The two prisoners replied that if the British officer came to them they would join the band. Nothing more was heard of the Italian. Much later, after I had left Tuscany, I met several men who had received similar approaches and who, after they agreed to go along with the request, had just been handed to the nearest German unit. Very likely those occasions were the result of the leaflet I found offering a reward for handing over prisoners.

On the approach to the village of Solata there was a solitary house, La Verghaia, alongside the track. It was the home of a very impoverished family consisting of elderly parents and a daughter named Gina, who was about eighteen. There had been reports of one or two incidents in which a person wandering in civilian clothes and claiming to be a British escaped prisoner was seeking to be put in touch with other prisoners. No wandering stranger was trusted by anybody in case he was trying to trap escapees. Although Gina's house was two miles from

Montebenichi, it was situated at the top of the hill overlooking the valley in which Valentino Giovannini had put a shack for the three prisoners he sheltered.

Once Gina was out walking down in that valley and met a man seeking such information. In her innocence she told him that she thought there were some prisoners but she did not know where they were living. I had met Gina and her parents on one occasion when I was passing the house. We chatted for a while and they gave me a drink of water. I was certain she did not know where my shack was. I was the only prisoner who wandered about the countryside, and she had almost certainly not met any others. I felt sure she could not have compromised anybody.

No more was heard of the wandering stranger who had spoken to Gina, and nothing would have been known of the incident if Gina had not herself mentioned it to people. Once she did, however, the word spread like wildfire and Gina was ostracized by the whole community. Thereafter she was no longer referred to as 'Gina della Verghaia' but 'Gina la Spia' (Gina the Spy).

Strangely, Gina later became a real-life 'rags to riches' girl. It transpired that her mother's husband was not Gina's father. Her real father, who lived in Ambra, was an extremely aristocratic and well respected man, and when the war ended he claimed Gina as his daughter and she moved from a life of poverty to one of luxury. After the war I went to have lunch with Gina and her father at his home in Ambra, in a room with beautiful life-size mosaics of family ancestors dressed in full ceremonial uniform. It was in direct contrast to the abject poverty at La Verghaia, which was the only house where I was offered water and not wine.

There was only one occasion on which any visit I made ended unhappily. It happened when I was making my way from the farm at Colli to the village of Solata, a distance of about a mile, along a track I had not previously used. I visited a remote house which was the home of Sesto Migliorini, his wife and two daughters, Assuntina aged eighteen and Mirella aged twelve. Their living conditions were rather similar to those of the family at Colli. They had not previously met any escaped prisoners and were keen that I should stay with them a little while. I agreed, and we were soon sitting down enjoying lunch. For two days all went well. I was sharing jobs like tending the sheep and carrying water from the spring, sometimes with both girls and sometimes just with Assuntina.

When I arrived back at the house on the second day, accompanied by Assuntina, Sesto had become worried about what his daughter had been up to. He was furious with her and berated her fiercely but said nothing to me. I protested that Assuntina had not been up to anything improper, but her father ignored me. There seemed nothing for me to do but leave, and I went back to Colli. I told the family there of my stay with the Migliorini family and that Sesto had been upset about my going out alone with Assuntina. Iolanda knew Assuntina and when she heard my story immediately showed that she was jealous, so I was losing out all round.

Chapter 11

The Decision to Leave

I was worried about the absence of news of any significant advance by the Allied troops fighting in the south. The euphoria which we felt after breaking out of Laterina and the early hopes of the arrival of Allied troops from the south had long since disappeared. Radio London had never offered encouraging news on any occasion I had the chance to hear a news bulletin. The Apennines running down the spine of Italy split the front into two sectors, and the Adriatic coast on the east seemed to offer a better opportunity for progress than our western side. The main impediment to any Allied advance appeared to be the strong German resistance at a line centred on the monastery of Montecassino.

When I had come out of Laterina with three companions immediately following the Armistice in September 1943, it had been our intention to head for the line and to keep moving. Unfortunately, after suffering repeated serious nose bleeds, I had felt compelled to drop out from that march. Now, thanks to the goodwill of the people of Montebenichi and surrounding villages, I was well fed, active and as fit as I had ever been in my life. Furthermore, winter was over. It was the spring of 1944 and I was becoming impatient. I felt certain that whatever had caused the nose bleeding of some months earlier, the matter was no longer a problem.

My parents had tragically lost my twelve-year-old sister, Betty, when the SS *City of Benares*, engaged in the child evacuation scheme to Canada, had been torpedoed and sunk in the Atlantic in September 1940. My brother Les was in India with the Royal Air Force and my other sister, Maude, was on a radar station in Cornwall with the Women's Auxiliary Air Force. Added to this, my name must have been on the missing list for five months since my escape from Laterina, so my parents remained entirely without any news of me, unaware even of whether I was alive or dead. With all this in mind, I now felt I had no alternative but to do something about trying to get home.

I had got to know Roy Page at the mill in Pietraviva quite well and I felt he might be prepared to join in a venture to go south, so I decided to visit the mill. I took Frank with me, and we were well received at the mill. I took Roy aside and asked him if he was interested in my proposal. Without hesitation, he said he was. We thought we would put the idea to the other fellows, and I pointed out to them that we had waited five months for the Allied troops and might well wait another five before they arrived to rescue us. Some of them put the idea to scorn, saying that they felt safe at the mill and were prepared to wait as long as it took for the Allied troops to fight their way up to us. However, one of them, Don Wigley, said at once that he was keen to join us.

Life had become much more relaxed for the fellows living in the mill. Originally the miller had insisted on their staying hidden inside all day and only going on an escorted walk after darkness fell every evening. German trucks were likely to pull into the mill at any moment to purchase flour, so the men there had to always be on their guard. During the day there was a permanent watch on the approach to the mill, and once a German truck was seen approaching the men hurried to their prepared shelter and maintained silence. Nothing that could betray their presence was left in view. Once the Germans had collected their flour and left the area, the all clear was given.

The miller now agreed to the men occasionally going into the village alone towards evening to visit the small bar. They were given a few centavos each by the miller. It was much more like a normal bar than the wine shop in Montebenichi. The local Chianti was very cheap, and the limited amount of money the prisoners ever had ensured that they followed the practice of the Italians and never drank more than one or two glasses. The bar, which was run by a young fellow named Toni, had become a regular haunt for the prisoners.

Any time they attended the bar in the evening there was quite a party atmosphere. The young population of Pietraviva was much like that of Montebenichi, with a fair number of girls but an absence of young men. So once the prisoners started to go to the bar it was not long before the girls appeared. The bar was quite small, but there was a gramophone which played dreamy Italian records, and the small space available for dancing was generally occupied by two or three couples.

That evening I went to Toni's bar with the fellows from the mill. It soon became apparent that some of the men were not following the monastic lifestyle that I had adopted. Occasionally a couple would leave the bar for a time and come back in an excited state. Some time later this sort of assignation led to calamity for one girl. The man thought to be responsible, although this was never certain, was a chap from the Essex Regiment known as Carnera because of his huge size and similarity to Primo Carnera, an Italian heavyweight boxer of the time. Apparently, by the time the pregnancy became known Carnera had already left the district and may not have known about it, whether or not he was responsible.

A postscript to that story happened some years later when I was posted to Chelmsford by the Ordnance Survey. One day, while walking along a main street in the town, I was passing a tailor's shop. To my surprise, there was Carnera standing in the window stooping over a tailor's dummy while he adjusted the clothing on it. I entered the shop and we chatted about Pietraviva for a time, but I did not refer to the outcome of events at Toni's Bar.

*

Now that Roy, Don and I had decided that the three of us would consider a move to go south and attempt to cross the line, it seemed better that Roy and Don should leave the mill and join me in Montebenichi. Frank, who had never settled in Montebenichi, was only too happy to accept an offer to join the group at the mill. This left the three of us free to use my shack whilst we thought the matter over.

The arrangement was soon a success, and we became a strong little trio. The one problem was that there were only two bunks in the shack. The third man had to make do with a heap of brushwood in the space between, but Don quite happily chose to accept that and he slept comfortably. I told Onelia and Corrada in Montebenichi of the changes and they expressed no regret at Frank's departure. They told me the villagers would carry on supplying us with food.

I did not tell Onelia or Corrada the reason behind the change. For a long time we had all been expressing impatience at the slow progress of the Allied forces and had spoken to the villagers of going south. This had come to be treated by them as something of a joke, and they just scoffed every time it was mentioned. We did not know what their reaction would be if we finally said we were leaving.

I should put something down about the two chaps with whom I had decided to throw in my lot, should we eventually decide to set off south. Roy was in the 2nd Regiment, Tank Corps, a London TA unit. He was twenty-one, a year younger than me. Like me, he had joined the TA some months before the war and had also been taken prisoner at Tobruk. Roy had been born in London but his family had emigrated to Canada during his childhood. His father had died, his mother had married a Canadian soldier and the new family returned to England before the war.

Don was from the 1st Battalion, the Parachute Regiment. He was born in Sheffield and was just twenty years old. Leaving school early, he had led a fairly boisterous life, enlisting in the army as a boy entrant with a Scottish Infantry Regiment. When the Commandos were formed in 1940 he volunteered for that regiment but was soon expelled from them, being held responsible for the collapse of an inflatable boat full of men on a lake in Scotland while training for the invasion of Norway in 1940. It happened that at that time the Parachute Regiment was being formed and needed volunteers, so Don immediately joined them. He was taken prisoner in Tunisia during the North African campaign early in 1943. He was a short but stocky chap, with curly hair, a twinkle in his eye and an engaging smile that never left his face. He had also had time to marry and have children before leaving England.

These were two men who I was happy to have as my companions if we finally decided to head for the line. Over the previous few months I had got to know Roy well. Don had been living for the early months with a small group in an isolated house in a valley half a mile or so to the north of Montebenichi. I met him when he joined the mill group in Pietraviva, and we had got on well together from the start.

It was now some time in the spring of 1944, the weather was improving and we were all in excellent health. Roy, Don and I gave much thought to our scheme, taking everything into account. We all felt committed, and so we made the decision to leave and try our luck heading south.

*

The time had come to tell the villagers of Montebenichi and Pietraviva of our decision. My announcement in Montebenichi was met with disbelief and caused an enormous amount of consternation in the village. Without realizing it, I had become part of village life.

Corrada, one of the two girls who had originally invited me to stay in Montebenichi, cried bitterly, saying, '*Franco, non devi andare. E come mi' fratello chi parta. Non troverai casa, troverai la morte*' ('Franco, you mustn't go. It's like my brother leaving. You won't reach home, you'll meet your death').

She went on to say that we might think Italians were all kind like the villagers had been towards me, but when I got 50km south I would find they were all thieves and vagabonds. She was very distressed. This seemed a rather harsh condemnation of Italians in general. Nevertheless, once word got round, I realized that it was the general opinion of all the villagers.

Another most important farewell call would be to the Becucci family at the farm at Colli, and we could call at Poggialto on the way to salute Vittorio, my first host in Montebenichi. Roy and Don knew none of these people, and I was looking forward to introducing them. We found Vittorio at home and I thanked him for his hospitality and kindness. We both regretted the infamous night at Ambra when he had taken me to the cinema only to finish up with a pub crawl of the village. Our most foolish actions that evening had put people at real risk and had threatened to cost me the hospitality of the villagers of Montebenichi.

There was a happy welcome when we arrived at Colli. I introduced Roy and Don and they were made most welcome. The atmosphere became more sombre when they learned that the reason for my visit was to say goodbye, but when Ginestrino suggested a glass of Chianti all round, good spirits soon returned. The family insisted that we could not just turn round and go and that we must at least spend some more time together. So we spent two nights there.

This was a very convivial stay at Colli. Without any advance notice, Rosa was able to serve a plain but tasty dinner. We were offered thick slices of bread, first rubbed with garlic and then covered liberally with olive oil, fresh herbs and a little salt. It was a very basic form of *bruschetta*. Roy and I tucked in, but unfortunately when Don saw it he said scornfully that he was not eating that stuff. The family was very upset, not in an angry way but filled with regret that they could not please their guest. They suggested that they could fry the bread, and Don agreed. The family accepted that but remained very hurt. Later I told Don he should realize that was probably the only food they had in the house. The incident was soon put aside, and we settled down to a comfortable evening chatting together. Roy and Don both spoke good Italian, so there was no pressure on me to act as translator.

The following morning we were up and about doing jobs and carrying water. Later Don and I headed off towards Cennina, an attractive, very small village with a magnificent ruined castle. I recalled the time when, travelling with my three original escapee companions after leaving Laterina, we had met a peasant who had been working in his vineyard. He had taken one of my companions up to Cennina and they had returned laden with food for us. I wanted to find this man and thank him for his generosity. Don and I enquired at some houses, and one lady with whom we chatted presented us with a bottle of wine. However, I was unable to find my benefactor.

The return journey was uphill and the day quite warm, so we sat down and rested a few times. The bottle had the usual folded chestnut leaf as a stopper instead of a cork, so the wine was accessible and we took a swig each time we sat down. By the time we reached Colli we were both rather tipsy, which was not the state of affairs that I had wanted. We just lay on the grass for a while to sleep it off and were soon back in form. Roy was aggrieved that he had not come with us, but I cannot recall the reason for his absence.

At Colli Roy wanted to take a bath. Only Primetta, the elder daughter, was present at the farm. We found a large zinc bath in one of the ground floor stalls and asked Primetta if we could fill the cauldron over the fire to heat the water. Primetta was distraught when she heard we were considering a bath. She claimed she dare not authorize such a thing because it was certain the person taking the bath would suffer a severe chill or worse. The weather was mild but in view of Primetta's concern Roy decided to forgo his ablutions. The next day we were back at my shack and we all bathed at the nearby Horseshoe spring.

When it came time to leave Colli the family were in a state of great emotion. The first time I had left, five months earlier, I had fallen ill again and been forced to drop out and leave my companions. That had resulted in my remaining in the area and visiting Colli on numerous occasions in the subsequent months. They had come to look upon me as a permanent fixture. Now I had told them that, together with Roy and Don, I was leaving to try to rejoin the Allied lines. Rosa, Primetta and Iolanda were weeping and, one by one, the whole family embraced me. Iolanda made no secret of her feelings, and as we were leaving I softened a little so as to part on good terms.

Ginestrino gave me a special hug and wished me good luck. I thanked him and the family for their friendship and their care, and then we set off. It was a repeat of the previous departure as we walked along the long grass ridge. There were occasional looks back and waves to the family, still standing grouped in front of the house, until we reached the end of the ridge and they were no longer distinguishable. From the outset they had so readily shared their few meagre resources with me and had welcomed me as one of their family. Having been away from my own family since 1939, serving at the front, being held as a prisoner of war and then on the run in a foreign country, their generosity and care all meant a great deal to me.

*

When we got back to Montebenichi I found that the villagers had called a meeting for a day or so ahead and that we three were invited. The meeting was to be to be held in the *Dopolavoro* and its purpose was to dissuade us from leaving. When we got there we found that a great many of the villagers had come. One by one the men spoke, emphasizing the distance, the unknown terrain and above all the difficulty of getting through the German lines.

They pointed out that at the time of the Armistice, when we had escaped, there had been total confusion in all Italy and escaped prisoners wandering in the countryside met with friendship from everybody. But now, many months later, there were Germans posing as escapees hoping to be introduced to their so-called fellow prisoners. As a result, no stranger could be trusted at all. The women spent the time assuring us that what the men had said made sense and we should listen to them. They pleaded with us to stay where we were and give up this foolhardy idea. Some of them were in tears, and as the evening drew on it became hard to reject their arguments.

However, we had not come to our decision lightly, and the thought of our families having no news of our fate for so long was not to be put aside. So we told them that we appreciated all they had said but it had not lessened our resolve to go ahead with our plan. We also offered our heartfelt thanks to them for the care and sustenance they had given all of us, especially myself, in Montebenichi.

The meeting finished with the villagers accepting that we were determined to go. They told us that they would provide some freshly cooked food for us to take once the date was fixed. We thanked them and said that we would go round saying goodbye in the following day or so.

The next day we had a message that the people of Pietraviva, Roy's base, wanted us to attend a meeting there. When the time came the evening proved to be a repeat of the Montebenichi gathering. There was one extra item, in that they produced a little Italian fellow who claimed to have tried to cross the line himself a short time before. Being Italian, he had no difficulty travelling by train to a town not far from the front line, but it was at that point his problems had started.

He reported that as he approached the battle area there were checkpoints and roadblocks everywhere, and when he had tried the countryside he had been afraid of minefields. So he had given up and returned to Tuscany. After all the arguments had been aired we told the gathering we were not deterred and still intended to go. We told them all that we were young and we wanted to try. There was the same anguish as in Montebenichi and once again tears were shed, but they reluctantly accepted that we were determined to go.

The meeting ended quite late and the long walk up the hill to Montebenichi did not appeal to us. We could not call at a house at that hour so we decided to find a sleeping place nearby. As we approached the edge of the village we saw a door which obviously did not lead into a dwelling. We opened it and found ourselves inside what seemed to be a small room, although it was pitch dark. We just spread our greatcoats on the stone floor and lay on them alongside each other. The silence was total, but the stone floor was hard and sleep did not come easily. It must have been towards dawn when we woke and heard heavy footsteps approaching down the slope from the village. We immediately jumped up quietly and huddled behind the door.

We were well attuned to suspicious or dangerous situations and although we trusted the villagers implicitly we had to remember that we could at any time be betrayed by someone. So we stood in silence behind the door and waited. As the footsteps reached the door they stopped. We heard the latch and stood with bated breath, ready to pounce on anyone who entered. Then, as the door opened, in the dim, pre-dawn light we saw that the person entering was a hunched old man staggering under an enormous bundle on his back.

He took a pace or two into the room and tipped his load on to the greatcoats on which we had been sleeping moments before. When we moved, he had the shock of his life. He turned out to be a peasant from the village, and we learned that we had been sleeping in the place that held the wood-burning oven that the villagers used for baking their bread every day. The load he had brought was a great amount of brushwood to start the fire in the oven for the day's baking. Once his surprise was over, we shared a laugh with him and then set off on our way.

The incident gave us the chance to make an early start and we were soon on our way up the hill to Montebenichi. One farm we could not avoid was Montesoni, and as usual we were invited in. When wine was offered we declined because it was too early in the morning, but some bread and bunches of grapes were produced for us to eat. However, we then took a glass of wine as a farewell toast to each other. Before leaving we washed at a trough outside the house then carried on up the long slope to Montebenichi.

When we arrived at the shack we spent a little time resting as we had not slept too well. Once rested we spent the rest of the day going round the houses of all my benefactors in the village so that I could express my heartfelt gratitude for the selfless care and wonderful friendship they had extended to me over the previous five months. Inevitably, in each house a glass of wine was pressed on us. This time however it was *vinsanto*, the stronger but smoother dessert wine. The measures were smaller, but by the time our visits round all the homes were done we had drunk quite enough. Before we left we were promised food to last for some days on our journey. We then retired to the shack and slept.

Corrada and Onelia had each given me a little token as a good luck mascot. Corrada gave me a small religious tract in the form of a triptych. On the centre piece was the Madonna with, on the left a soldier and on the right a sailor, of the Italian forces. In the centre Corrada had written '*Buona fortuna durante il tuo viaggio*' ('Good luck on your journey'). Onelia gave me a brooch of a little spray of flowers, which sadly disappeared along the line some years ago. They had been two very good friends and I was pleased that we had managed to keep our friendship platonic.

The following morning we searched out the men we had not seen the previous day because they had been working in their fields and vineyards, and said our goodbyes. Then we set off for Pietraviva to repeat the whole process. Our first call was the outlying farmhouse, Poggigiobi, to see the Meliciani family of three brothers and two sisters. It was in this family's vineyard that I had first met Roy, and I had slept in the little shack there for a few nights before I was invited to stay permanently at Montebenichi.

We found all the Meliciani family at home except the eldest brother, Anselmo. He was working in one of his fields so, after saluting the family, we set off to find him. He was ploughing with his two magnificent white oxen. It was backbreaking work because the plough was a very primitive appliance. When we told him we had come to say goodbye he was extremely upset and tears came to his eyes. He crooked his right forefinger, put it in his mouth and bit until he drew blood, then implored us not to leave. He and the rest of the family had always been kind to us and made us welcome, especially when we had been living in their vineyard. One of the four brothers was a prisoner of war in Sussex and I think that was partly the reason for the family being particularly sympathetic to our plight.

At Pietraviva we spent the rest of the day going round Roy's village friends. I knew some of them, but Roy was a great favourite with them all. When we had finished the round we set off for our shack. We had decided to spend the following day resting up in the shack then set off the next day. We passed this news to Onelia and told her we would collect any prepared food as we passed through the village. So we settled down to our rest day. This was the last time the villagers brought food to the shack.

Chapter 12

Departure from Montebenichi

It was dusk on a glorious cool crisp day, my last day in Montebenichi, when Roy, Don and I left our shack in the woods for the last time. As we approached the village we saw there were people waiting in the lower piazza to see us off. There were lots of final kisses, handshakes and embraces with many of my friends. Onelia and Corrada walked with us past the Castello to Corrada's house, where we collected prepared food that was ready for us. Then we said farewell for the last time to both girls. Onelia and Corrada each in turn embraced me very warmly and I realized what wonderfully good friends they had been. It was an emotional moment, but Roy, Don and I were all in good spirits and feeling ready for whatever lay ahead of us.

We had decided to travel by night and keep off the road during the day. The evening was perfect, with mild weather and a clear sky, the moon and stars shining brightly. We had no map but we knew we just had to keep going south and the stars could lead us. So we took to the road and were soon walking past points we knew so well. First the village cemetery and then the church itself. A mile or so further down the hill we passed the Villa La Selva, where Roy and Don had been imprisoned with their working party. Then the cluster of two or three houses at the junction with the main Ambra valley road. As we turned right towards Siena, instead of our usual left turn for Pietraviva, I knew I was really saying goodbye to Montebenichi. The last two points we recognized were the road on our right leading to the Castle of Montalto and that on our left to the village of Rapale.

After the Rapale turning we were entering unknown territory. Not only was the immediate territory new to us, but as we moved ahead the whole world appeared uncharted. The silence of the night was broken only by the woodland sounds of occasional birds and animals. All three of us were in a good state of health for walking and we made good progress. On arriving at the T-junction of the Siena to Arezzo road we quickly crossed the junction. There seemed to be scarcely any traffic, even on that main road. Civilians received hardly any petrol anyway, and military vehicles were almost totally absent at night. When we did see a vehicle, the headlamp masks, because of blackout restrictions, only let out minimal light. This also restricted vehicles to a moderate speed, and on the few occasions we met one we had plenty of time to get out of sight.

We kept to minor roads and tracks as much as we were able and used the clear sky and bright stars as far as possible to guide us south. The ground was a series of gently sloping hills, which was typical of the terrain around Siena. Shacks built of brushwood or stone were dotted about in the fields, so well before dawn we picked one with a copse of trees alongside. We knew we would have to lie up during daytime, and the few trees would give us cover to stretch our legs a little. The previous day had been strenuous enough, and after walking for hours through the night we were ready for a good sleep. After a swig from our water bottles and a bite of food, we lay on the ground and were asleep at once.

The sun was already high when we woke after a sound sleep and got up to assess our surroundings. We saw one or two buildings but we settled down to an undisturbed and restful day. We felt we had not come many miles but we knew we were on the right track. As twilight approached, we took to the road again. That night and the next one or two were equally successful, and we were getting into a good rhythm, feeling that we were making good progress.

*

We had one alarm that turned out to be a lucky escape. As dawn approached one morning we spotted a shack 30yds or 40yds from the road, alongside a hedge on the right that sloped uphill. We decided that that would be our lay-up point. On entering the shack, we found the floor was littered with a deep jumble of pantiles. We were too tired to worry about this setback and decided to make the best of it. We made the place as comfortable as possible and lay down for another sleep. It was not as comfortable as earlier days, but we awoke refreshed.

The shock came when we surveyed our surroundings. We saw to our horror that a couple of hundred yards further down the road there was a German checkpoint. Another few minutes walking that morning and we would have blundered right into it. We had not been able to see it in the darkness, but from inside their hut the Germans would have heard us approaching. As soon as we realized what it was, we dropped to the ground. Fortunately, we were on the right side of our hedge and could not be seen from the checkpoint. We did not want to sit on pantiles in the tiny shack all day, so we crouched behind the hedge wondering what to do. The road ahead was sloping gently down and the checkpoint was very clearly visible, with a couple of men standing outside the hut. Immediately by the checkpoint a stretch of woodland began on each side of the road.

The hedge by our shack ran uphill a short distance then disappeared over a crest. We decided to crawl up alongside the hedge and, once out of sight over the crest, to weigh up our next move. Out of sight of the checkpoint we felt safer and we decided to make a wide circuit and come back towards the road when we were past the woods and safely beyond the checkpoint. When we were happy with the position, we could rest before setting out on the evening's march. The going was difficult for a while, but we tried to keep roughly parallel to the road and eventually found a track heading our way, so we moved swiftly. We had seen occasional vehicles moving so we knew where the road was, and when we found a track in the right direction we took it.

Then as we approached the road we found a comfortable spot and sat down for a break until the right time of evening to take to the road. We did not know at what time the guard changed at the checkpoint, and it could be that a truck would arrive with a new guard, so we did not want to start before dark. Once it was dark we would be able to see the dim lights long before the truck spotted us. So we relaxed and felt that we had had a lucky escape.

*

We were fairly happy that having just passed a checkpoint there would not be another for some considerable time. We now had to face up to a serious problem because the food we had carried was practically exhausted. We had known this moment would arrive and now we had to do something about it. Our best option seemed to be to give ourselves enough time just before dark to find a farmhouse and simply throw ourselves on the family's mercy. It meant a slight change of plan, and we started a little earlier than we had meant to. Nevertheless, there was still a glimmer of light in the sky when we arrived at a roadside farm. Made up of big barns and outbuildings and a very large farmyard, it was a much bigger concern than the small peasant farms of Montebenichi and the other villages in the Valdambra. As we entered the yard a young girl was crossing its far side. When she saw us she hurried forward and disappeared into the house.

Now Corrada's words of warning to me about the character of people to the south came to mind. As we reached the door a man appeared. We came straight to the point and told him we were English and needed food. He hesitated, looked very worried and told us we should not come to his house. Then he told us to come in quickly and sat us down at a table, with the family standing silently watching. They were a much more prosperous looking group than the peasant farmers of the Valdambra. He asked that food be brought, and his wife produced some bread, cheese, salami and a flask of wine. We had been sparing with our own food and now we tucked in hungrily under the silent gaze of the family. As soon as we had finished he said he would give us food for the road. He also let us fill our water bottles.

We must have looked pretty scruffy, because he then asked us if we would like a wash. We accepted gratefully and were taken to another room, where we found an enamel basin on an old-fashioned iron frame, buckets of cold water and the very poor quality Italian soap. When we had cleaned ourselves up, we felt like new men. As soon as we had finished, the farmer told us we had better go. He and his family had been very frightened of us being in his home, and when we left our thanks were heartfelt. They were not Corrada's so-called 'thieves and vagabonds', but their fear was real, because they knew there were Germans in the neighbourhood and the farmer feared for his family's lives.

It was dark when we left, and now we met our first major setback. The clear sky with its multitude of stars was no longer with us although the moon was strong enough to be visible. Instead, there was a fairly thin layer of cloud, so we had lost our direction-finding stars. We carried on just trusting to instinct, but when morning approached we were not sure whether we were any further south than where we had started. This left us downhearted, and unless conditions changed the outlook was bleak. We then spent a worrying day lying up. Towards the end of that day, as darkness was approaching, conditions had not changed. We could not afford to stay still, however, and we thought maybe our worries might be unfounded and we might still be progressing south.

That evening we had our first encounter by night, and a most strange one. We were walking not on a road or track but through an area of waist-high bushes. Suddenly a figure was coming towards us in the gentle moonlight. It turned out to be a priest and he immediately asked us if we were English. Surprised at this almost surreal encounter and the priest's instant assumption, we admitted that we were. He told us that if we kept on for a few hundred yards we would come to a house where the family would help us and give us food. He then went on his way, wishing us good fortune, but the meeting left us quite bewildered.

We soon arrived at a house and decided to take our friendly priest at his word. Wondering what sort of help they could give us, we knocked on the door. After some time, because it was now late evening, the door was gingerly opened. Again we introduced ourselves as English and in need of help. We were invited in and found a large family there. We told them of our meeting with the priest and his advice that we should call. It seemed he had left their house shortly before we met him. As we had eaten not too long before, we sat down to a token meal of bread and salami, with a drink of coffee. Their reaction was different from that of the previous family. Some seemed worried, but others chatted freely with us. This time we did not need telling we should go, because we were keen to be on our way. They too gave us food for the road. This now meant that we had food for some days. The family knew we wanted to go south and gave us some directions and tips. However, when we got outside in the dark we found it impossible to sort out the advice, so again it was a case of following our instincts.

*

That night we were able to travel by small country roads and we hoped that we had made progress in the right direction. Our uncertainty was worrying, though, and we knew it could not go on. We realized we had to change our plan. Before we started we had decided that we would try not to walk in daylight at all. But now we had no choice while the night sky stayed cloud-covered. The only option was to travel by day, and we reluctantly decided to do that. We hoped that the clear nights would return, maybe even after just one day's walking. As soon as we found a suitable place we bedded down and were able to get some sleep.

We started our first daylight march early and were now able to make good progress on empty roads and felt reasonably confident that we could keep our bearings under control. For some time we were on minor country lanes and tracks and, with the help of the sun, we could roughly control our direction. We only met one person on the road. He was an elderly man and, in a totally rural area with no habitation in sight, he was sweeping the roadside with a very large brush. He proved to be simple-minded and when he spoke, his words were incomprehensible. We could not tell whether he understood us or not and we were unable to get any useful information from him. We felt sympathy for him but just had to carry on. We eventually came to a T-junction with a major road. Unfortunately, there was no signpost that might have given us any helpful information, but to turn left on that road took us pretty well due south, so that was our obvious choice. We decided to risk it and take a chance on a main road in daylight.

Fortune seemed to be on our side, and the road was empty of traffic. We covered a mile or two and then the road began to run alongside a railway line. The railway was constructed on a grassy embankment about 10ft high, with the boundary fence only about 30yds across the grass from our road. We had not been alongside the railway for long before we heard a train approaching from behind us.

It was a goods train and was not made up of normal goods wagons but of a long line of low-loaders. It was a train of reinforcement supplies for the *Wehrmacht*, the German army. On each wagon was an artillery gun, a heavy tank or an armoured troop carrier. We silently wished the guns and tanks no luck when they reached the battle zone. On many of the wagons a heavy machine gun had been mounted, with a German soldier sitting behind it, some facing us and some facing the other direction.

The train was only about 40yds from us and we waved our arms wildly in a mock greeting. Our minds had been tense for so long, but now this scenario seemed hilarious and all the tension fell from us. The German soldiers must have been bored stiff trundling along on a goods train all day and they, without enthusiasm, waved back. If they could have known who we were they would probably have turned their machine guns on us. This put a spring in our step as we walked on. It was not long before another train passed us and we enjoyed going through the same routine. The road had been kind to us as we had been walking for some time and we had not seen a vehicle or a roadside house.

For some days the landscape had been quite different from that around our villages of the Valdambra. The rolling hills were much lower than those around Montebenichi and the countryside was grassland with a few crops here and there and some patches of woodland. We saw no vineyards or livestock. Soon after the second train had passed us we came to a minor road turning left which passed under the railway embankment. We were able to see that it carried on straight for a couple of hundred yards beyond the embankment, but we chose to trust our luck on the main road for a little longer.

Just as we passed the side road we all decided it was time for a relief halt before we went any further, so the three of us walked across the grass to the railway fence and stood alongside each other, relieving ourselves. The road ahead was an unknown quantity because a couple of hundred yards ahead it swung right and disappeared out of sight behind a sharply rising hill. This hill was very high, an exception to all the other gentle slopes around us.

Then suddenly we heard the first vehicle moving on the road. It came speeding around the bend ahead from behind the hill. To our horror it was a German open-topped, jeep-type vehicle. The grey-green uniforms and the silver braided peaked hats of the four occupants told us that they were German officers. We were glad we were not still on the roadside. Even so, they were going to pass very close to us and our hearts were pounding. Worse was to come when they were a few yards past us. We heard a screech of breaks and the jeep squealed to a halt. We hardly dared to look but we saw them for a moment looking our way and the four of them dismounted.

At that moment a return to the barbed wire of Laterina seemed to be looming very close in our minds, and that was just the best scenario. However, we gazed in amazement as the incredible happened. Once dismounted, the four of them each stood by a wheel of the jeep and relieved themselves, then remounted and drove off. We could not believe our luck, realizing that we had unwittingly sponsored a little auto-suggestion. We could imagine the conversation that had gone on in the jeep: 'Isn't it time we stopped for a piss, Hermann?' We laughed when it was over, but it frightened us off the main road.

*

We decided we must change to the minor road passing under the embankment. So off we set along this side road and, as we approached the embankment, there was a priest accompanied by a lady and two small girls approaching from the other side. I thought he might stop to chat, as priests usually recognized us for what we were, but as we passed each other we merely exchanged a short greeting.

We carried on along the couple of hundred yards of straight road that we had been able to see from the main road. There was then a dense high hedge growing on the right of the road, an unusual feature of the land around there. As we neared the end we saw that the road bent sharply right. This was what we wanted, because turning right meant we would be heading south. We were about to take the turn when disaster struck. We came face to face with two Italian policemen, *Guardie Civile*, not 20yds ahead, rifles slung over their shoulders. There was no place to hide. We had not seen them because of the thick hedge. The hedge was impenetrable, and to have run back down the road would have been suicide, so there was no escape.

Both parties kept moving without making any sign. We were alongside each other, on the right of the road. I was the left one of our three, and the police were approaching on my left. I was thinking this was a good thing because I had the best command of Italian, but my heart was beating wildly. When they passed my shoulder I was beginning to think that this was another miracle. Two such episodes so close together were an enormous strain on the nerves, and I was praying that, now they were behind me they would take no action. However, there was to be no such luck.

From just behind me came the dreaded words '*Un momento*'. The three of us knew at once that all was lost. One of the police asked me who we were. I told them we were refugees bombed out from a town in the Arno valley and were going south to stay with relatives. They looked at each other and said nothing for a moment. I began to hope that we might have got away with it. Then came the killer word: '*Documenti*'.

There was no answer to that as we had no documents, and we knew we were sunk. Their rifles immediately came into action and were pointed at us menacingly. They ordered us to turn and walk back down the road, following just behind. As we walked back under the bridge my thoughts turned to the priest we had passed at that point and I wondered whether he could have warned us about the police. Then I realized the police were well behind him and he would not have seen them. It had been an awful piece of ill fortune spotting them when we were hardly 20yds apart.

They marched us along the main road for some way until we arrived at a small town and were directed to the town's *Carabinieri* station. Our captors were in the uniform of the civil police but the station chief, an elderly, white-haired man, was in the uniform of a *Brigadiere* of the *Carabinieri*. We were escorted immediately to a cell and ordered in. The door clanged behind us. We could find no light switch. Daylight was fading and there was only a small barred window, so we could see very little.

Fortunately, we had been locked in our cell without having been searched. We were extremely worried that we had between us a number of photographs of friends from Montebenichi and Pietraviva. We knew we had to destroy them before they were found on us, and luckily we had matches. The photos were printed on very thick paper and when it burned, a great volume of acrid smoke was produced. The small window let in hardly any air and there was little wind outside anyway to blow air into the cell. We coughed and spluttered as the smoke got thicker, but we were glad of the opportunity to destroy the photos. We were afraid the police might come to check what was making so much smoke, but the exercise passed off unnoticed.

Later a *Carabiniere* opened the door and asked who spoke the best Italian. As I did I was escorted to the charge room. The *Brigadiere* asked me to enter my particulars in the charge book. I entered my name and then put my age as twenty-two.

Seeing this, the *Brigadiere* raised his arms in dismay and echoed in Italian, 'Twenty-two! Still a boy, and he's going to Germany! You can't have been wandering around all these months. You must have been with friends, so why did you leave them?'

I ruefully thought of the insistent advice given to us in Montebenichi and Pietraviva. He then told me to enter my companions' names. He was even more distressed when I entered Roy's name and his age as being twenty-one. Worse was to come, though, as Don was only twenty. The *Brigadiere* seemed close to tears and would certainly have been pleased to tell us to clear off if he had been able to do so, but with the entries in the charge book it was too late.

*

The following morning we were given breakfast and put in an open truck with two armed guards and driven north. It was a beautiful spring day and the countryside matched the weather in beauty. Our destination proved to be Siena, where we were driven to the civil prison of Santo Spirito. After undergoing formalities inside the main entrance, we were escorted through a number of steel-grille gates until we arrived at a corridor with four or five cell doors on each side. We were ushered to the last door on the right and heard the depressing clang as it slammed behind us. There were two beds in the cell that were hinged and fastened to the wall which we could bring down to the horizontal. There was also a camp bed and blankets. After a while we noticed a small door about a foot square in the wall at floor level. When we unlatched it we found it contained a little pot for our toilet. So we were well catered for.

After a while a warder arrived with a meal. The door opened only a few inches and the thinnest man one could imagine squeezed sideways through the gap. His peaked hat seemed to be as wide as any part of his body. Once he was in the cell he looked at us and, lifting his head, burst into a passage from the song 'Yes, We Have

No Bananas, We Have No Bananas Today'. It was so surprising that we just burst into laughter. The performance was repeated on almost every visit he made to the cell. These were his only words of English but he was very proud of them. We gave him the nickname 'Bananas' and during our stay we looked upon him as a friend.

Before leaving the cell Bananas asked, in Italian of course, whether we wished the door to be left open or not. We were incredulous because we had thought it had been locked all the time. He explained that the grille gate at the end of the corridor was always locked but that good conduct prisoners were allowed to have their cell door unlocked. The prison governor had decided that as we had not committed a criminal act we could be considered good conduct prisoners.

It was not long before the first neighbour walked in and said he had come for a chat. He was an enormous man, and we conversed happily for a while. We then gingerly asked the reason for his imprisonment.

'Oh,' he said quite nonchalantly, 'I'm in for twenty-one years for murdering my wife.'

We all drew breath and decided the less we knew about our fellow inmates the better. From then on we kept our door closed and met no other prisoners.

Our next visitor, a couple of days later, was the prison governor. We were obviously his star prisoners. He brought with him two beautifully dressed Italian ladies, his wife and a friend. It was like having a party, and the chatter was fast and very friendly. They sat along one bed and we sat on another. They sympathised with us over our predicament and told us that they also were aiding escaped prisoners. I am sure they told their prisoners of our plight and that those fellows just as surely got the message to stay put where they were. The governor apologised for having to hold us in such conditions, then he and the ladies left.

Not all our visitors were so cordial, and we got a nasty surprise on one occasion. The door opened one day and Bananas slid in, but this time he did not sing. He was followed immediately by a small man dressed in the black uniform of the Fascist Militia. We knew that those men were the nasties of the Italian military. He seemed to weigh us up for some moments. Then we saw that he was holding a metal truncheon in his hand. It all felt very menacing, and we wondered what we were in for. He then walked to the cell window behind us. The window was large, and sunk into the wall was a grille of heavy horizontal and vertical iron bars covering the window. He raised the truncheon and drew it backwards and forwards swiftly across the bars of the grille. Each bar rang loud and clear like a carillon of bells, and he was evidently satisfied none had been tampered with.

The two left without further ado, without a word having been spoken, and we drew deep breaths of relief. Moments later we heard the same drill coming from the next cell and then successively in each cell along the corridor. We happened to be the last cell in the corridor and the Militia man had come to the end to start his checks, so we had had no warning. If we had not been the first to be done we would have been saved our moments of panic. We wondered why a military figure had come to check cells in a civilian prison. We thought it might have been because we were military, but all the other cells got the same treatment.

*

One day the message came through that the following morning we were to leave the prison, but there was no mention of our next destination. Being forewarned, we were ready in good time when the call came. We were escorted to the reception hall near the main door where we found a couple of warders, two German soldiers and the prison governor.

The senior of the two Germans was a tall, burly man whose grey-green great-coat reached almost to the ground. His belt held a holster which housed an enormous pistol, and he was also armed with a large Mauser rifle. Around his neck a long chain of metal links stretched down to his chest to support a heavy metal plate on which the word *FELDGENDARMERIE* was emblazoned in relief. He made the Redcaps, our military police, seem like Sunday school teachers. The Germans and the governor had no common language to discuss the handover, so it was all done in sign language. The three of us had to pass between two points across the room through a metal-detecting ray, which we managed successfully. That was the end of formalities, and we were now in German hands.

At that point the governor went into his office and emerged holding three large cartwheel-shaped loaves of lovely fresh bread. As he handed one to each of us, we could see that he was quite upset. It was a very touching gesture and we were very grateful to him. He was obviously concerned about our future welfare and brave enough to make no secret of his sympathies. It had all the atmosphere of an Italian opera. The two Germans then led us through the small wicket gate in the large prison door. It was so good to emerge from the dingy electric light of the prison interior into the special light of an early morning in Siena and take great gulps of the clean fresh air.

Here I must digress a moment. Stretching from the main prison entrance along the front wall of the prison was a narrow alleyway named *Vicolo di Finimondo* (World's End Alley). I was not to know that thirty years later my daughter Betty, during a year studying at Siena University, would rent a room at the far end of this very alley. *Vicolo di Finimondo* runs along the front wall of the prison, with two barred windows overlooking the alley. It was never possible to see out of the cell windows when we were inside, so I do not know whether one was the window of my cell. But day after day, morning and evening, Betty was to walk past my infamous former abode.

Now back once again in spring 1944, a taxi with a mild-looking little Italian driver was waiting for us outside the prison. As we reached the taxi the bigger German pointed to his pistol and made it plain that he would not be afraid to use it if there should be any messing about. He then ordered us into the car. I found his manner and orders curt and gruff, and his voice detestable. We got into the back seat while the other German, who fortunately was slim, squeezed in beside us. The boss fellow was in the front with his Mauser rifle pointing at us and the other guard had his rifle across the back seat under our noses. They had no cause to be thinking of using them, but it was disturbing to have the wrong end of both weapons pointing at us.

We had no idea where we were going but we hoped it was not too far, because it was desperately uncomfortable in the back seat. We were in fact heading north towards Florence, skirting the western edge of the *Chianti Classico* wine region. Once again, it was a perfect spring day, and the picturesque scenery of the Chianti hills was something we should have been able to sit back and enjoy. The road was almost empty as we cruised along, with hardly any more traffic than occasional peasants with their creaking ox-carts pulled by the usual pair of white oxen. At that moment, though, we were all somewhat apprehensive about what the future held, and it was just not the time to sit back and enjoy the scenery.

We did not speak much to each other and when we did it was in a hushed whisper. The Italian driver was clearly frightened of the Germans but at one point he plucked up enough courage to say that he was sorry he had to drive us to Florence but if he refused to do so his family would suffer. Then, as we were nearing Florence, with attractive villas dotted about the hillsides, he commented that before the war all those villas had been occupied by English families. He spoke in Italian but the German picked it up and snarled '*Nein, alle Juden*' ('No, all Jews'). We passed no comment, and that ended all conversation. Apart from that one outburst, neither German uttered a word.

Chapter 13

La Fortezza da Basso

As we entered the outskirts of Florence the streets seemed empty of people. The taxi continued into the city and it was not long before we drew up outside the main entrance of the daunting, impregnable looking Renaissance Fortezza da Basso (Basso Fortress), built for the Medici family in the 1530s. The taxi was cleared to enter and drove into a large courtyard that contained several two-storey prison blocks, before pulling up outside the door of one of them. As we were ushered out of the taxi we said goodbye to the driver, wishing him well and telling him that we harboured no grudge against him.

On entering the building we found ourselves in a narrow, stone-flagged corridor stretching both left and right. To the left, about 10yds away, the corridor ended at a heavy metal-grille gate with a room beyond it. We could see a lot of young German soldiers in the room, brawling with each other and kicking up a great din. Soon they spotted us in the corridor and realized at once that we were British.

Immediately they rushed to get to the gate. Arms were thrust between the bars waving threateningly with fingers pointed towards us, and legs came through aiming equally threatening kicks in our direction. The screams of a dozen voices rose into a crescendo of abuse in German. It was frighteningly clear that if they could have got at us they would have torn us apart. The three of us were in a state of shock because we did not know whether or not we were about to be put in with this bunch. Even our German escorts were taken by surprise and were moving towards the gate to calm things down. Then a gaoler arrived to take charge of us. The handover needed only moments, and we were whisked away from the young Germans. We later learned the German soldiers were themselves in detention. To our relief, we saw no more of them.

Our gaoler, a German soldier, was a strange fellow. He was a little old to be in the military, short and rather hunched. His features were almost grey and dry, like faded parchment. He was obviously not fit for service at the front and was probably condemned to service in the Fortezza for the duration. He never uttered a word and ignored any questions we asked him. He did not understand English anyway, but his silence seemed to go beyond that point. Hanging from his belt was a huge key ring with an enormous number of keys. Each time we saw him open a lock he knew precisely which key to use. It was quite likely it had been drilled into him after doing it for some years.

He escorted us along the corridor and up a flight of stairs to the upper floor. There we were confronted by another metal-grille gate opening on to a long corridor which had other corridors leading from it on both sides, each starting with a similar gate. There were about five cell doors on each side of our corridor, and our cell was half way down on the left. The door had a small aperture at about eye height, with a metal cover which swivelled up to allow inspection of the cell from outside. We were ushered into our cell and the door clanged to behind us. I was now so used to cell doors clanging shut behind me that I was beginning to feel like an old lag. It was an ignominious way to arrive at our first home in Florence.

All three of us were exhausted by the events and the tension of the day. We sat down to take stock of our predicament. The cell was about 12ft by 10ft with a concrete floor, white painted walls and a very high ceiling. On the outside wall opposite the door was a window which had quite an unusual construction. The fortress wall was about three feet thick and on the inside face of the wall the windowsill was about five feet above the floor. The sill was not horizontal but sloped steeply upwards towards the outside face of the wall. This meant that although the window space on the inside of the wall was about five feet high it was only about two feet high at the outside of the wall. So the only view of the world outside that we could have was a small patch of sky through a hole high in the wall and that hole held a grille of thick metal bars. There was a glass-panelled, hinged window on the inside wall which we could open or close as we wished.

The only pieces of furniture in the cell were two iron bedsteads, and there were three straw-filled palliasses and six blankets of surprisingly good quality. We were thus one bed short, but we each had a palliasse and two large woollen blankets with a different colour on each side.

It was now late afternoon. With the pressures of the day we had never felt like eating, but now we realized that we were hungry. There was no prospect of any food arriving, but we still each had the loaf which the governor of Santo Spirito gaol had given us when handing us over to our German escort. So dinner that evening was dry bread, but it was still fresh and we appreciated the thoughtfulness of the governor. We had not heard a sound since arriving in the cell so we had no idea whether or not we had any company in the corridor. Don settled the problem of the missing bed by volunteering to sleep on the floor. It was not long before we were wrapped in our warm blankets, and we slept soundly.

*

Next morning did not bring much enlightenment as to our future. There was still total silence and no knowing whether or not we had company in the other cells. Nor had there been any indication of when we would be given food. So the morning dragged on, and we just had to show patience. Eventually, towards the middle of the day, we heard the rattle of keys in the grille gate at the end of the corridor. Moments later, much to our relief, our door was being opened. As it swung wide, our same gaoler, whom we had by now decided to call Fritz, was standing there looking as impassive as ever. As we stepped out, Fritz went to unlock the cell door opposite ours.

In doing so, he seemed apprehensive and jumped aside as the door opened. We then saw three Indian prisoners inside, squatting cross-legged on the floor. Each of them was entirely swathed in a large blanket, staring forward impassively with only their face and turban showing outside their blankets. This bizarre sight every day was too much for Fritz. Two other cell doors were then opened, the first producing three British prisoners and the second two black South Africans, making eleven in all.

Fritz escorted us all downstairs and outside to what was to be our exercise yard. This stretched about 30yds along the building and was about half as wide. The three surrounding brick walls were about 12ft high. We were to spend around an hour there every day, during which time we would eat and take some exercise. We soon got to know each other's history and how we had come to be in the Fortezza. Some men took advantage of the fresh air with a spell of jogging or walking around the boundary walls, while others just stood talking to fellows from other cells.

The food usually arrived soon after we reached the yard so it was still slightly warm. It came in a small milk churn containing a watery pasta with no flavour to it. The contents allowed for a large ladleful for each man, with just a little extra left over. It was usually left to any two fellows to scrape out this extra portion and there was never any squabbling. We were also able to fill our water bottles at a tap before leaving the yard, and on that first day we were given a bucket to look after our toilet needs whilst in the cell.

Besides the pasta, we each received a large hard-tack biscuit similar in looks to its British Army counterpart. Whereas the British version, even though not very interesting, was full of nutritional value, our Italian version was more like a dog biscuit and offered very little nutrition. The biscuit was our food for the rest of the day.

One grim aspect of the yard was the bullet holes on the end walls, about chest high, in the ancient brickwork. This was obviously where executions had taken place. An Italian man appeared at a ground floor window one day and told us he was going to be shot. Although we believed our cell window might have been above our yard, we neither saw nor heard any evidence of such events during our stay in the fortress.

However, on one occasion we saw clear evidence of a terrible atrocity. The heavily barred ground floor windows started about 6ft above ground level in the yard.

During one exercise break we heard the sound of blows and terrible screams coming from one of the open windows. Everyone stood still and mute for some time while this lasted. When the screams gave way to sobs and moans, one of our group grabbed the metal security bars of the window. They projected out from the wall of the building so he could grasp the short horizontal length and heave himself up.

He dropped back almost immediately and reported that he had seen two German soldiers and a half-dressed man covered in blood. Some minutes later we saw two bloodied hands come up to grip the bars and moments later a man's head slowly came into view. There was blood all over his face and his right ear was hanging off. His eyes were staring but I do not know whether he could see us. He babbled something incoherently for some moments and then fell back. This was evidence that there were people here in the Fortezza who were experiencing dreadful atrocities, and it was a very chastened bunch that filed back to our cells.

We soon became used to the same regime every day. We did not know the date but we decided to keep track of the length of our stay with the time-honoured prison method of a pencil mark for each day, drawing six vertical strokes then a diagonal through them to denote a week. Don showed himself to be quite an artist by pencilling the figure of a woman on the wall. In the following days he added items of clothing until we eventually had a passable mural. Then Don gave a remarkable display of generosity. He said that as near as he could tell it was his birthday and he wanted to give his biscuit to Roy and myself to share. We protested that this was the wrong way round for a present, but Don was adamant so Roy and I had an extra half biscuit each.

*

After some days in the Fortezza the three of us were told we were to be taken somewhere for interrogation. When the call came we were escorted by two German guards to a Headquarters set up in a magnificent villa in the hills overlooking Florence, though I was in no state to appreciate that aspect at the time. This time we travelled in the back of a military lorry.

From the tailboard of the lorry we were able to see more of Florence. Once again there was a noticeable absence of people on the streets and very few vehicles on the road. Florence was basking in a lovely light and it was so good to have a break from our claustrophobic cell and enclosed yard. I now know that we were going round the north-west outskirts of the city, and soon afterwards we turned north on to the hill probably leading towards Fiesole, high above the city. After a short distance on that road, we turned into the grounds of a large villa.

When our escort led us into the villa we found ourselves in a large circular hall. The floor was of gleaming polished marble. The decor, in light pastel colours, reinforced the silence enveloping the hall. The high walls were a light grey. It is strange that I cannot recall what was overhead, but it will have been a beautiful painted ceiling as such a place would warrant. There were numerous doors, all painted white. Opposite the entrance was a staircase, with the pillars at the base of the stairs also in white. An idyllic sort of place and even a feeling of privilege to be there, but such feelings dissipated the moment I thought of our circumstances and the reason for our presence.

Outside every door and on either side of the stairway a sentry was stationed, although the word sentry seems to demean them. They were magnificent men dressed in the uniform of the prestigious and ultra-smart Hermann Goering regiment. We had heard of these people but never thought we would come face to face with them. Towering fellows, they scarcely needed any identifying features, but for good measure each cuff of their grey-green uniform was embroidered with two narrow silver bands. Between these bands, also in silver, was embroidered in bold letters of German script the name 'Hermann Goering'. Each man was armed with a pistol. Their very presence was suffocating, and after having spent some days in the Fortezza, allowed out of the cell into a yard for an hour every day, with poor facilities for washing or laundry, I do not think I have ever felt so scruffy and unkempt in all my life.

In the English Penguin book by Robert Graves an Italian girl had given me during the grape harvest in Montebenichi I had come across Dante Alighieri's oft quoted phrase, '*Lasciate ogni speranza voi ch'entrate*' ('Leave behind every hope, you who enter here'). It had struck me as really pithy at the time I read it, but, standing in that hall it just seemed that there could be no more appropriate phrase to highlight my predicament.

With our escort from the Fortezza looking hardly less scruffy than ourselves in comparison with the Hermann Goering soldiers, we stood in the centre of the hall for what seemed an age. The silence was total and the only movement was military officers quietly going about their business. Looking back, it must have been that long wait which etched the scene so indelibly on my mind.

Eventually, three men dressed in civilian clothing arrived. They all wore long raincoats and one wore a trilby hat. They stood inside the entrance for a time contemplating the scene and watching us. Then they moved over to us and, one by one, we were each put under close scrutiny. They were commenting in low tones in German until they came to me. Then the trilby-hatted fellow fixed me with his eye and ground out the words '*Ach, hier ist ein typische Engländer* ('Ah, here is a typical Englishman'). I understood scarcely a word of German, but his meaning was all too clear. My spirits were already at a low ebb but at those words I was filled with despondency.

The three men then disappeared into a room and we guessed our interrogation was about to begin. They may have been Gestapo, but as they were not in uniform they may have been from the Todt Organization, the body responsible for slave labour. Eventually, one of the others was taken into the room. We had assumed that the information they wanted would be the particulars of people who had sheltered us for many months, and since recapture we had carefully rehearsed an appropriate story. This would be along the lines that we had escaped from a large PoW concentration camp somewhere up north. We vaguely thought that it was somewhere near Bologna.

We would appear to have learned no Italian. Our lack of Italian would be quite understandable if we had been in the complete segregation of a concentration camp, as against being in a small working party, where there would have been close relations and familiarity with Italian workers. Then we had made our way down through Italy, never stopping more than a few days in any one place, not getting to know people's names and not remembering any villages we had visited. Sometimes we had been offered a lift on lorries for some way. We had decided that the story should be slowly dragged out of us, and our fumbling, head-scratching answers would reflect sadly on us as three members of a fairly dim soldiery. Such was the story we had concocted between ourselves. One thing we hoped for was that we would not contradict each other's stories too much.

The second chap was then called in, although the first did not rejoin me. This left me standing alone in the splendour of the hall with our two escorts and the Hermann Goering watchdogs. My stomach was churning as I waited, wondering what was happening. It seemed to me we were being kept apart so that we could not ask any questions about what form the interrogation had taken. Then after some time Roy and Don both appeared and we were handed back to our escort. I was not going to be subjected to any interrogation at all. I could not imagine why, but this was an enormous relief. Outside the air smelt sweet and I was singing inside. I almost felt well disposed towards our scruffy old escorts as, with Fiesole above us and Florence below, we climbed into the back of our vehicle and set off back to the Fortezza.

*

Every few days more prisoners would arrive at the Fortezza. Sometimes they were British, and on one occasion a young Belgian was among them. He was not in uniform but wore a light grey civilian suit. He said he was not military, but we never quite worked out what he was. It seemed unlikely he was a plant among us but we just accepted him.

One morning the group had quite a surprise. We had heard nothing during the night but fairly early the next morning a shout echoed along the corridor: 'Hey guard, when do we eat?' The accent was unmistakeable and we realized that during the night some Americans must have arrived. We guessed that they were newly captured prisoners and sympathized with them because they would be going through the traumatic early days of captivity.

The shouted request was repeated endlessly and became ever more impatient and angry. Finally, in another cell somebody's patience gave out and their answer was fired back: 'On Thursday afternoon. Now be quiet.'

This must have given the Americans something to think about and a period of silence followed. However, the silence did not last long. When the next cry started, it was, 'Hey guard, where do we shit?'

Like the previous cry, this was repeated and repeated until somebody's patience once again gave out. This time the terse rejoinder was, 'Kick it round the floor till you lose it.'

It was then not long before Fritz arrived and gave us our temporary freedom from the cell. So for our exercise period we had the excitement of meeting the Americans, as none of us had met any before. They were dressed in a one-piece combat uniform, in a yellowish off-white colour.

We were able to describe the routine of the place to them. They wanted to be first in everything and jostled round the German guard serving the pasta. At meal-times every day we picked up a basin, a fork and a spoon and left them on a table before returning to the cells. The Americans picked up the drill right away. The moment the guard had served the last man the Americans took over the milk churn and the three of them were scraping away inside, fishing out the last shreds of pasta. They then went back to their cell armed with a bucket and in a more relaxed frame of mind.

When we met them the next day they complained of the cell being cold during the night. They also told us that they had two two-tier wooden bunks for sleeping. When we woke the next morning there was a smell of wood smoke, and smoke was seeping into our cell. Questions, coming from other cells, began to be shouted along the corridor. The Americans joined in the shouted conversation to tell us that there was no closable glass window in their cell and to keep warm they had made a fire with the wooden cross pieces of one of their bunks. They also said they were suffering a little from smoke inhalation but at least they were warm. There was no sign of Fritz, and we had to wait for exercise time. Once the day was warming, we opened our window, and the smoke which had penetrated our room soon cleared.

As a result of this situation the men in three of the cells each invited an American to move in with them. We were one of the three. The chap who came to our cell had no kit whatsoever. He just brought his blankets and palliasse with him and we made some floor space for him. His hair was reddish and his name was Renard, so he was known to all as Foxy. This proved a good move because the constant chatter with a stranger and the exchange of news and views greatly relieved our boredom in the cell.

It turned out that a Rangers battalion, who I think were the equivalent of British Commandos, had landed at Salerno or Anzio in the south of Italy. We learned from Foxy that his unit had suffered such severe casualties that he knew of no survivors except himself and his two colleagues in the Fortezza with us. They had survived by standing in a river up to their necks in water and had not been spotted. When they later tried to move they had been taken prisoner and escorted north through Italy until they arrived at Laterina. Security at Laterina had become very poor and they had been able to escape soon after arrival. They were unlucky, however, and were recaptured very soon afterwards. As they were now classified as returned escapees they had been sent up to Florence, to the more secure conditions of the Fortezza.

Foxy's two companions were a very large man from New York, named O'Dell, and another whose name I cannot remember. Being in with more seasoned prisoners helped them settle into the life, although they still seized the milk churn and scratched for any pasta leftovers. It was not long before they were due for interrogation. Being new prisoners and much more au fait with the goings on of the war, their questioning was likely to be more rigorous than ours.

When they returned they told us O'Dell had been magnificent in tongue in cheek exaggeration with his answers. He was asked the hypothetical question, 'If the Allies were to invade Europe, what number of forces would be available for the operation?'

After pausing for some moments of thought, his laconic answer was, 'Oh, on the first day there would be a million, then they'd take it from there.'

When it became obvious the three knew nothing of any value, the interrogation came to an end and they were returned to the fortress. Hearing O'Dell tell his story the following break time, we all had a good laugh.

Soon after that we were told we were to leave the Fortezza the following day. We had then clocked up three weeks on our wall calendar. In that time the conditions and lack of exercise had taken a heavy toll on our fitness. The eternal hope of PoWs is that the next camp will be better, so we consoled ourselves with that thought. The reason for the move proved to be that our numbers were now sufficient to fill a railway wagon to take us north towards Germany.

*

During my imprisonment in the Fortezza da Basso I simply considered it to be an inhospitable and inhumane institution. In later years I looked into its history. It appears that it had always been such a place. Many generations of Florentine notables and enemies of the State endured their final sufferings there.

Construction of the Fortezza began in 1534. It was the first of the fortresses built in the warring towns of Tuscany and was the brainchild of Pope Clement VII, the Medici Pope. He had proposed building it to enhance the reputation of the Medici and as a family sanctuary in times of civil unrest. Over the centuries it has served as a garrison, a foundry to manufacture arms and a house of correction. In the Florence floods of 1966 the Fortezza suffered extensive damage and the prison buildings, including the building where I was held, were destroyed. Only the for midable ramparts and the moat remain. The interior has now been developed as an international exhibition centre for artisan products.

In post-war years, during any visit to Florence, I have often taken a stroll behind Santa Maria Novella railway station. There I can gaze at the impregnable looking ramparts of the Fortezza and thank my lucky stars that the horror is all in the distant past.

Chapter 14

The Transit Camp at Mantua

Together with Roy and Don I became part of a group of about forty prisoners, enough to fill a goods wagon. We were taken to a railway siding at Campo di Marte railway station in Florence, where a train was waiting. We boarded our wagon and it was not long before the train left. The train trundled along but we could never see where we were going. A number of times we pulled into sidings, presumably to let fast trains through. On one occasion we were allowed out of the wagon to relieve ourselves.

As night fell we prepared to lie down and sleep. I then made a mistake which saddened me greatly. In my kit was the bevelled glass and ebony hand mirror from my mother's dressing table which I had carried around England, camps in Egypt, the Libyan desert, Greece and Crete. It had served me well in Laterina for a year, and while I was loose in Montebenichi it had hung for months on a small pine tree outside my shack. The frame had lost a little colour but otherwise it was as good as new. I must have had about 1,000 shaves in front of it. It was to be my lifetime souvenir of the war.

In the goods wagon travelling north from Florence the mirror was in the pocket of my greatcoat, which I had folded to use as a pillow. When I laid my head on the pillow, the mirror, being under my head, caused me some discomfort. It was totally dark in the wagon and I was very tired, so I just fumbled it out of the pocket and slid it under my greatcoat on the floor. The moment I put my head back on to the greatcoat I was asleep. Later everybody was wakened by the wagons jolting to a halt as the train stopped. Moments later, the Germans opened the doors and urged us to get out. It was still dark and I hurriedly rose, put my boots on, picked up my greatcoat and kit and jumped out of the wagon. I had not given a thought to the mirror, and it was only some hours later that I realized what I had done. I knew there was no going back and that I had lost my talisman forever.

Daylight was coming as the Germans got our little squad into some sort of order for marching away. We were in a fairly large town in northern Italy which turned out to be Mantova, known in English as Mantua. Again there was little movement in the streets, so there were not many people to take notice of us. Our destination was right on the edge of the town, and our first view of the camp was across a wide open space.

As we walked across that area we could see the inmates gathering inside the main gate eager to see if they recognized anybody among the new arrivals.

Then near the gate our three Americans rushed forward shouting, and the shouts were taken up by many of the men inside the gate: 'Hey Foxy, where did you get to?' The shouts went on as the gate opened to let us through. There was much back-slapping with other Rangers as they were reunited with our three.

The site had previously been an artillery barracks, and to form our compound a wall of barbed wire had been erected around a few amenity buildings and two enormous single-storey gun sheds which were now empty. There was another line of barbed wire across the middle of the camp passing between the gun sheds. This line had an open gateway in it so the whole camp area was accessible to everybody. The open plan floor areas of both buildings were covered by a forest of two-tier wooden bunks. For those sleeping near the centre of a barrack, finding one's bunk was an ever present challenge. Toilet and ablution facilities were housed separately. Our group were all assigned to the same shed. We had soon sorted out bunks for ourselves and been issued with blankets and eating utensils.

For the first time I was in a camp guarded by German sentries. They patrolled the wire night and day. Everybody had to be inside their shed and the doors closed by dusk. An added deterrent to escape was a team of Alsatian dogs which were let loose at nightfall and roamed the compound till daybreak.

Life in the camp was not too hard, and in general the Germans left us to ourselves. Food was not plentiful but it was reasonable. However, we had a shock when we looked in the cookhouse and saw two horses' heads on a meat slab. Meat dishes were few and far between and were regarded with suspicion after that.

Spring was well on and the weather became pleasantly mild. Roy, Don and I now had lots of new people to meet, so the days passed more easily. The prisoners in the camp were of many different nationalities. Many had been on the loose for some time and had learned some Italian. We chatted a good deal with two young Russians. One had been a student and the other an engineer. They reckoned that they would be shot for having surrendered if they returned to Russia. One asset in our shed was an Italian who was a true virtuoso on the piano accordion. Every evening, before we slept, he gave superb recitals of Italian and classical music.

We had been told that all the barbed wire of the compound, including the centre strip, held an electric charge. On one occasion we were talking to the Russians while we stood by the open gateway in the centre section of the wire. The engineer was standing near the wire and asked us if we knew that the wire was live. We scoffed at the idea, but Don was teased into testing it. As his fingers touched the wire he yelped and threw himself away. We did not know what to make of this, but none of us tried it again.

After about a week the Germans announced that two American soldiers had died and that volunteers for a funeral party were needed. We did not know their names, anything of their history or the circumstances of their death. With my mind still set on pursuing every chance of escape, I realized that volunteering to be part of the funeral party would take me outside the camp. The difficulties of escaping while one was inside the barbed wire were immense, but once outside that wire there was no knowing what opportunity might present itself. So with just a spark of hope in my mind, I volunteered and was accepted for the party.

As was customary on any occasion such as the funeral of a fellow prisoner, it was policy to try to outshine the sentries in smartness. Boots were polished, cap badges burnished bright and the smartest uniforms borrowed from colleagues, with the result that we did ourselves proud. When the time came, the funeral party formed up outside the camp and the two coffins arrived, escorted by an American chaplain. The coffins were roughly made from pine, but what cut through to the heart of each one of us was that wisps of blond hair were protruding from one of them. This brought home to us exactly what ceremony we were partaking in, and I dismissed all thoughts of escape from my mind. We marched off with some chastened spirits among the party.

At the cemetery a simple burial service followed, after which we marched back to the camp. During the march, the sentries had made sure there was no chance of anybody leaving the party. This had been made easy for them anyway because the sight of those wisps of hair, so suggestive of a young fellow, had told us that this was not the occasion for an escape attempt.

Chapter 15

Leaving Italy

The day then arrived when Roy, Don and I learned we were to be members of a party leaving for Germany the next day. The realization came that Germany was now only a matter of hours away. We had lost all sense of date and time and were just living from day to day. By now it was probably May of 1944, and we hoped the worst of the German winter was over. Once over the border, the situation would change dramatically. Everything would weigh against us: the efficiency of the German army, a hostile civilian population and no chance of the co-operation I had received when I was on the loose in Tuscany. So no more than a glimmer of hope of escape lingered for those remaining hours.

In preparation for our departure the party assembled near the main gate of the camp. Quite near that gate was a wooden building straddling the barbed wire, half inside and half outside the camp, with a door at each end. This building was used when, as on this day, groups of men were leaving the camp in transit to Germany. The groups usually comprised several hundred, enough for a train of goods wagons. Any men still harbouring thoughts of escape knew that it was almost certainly their last chance before leaving Italy.

The purpose of the hut was to enable the Germans to carry out a strip search of everybody as they left the camp. On entering, each man's identity was verified. The whole floor space inside was bare, and German soldiers were positioned all around the room. I did not have anything likely to be confiscated, so when my time came to enter the building I was not worried. Each man was sent off to a soldier, who then carried out the search, which required stripping down to vest and pants and then a thorough ransacking of all clothing and kit. It seemed as though nothing subversive could possibly escape detection.

When my searcher began his routine all appeared to be going well, and I was looking forward to dressing again and escaping the indignity of it all. He cast an eye over me and rummaged through my clothing and belongings. All seemed satisfactory. Then he dropped his bombshell by picking up my greatcoat and dropping it on the floor behind him. Seeing my consternation, he spread his hands and said very firmly, '*Nein. Kaputt.*'

Eventually, I followed his thinking. Soon after my escape from Laterina camp, Primetta and Iolanda Becucci had dyed most of my outer clothing. This meant that everything except my battledress was now green, brown or black, and my black greatcoat was completely different to the many other khaki greatcoats lying about the floor and not, in the eyes of my searcher, an item of British uniform.

Having spent most of the three previous years in the climate of the Libyan desert and then in Tuscany, the thought of facing Germany without a greatcoat was daunting. I had to think quickly and decided to base my objections on the colour of the uniforms of different regiments. I knew that the German tank regiments wore black, including their greatcoats. I also knew the word in German for tank, *Panzer*. So I insisted I had been a member of a tank crew and that before capture my uniform had been all black, although the only remaining black garment I now had was my greatcoat.

In support I pointed to the military buttons on the coat. The fellow obviously knew nothing of British uniform and, after a little more protestation from me, he relented and agreed I could take the coat. My sense of relief was enormous. Once that was settled I dressed, repacked all my bits and joined the others proceeding through the far door into the roadway outside the camp. As we left the hut, each man was given a large piece of fat German sausage and three not very large loaves. We were told that this was three days' rations, so as we marched off to the railway station we knew that we were in for a long train journey.

*

At the station I was among the first to go on the platform. There was no sign of a train, but I was in a position about where the first goods wagon would pull up. At the very end of the platform, just a little further ahead of me, were German guards, each with an Alsatian dog held on a tight lead. Eventually a train approached and, as it neared, there were gasps of dismay from those of us near the front. To our horror the first wagon was made of metal, followed by a long line of wooden ones. Everybody knew that even though the chances of breaking out of a wooden wagon were desperately slim, there would be no chance whatsoever from a metal one.

The platform was tightly packed with men. As the engine was drawing to a halt beside us there was a desperate scramble by most of those at the front to get further back down the train, away from the metal wagon. Confusion reigned, and people were falling in the crush. At that point the Germans went into action and came forward with their dogs. I tripped on somebody and when I regained my footing one of the dogs was at me. I was not able to move either way and pressed myself back against a wall as the handler held his dog back from me. Its outstretched paws were only inches from my chest, and its snarl and bared fangs told me what the dog would do to me. That situation only lasted some moments before the German pulled his dog back, but the horror seemed to have lasted an age. I began to breathe again. My one consolation was that I had got far enough along the train to be past the metal wagon. However, I had become parted from Roy and Don.

As the train came to a halt and calm reigned once more on the platform, the sliding doors were opened and the Germans began to herd men into the wagons. This went smoothly at first but became intolerable as the wagons began to fill and the urging became more intense. The men already in were protesting against the crush and the men still on the platform were being prodded with rifles to squeeze in. By the time the Germans were satisfied, there must have been more than forty men in the wagon. The doors were rolled closed and we could hear sounds of them being sealed. Soon after, we were off.

It took some time for the mass of men in the wagon to sort things out. Each side of the wagon had two windows, one at each end. These were high on the wall and about 18ins long by 8ins high. All four windows had been boarded over with a piece of wood, each with two circular holes about 6ins in diameter cut into them. This meant the wagon was pretty dark and with very limited fresh air. In the centre of the floor was a box about 2ft square and 18ins high. We realized this was our toilet for the duration of the journey. We could all sit on the floor, but it was obvious there was not room for everybody to lie down at night. Who was to lie down and who sit with their back to the wall could be sorted out later, so that was left for the time being.

As soon as all were sitting, a group of four chaps said, 'Right let's get going.' Two of them stripped off their shirt and vest. To everybody's amazement, this exposed a large folded map stuck on one back and a small axe strapped to the other. We were all staggered and thought, 'So much for the strip search at Mantua'. We made room for the men to work, and once the train started they selected a point along the side of the wagon and pencilled in a 3ft square from the floor upwards at that point. They then set to work with the axe, with several of us taking our turn at the task. The wood was tough, and the axe small, so it proved difficult, particularly as the cramped space made any movement very difficult. The plan was not to break completely through the wood but to leave only a thin film holding the panel in. This could then be quickly kicked out as soon as an opportunity presented itself.

All was going well with the work, when the train suddenly jolted to a halt. We guessed we had come into a siding. Work on the panel stopped at once and we sat waiting for the journey to start again. We could see we were alongside a platform, with a guard stationed at the front end of each wagon. After some time we heard, to our dismay, the sound of their boots crunching on the ballast alongside the line. Then there was much shouting as orders were barked out. Our hearts sank as we heard the seals on the door of the wagon being twisted open. Immediately a number of men huddled together in front of the splintered panel to keep it from view.

This proved a futile precaution because the first order as the door slid open was '*Alles aus!*' ('All out'). We knew then that we were in deep trouble.

The guards, rifles at the ready, lined themselves alongside the train as we scrambled down to the track. Each wagon was being inspected to check that all was in order. As soon as a guard arrived at our wagon pandemonium broke out. Other Germans came hurrying to find the reason for this, and the officer in charge was called. The sight waiting for them was a panel in the wall almost ready to be kicked out and splinters lying all over the floor. There was no sign of the axe. The officer was furious and scrambled up into the wagon to inspect the damage. Then he barked out some orders and a couple of his men went running back along the train. A number of guards formed a ring around the men from our wagon to ensure nobody left the scene.

After a while the sentries returned carrying a roll of barbed wire and hammers. They climbed into the wagon and set about making it escape proof. Three strands of barbed wire were firmly nailed around the inside wall of the wagon, the top one being about two feet above the floor. With the task completed, the officer came to address us. First we were counted and then the message, translated by an interpreter, came loud and clear: 'If there is any further attempt at escape, for each man that escapes ten men will be shot.'

We were then ordered back into the wagon and the door was closed and sealed again. This was a bitter pill to swallow. Those men having no intention of escaping made it plain that the majority would not stand any further escape attempt. The other wagons had long been ready to move. Soon afterwards, the train began its journey once more. There was a general feeling that it may all have happened before and that the Germans had been prepared for it. This was supported by the fact that the barbed wire and hammers had been on hand to repair the damage. We were dismayed at being discovered but we thought it a praiseworthy effort and we took comfort in the thought that we had at least been able to make an attempt at escape. We had lost this battle, but I was determined to keep looking for any further opportunity which presented itself.

*

Conditions in the wagon were now almost intolerably difficult. It had been bad before, when not everybody could lie on the floor. Now those sitting with their back to the wall of the wagon could not avoid discomfort from the barbed wire. The air was stifling and everybody wanted a spell near one of the tiny windows to be able to take a few breaths. I became hungry and thought I would try a piece of sausage, but it seemed only half cooked and the taste was foul. I persevered for a time but soon began to feel unwell.

The journey seemed endless. Often the train was shunted into a siding for what seemed ages, and occasionally we were let out of the wagon for a short time. It was a relief to be able to stretch our legs and get a breath of fresh air. It was a depressing thought that the regular shunting into sidings was probably to clear the way for trains carrying equipment and troops southward towards the front line.

In the meantime my sickness persisted and I became quite ill. My trouble probably lay with the meat I had eaten. A few other fellows were complaining that they too felt unwell. The feeling did not leave me. There was nothing to do but try to dismiss from my mind the discomfort of the wagon and of feeling so unwell, together with the despair which came from the now inevitable prospect of my future in Germany. As day turned to night and night to day and the train trundled on, the realization came that the German border would soon be behind us.

It turned out that our destination was not yet Germany, but Stalag VIIA at Moosburg in Austria, a small transit camp for PoWs. The one good thing was that I was reunited with Roy and Don. We now found ourselves in an entirely different climate. Although the sky was a clear cloudless blue every day, the temperature was very low. I had not experienced cold weather since being in the mountains of northern Greece during Easter 1941, three years earlier, when we first came face to face with the German army. The Moosburg camp was closely ringed by pine woods so there was no distant view. Heavy snow had fallen, and the camp presented a very stark picture. The combination of the dazzling whiteness of the snow, the jet black of the surrounding pine woods and the blue sky above made an intense contrast strong enough to hurt the eyes.

Moosburg proved to be an unpleasant camp. Although the buildings and fittings appeared to be new and in good condition, things were not as they seemed. The sleeping arrangements were simply straw-filled palliasses on the floor in large dormitories. We were not given fresh straw for the palliasses and we found that the straw we had to use was lice-infested. So within a day or two, so were we. De-lousing had always been an unpleasant and tiresome job, entailing burning along all the seams of shirts and underclothes with a lighted cigarette, until all the lice and eggs were eliminated. However, nobody had any cigarettes, so we just had to stay in that state.

There was one pleasant event at Moosburg. The permanent prisoners in the camp had a concert party and one evening they put on a show for us. It proved to be a tremendous evening's entertainment. The stage props formed an excellent backdrop, the costumes were very well made and the acting was first class. Much of the equipment had come from the Red Cross in London. One fellow played the part of a female dancer. He was so convincingly made up it was hard to believe that we were not looking at a woman. It went down very well with the sex-starved audience. The show was a wonderful break from the claustrophobic atmosphere normally present in a prison camp.

Part II

GERMANY

Chapter 16

Stalag XIa, Altengrabow

Our stay in Moosburg was short. After a few days, together with Roy and Don, I was on another train for an uneventful journey to Stalag XIA at Altengrabow, an isolated place east of Magdeburg. Near the main gate a hut straddled the barbed wire, and we entered it via a door outside the wire. Inside the hut each man was photographed and fingerprinted, and that data, together with his personal particulars, was transferred to an identity card. This was to enable identity checks to be carried out at the time of any future transit between camps. Exit from the hut was then via a door that gave access to the camp. I only spent a matter of weeks in Stalag XIA, but it proved to be a most unpleasant place.

The camp comprised a number of very large compounds, one each for British, Italian and Russian prisoners, and a separate one for Italian officers. My billet was in one of two long brick buildings which we understood to have originally been stable blocks and which had accommodated prisoners during the First World War.

The conditions in our sleeping quarters were pretty awful. The only access was a very large wide-arched doorway at each end of the sheds. Inside, along both side walls there was a seemingly endless three-tier bunk the length of the building. This catered for about eighty men lying closely alongside each other on each tier. Hence there were nearly 500 men to each building. Other than three or four mess tables with benches along the centre aisle between the two rows of bunks, there was no form of comfort. Men slept so close that each palliasse touched its neighbour. I was fortunate to have a place on the top tier, which got more light and so felt less claustrophobic. One of my neighbours on the bed was Eric Sprawson, a chap who had been in the same tent as me in the desert compound at Benghazi in Libya.

There were other buildings for various purposes, including a large one used for concerts. The camp had been established for some years, during which time the British Red Cross had sent out many items. A large selection of musical instruments had been received and a very competent orchestra gave recitals. I attended one performance during my stay in the camp. I remember one short piece they played was 'The Mexican Hat Dance', which I have heard on the radio on occasions in post-war years. These concerts were very popular with the German officers, so the seats of the front row were reserved for them. The shows were always in the evening. By contrast, the days were extremely boring.

The most common pastime was card playing and the favourite game was solo whist. Games could continue for three or four days and nights without a break. When one of the four players became tired and wanted to drop out, his place was immediately taken by another man. Unlike at Laterina camp, there was no football field, and the only form of exercise was endlessly perambulating the inside edge of the compound.

One unpleasant daily routine was dog training. Every morning a dog handler with an Alsatian would be stationed in each corner of a small field. Not far from each of them was a German soldier dressed in a well-padded British battledress, to act as an escaper. The escaper would run away and the handler would then send the dog in pursuit. In moments the dog had caught the man by the arm and brought him down, standing menacingly over him until the handlers called it back. The exercise was repeated tirelessly, obviously aimed at intimidating us. I had had enough of Alsatians on the platform at Mantua railway station so, after witnessing the show once, together with most other fellows I chose to ignore the demonstration and be in another part of the compound whenever it was being performed.

Working parties were sometimes detailed to go on various daily jobs in the locality. Names of those detailed were posted up the evening before. One day the names of Don, Roy and me appeared, and the following morning we presented ourselves at the main gate. Here I struck lucky because the prisoner overseeing the working parties turned out to be the quartermaster sergeant of my artillery battery. His name was Mitten, but he was always just known as 'Q'.

When he saw me he said, 'Hello, I've got a good job for you. Do you have two friends?'

I assured him I did, and from the start we were on to a cushy number.

The location of the work was a remote windy place a mile or two from the Stalag. The task was loading steel plates on to railway wagons, which was a pretty heavy job, but we three were fortunate enough to be the tea boys, with nothing more laborious to do than unload from a truck firewood, a couple of large dixies, some jerrycans of water, tea and milk and then make a fire to boil the water. From then on we just squatted on our haunches around the fire and waited for the water to boil. Just the fact of being outside the barbed wire brought an exhilarating feeling. Everybody invariably carried some form of mug slung on their belt for the chance occasion when any food or drink might become available. When the tea break was called the gang came over and we dished out a mug of hot tea to each man. Later we dowsed the fire, loaded the kit and our job was done. What might have been a hard day's work had turned out to be a quite pleasant relaxation.

*

One experience in the camp seemed quite innocuous at the time; however, after the war I realized it had very sinister connotations. My name appeared on the notice board one day in a party of around twenty men to parade at the main gate the following day. It transpired that we were to be taken somewhere by lorry. The destination proved to be a solitary building not far away, where we were ordered to dismount and enter. Once inside we were taken into a room and told to strip naked. Having no alternative, we complied. We were then ushered into another room which had a tiled floor and was quite warm. It was fitted with a large number of sprinklers at ceiling height. On one wall there was an opening of three or four feet which gave access to another room. That other room was empty.

Suddenly, without warning, the sprinklers began to function and covered the entire room with warm water. It was impossible to escape the spray, so we all went through the motions of scrubbing our bodies. Although a shock, it was a pleasant one, as a warm shower was a novel experience. The spray continued for a considerable time, giving everybody ample time to finish their scrub down. We were left standing there and the warmth of the room served to dry us. Soon, after the water had all drained away, the floor dried and we became completely dry ourselves.

A German soldier came through the break in the wall and made it plain that, one by one, we were to go through to the adjoining room. When my turn came I walked through and came face to face with another German soldier squatting on a low stool. Alongside him was a low table bearing a mirror and a small pair of hairdresser's shears. I was ordered to stand in front of him, naked. Without further ado, he leaned forward, picked up the shears and shaved the hair from my private parts. This came as a total shock. It was a very degrading experience, but there was no chance of objecting. This happened to all of us. We were then led back to the room containing our clothes and ordered to dress.

This had been a demeaning procedure. In the lorry on the return journey there was much protestation and embarrassment at the indignity of such treatment. We wondered why we had been taken out of the Stalag for a shower when there were facilities, although not so efficient, in the camp. However, it had happened, and there was nothing we could do about it.

It was some years after the war that I began to believe there was probably something very disturbing about the event. I saw a television programme showing the gas chamber at a concentration camp. In the programme the building was inside the camp, whereas the one we were taken to was isolated and in open ground. However, the layout and set-up was precisely the same as our shower building. The television programme explained how Jews had been taken into a building and told to undress and were then directed into a room with a notice above the door reading 'Shower Room'. It was said to have been to keep them calm. If there was any such notice in our building I cannot recall it, and anyway it would have been in German. Once the Jews were inside the shower room and the door locked, the gas would be turned on.

Even today it is troubling to think that I may have been in a gas chamber during the Holocaust, but the similarity of my experience to the description on the television programme convinced me to think this is so. The circumstances of the building support it, since it would be quite unreasonable to build a large, complicated, purpose-built structure on its own for the sole purpose of people taking a shower. There were no human dwellings anywhere nearby. If the true purpose of our visit had been for us to have a shower, it is surprising that no soap was available.

I cannot help but believe that the place to which we were taken was a recently built untested gas chamber. The Holocaust authorities would not have wanted to advertise the true purpose of the building to the German population. So instead of using civilians or German soldiers for the trial run, I suspect that a group of PoWs were used as guinea pigs. The shaving of our body hair remains a mystery to me but could have been a red herring to focus our objection on that aspect of the visit rather than on the shower. To my knowledge, while I remained at Stalag XIA, nobody else was ever taken on any subsequent occasion for such an exercise.

*

For a short distance the British and Italian compounds in the Stalag shared a barbed wire boundary fence, so we were able to talk to the Italians through the wire. I became friendly with one of them and we often chatted together. One day he made a most generous and surprising move. He had received a food parcel from his mother in central Italy containing some cake-like delicacies of the region. When we met he offered one of them to me. I could not believe he was giving food away. Although the camp rations were sufficient to keep us above starvation level, they were far below the level of a basic healthy diet, so hunger was always present. Despite my protests he insisted, so I accepted the gift and appreciated it greatly.

The treatment of men in the Russian compound was an entirely different matter. The situation emphasized to us the value of the Geneva Convention, which included the treatment of PoWs. Although we felt that conditions in our compound did not fully comply with the Convention, we nevertheless managed to get by. The Russian authorities however did not recognize the Convention, so the Germans reciprocated, and the Russian prisoners suffered far worse conditions.

The open latrines in our compound were emptied at intervals by Russian prisoners. It was from short exchanges with these Russians when they were emptying the latrines that news filtered through about conditions in their compound. We heard reports that disease was rife and that the German guards scarcely ever went in. There was virtually no medical treatment. Rations, scarcely above starvation level, were put inside the gate and left there to be collected. Alsatian dogs roamed freely in the compound. Men died regularly and their bodies were kept in the compound for days to keep up the numbers for food rations. We could not check these accounts from the Russians, but we accepted them.

There was one particular event which highlighted the severe treatment of the Russians. A Russian prisoner was emptying the latrines in our compound when one of our prisoners offered him a cigarette. As the Russian was lighting it, a guard in a nearby machine gun tower picked up his rifle and shot the Russian dead. The latrine in question was situated alongside the dog-training field. Since I avoided that area, I did not witness this event.

Chapter 17

Jesabruch Factory

One day when we looked at the notice board, my name and Roy's appeared on a list of men to depart the following day for an *Arbeitskommando* (work camp). Sadly, Don's name was not on the list. Our little trio was about to be broken up. Over many months the three of us had been through so much together, and to be separated now came as a wrench. Despite the circumstances in which we found ourselves, there had been no bickering or arguments between us, and we had become a really strong team. We had come to assume that we would finish the war together, with no doubt in our minds that we would reach home together safely.

The following morning Roy and I said our final goodbye to Don, wished him good luck and a safe return home. We then paraded at the main gate in a party of about forty men. We did not pass through the main gate, but through the guard house alongside. Inside, our fingerprints and photographs were checked on our identity cards so there was no chance of any impersonation. Once again we had the feeling that we did not know what the future held for us as we headed for the work camp.

Leaving Stalag XIA we travelled by lorry to the nearest railway station and boarded a train. Our destination was Nienburg-am-Saale, a small town in Lower Saxony a few miles south of the River Saale's confluence with the Elbe. The party formed up outside the station and we were soon marching along a road out of town. A little to the south of the town we passed two cement factories, Anhalt and Concordia, each with its own stone quarry at the rear. An *Arbeitskommando* of about 240 prisoners from our Stalag at Altengrabow was already established in a compound just south of the town. Those men provided the workforce for the two factories and their respective quarries. A small crew of German civilians oversaw the work.

A little further out of town on the same road was an abandoned cement factory named Jesabruch, with its associated quarry, which was now flooded, some way behind it. It was to that site that we were marched. The sun was shining and the day was warm and pleasant. Along both sides of the road were apple trees, already showing their small fruit. On the left of the road there were just the isolated factories with their quarries behind them, while on the other side of the road fields sloped down for a short distance to the River Saale. We were in the middle of an enormous plain, with not a hill in sight. The flatness was emphasized by the absence of trees in the fields. The agriculture seemed intensive, the only crops being wheat, potatoes and maize.

On reaching Jesabruch, which lay alongside the road half a mile beyond Concordia, we learned that this was our destination. As we turned off the road, there was a single-track railway to cross, with a level crossing and a crossing keeper's bungalow. We took the track leading into the fields and as we passed the former factory building we saw the area around was littered with rusting machinery and a great amount of untidy rubbish. The factory building, with it wide open doors showing an empty interior, was obviously derelict.

Half a mile further along the track we arrived at the quarry. A steep track half-way down the quarry led to a small plateau on which the powerhouse had been built. This had been gutted and converted into two storeys of living quarters for prisoners and their guards. This was to be home for our party of forty. Below our plateau, a very large lake had formed in the bottom of the abandoned quarry.

Prisoners lived on both floors of the powerhouse, with the toilets, showers and ablutions rooms on the lower floor. The small plateau outside the main door was to be our roll-call and exercise yard. It was enclosed by a high barbed-wire fence stretching from one front corner of the building, running along the edge of the small plateau and returning to the other front corner of the building, with an access gate halfway along. On one side of the gate the ground outside the wire fell away towards the lake and on the other side of the gate a track rose up to the top of the quarry.

The guards were housed in a section of the upper floor. Their separate access was by means of a catwalk from the path coming down the quarry leading to a door in the upper floor of the building. The guards consisted of three soldiers under the command of a *Feldwebel* (corporal). A short corridor separated the guards' quarters and the prisoners' quarters on that floor. Situated on this corridor was a small storeroom for Red Cross food parcels and personal parcels from prisoners' families.

When rooms were allocated to us, mine proved to be on the upper floor. It had two doorways, both without doors, and a heavily barred window. There were four two-tier bunks, with a small wardrobe for each bunk. The room measured about 14ft by 12ft. As there was a small table in the centre, there was not much floor space for eight men to move around. I occupied one of the lower bunks, and above me was another Liverpool fellow, Tommy Clifford of the Irish Guards, who became a good friend. There was a constant traffic of six other fellows through our room from the adjoining room, as the only access to their room was by passing through ours.

*

It did not take the guards long to get us organized as a work force. The first day was spent sorting out sleeping places, allocating blankets and generally learning the rules of the place. In a work camp the German guard commander appointed one of the prisoners to be the 'Man of Confidence'. This was the person through whom all orders would be passed to us. In our case it proved to be Tommy Stewart, a tall, well-built fellow from the Scots Guards. As he spoke German, he was perfectly suited for the job.

A Liverpool chap from the Medical Corps was appointed as Medical Orderly. He held a small amount of medical supplies, which sometimes included a few vitamin tablets. As a fellow Scouser, he occasionally favoured me with a few of these, and I felt I survived a little better than I might have done without them. In the prevailing circumstances, a tiny benefit like that could make an enormous difference to one's morale.

The daily routine started at 5.00 am when we were awakened by the guards stamping around the rooms urging us to get cracking with repeated loud shouts of '*Raus, Menschen, raus! Weitermachen!*' This was the malevolent equivalent of our 'Show a leg, everybody'. We were given half an hour to use the ablutions and toilets, dress and then form up at half past five in our tiny compound outside. That half hour included retrieving our trousers and boots which had been deposited in a locked room overnight to forestall any night-time attempts at escape. Once out in the compound, a roll call took place. We were given no breakfast and, once the count was satisfactorily completed, we were ready to move.

On that first morning we were allocated to the three different factories. I found myself in a group of about ten bound for Jesabruch, the derelict factory, but Roy was with a larger group for Concordia, the nearer of the two working factories with its quarry. So we were not to be workmates. At 5.30 am three civilian quarrymen arrived at the compound. Each of them signed for the group assigned to their particular factory or quarry, and at the same time they were issued with a pistol for the day. We then moved off to begin our day's work.

The working hours were from 6.00 am until 6.00 pm, with a first break from 8.30 to 9.00, and a second from 12 noon to 12.30. It was a seven-day working week, with every third Sunday off. During the first break we were given a mug of almost tasteless ersatz coffee, and during the second we had a fairly large ladle of watery soup as tasteless as the coffee. The vegetables in the soup had been shredded to fine particles and could be identified only by their colour. So every day we had one from a selection of what we assumed was carrot soup, turnip soup, potato soup and an unidentifiable green soup we referred to as 'whispering grass', which was the name of a popular song at the time.

This food was brought every day from a communal soup kitchen in Nienburg. It was carried in a milk churn loaded on to a small cart, which was pulled for more than a mile from the town by a prisoner. So by the time it reached us it was never more than tepid. I do not think the civilian population drawing their rations from there got much better.

On arrival at the billet each evening we were issued with a small loaf to be shared between six men. On two evenings a week there was also a small portion of cheese for each man. On Sundays there was a small portion of meat in the soup. This completed our daily food ration. Sharing the loaf was a critical matter. Hunger was so acute that every man wanted to be sure he had a fair share, and fighting regularly broke out. It was not long before an acceptable but fiddly system was found, one about which nobody could complain. Each of the six men sharing a loaf had a number and that order was fixed. Every evening a different man would cut the loaf into six pieces, as near equal as he was able. Nobody could speak or comment until the cutter considered he had brought them as near equal to each other as was possible without the use of scales.

The cutter looked long and hard at his handiwork and inevitably decided that this piece looked bigger than that piece and maybe the piece on the end was the smallest of the lot. So a sequence went on of slicing a sliver off one piece and adding it to another smaller looking piece. The cutter knew that the other five had their choice before him and that he would be left with the smallest looking share, so he slivered away until he was satisfied. Each man in his allotted turn could take his time over choosing the best piece available. The cutter took the last remaining piece and could not complain if his piece appeared smaller than the rest. He just had to accept it. This was all over a portion of bread weighing little more than 100 grams. It was a demeaning and lengthy system, but feelings of injustice and fiery tempers could flare into serious fights, until we established this rule of law. These food matters were all unknown to us on that first morning, but they were bitter lessons we would soon have to learn.

*

When we were collected by our one-man escort for the day we set off up the path out of the quarry and along the track as far as the Jesabruch building. As we entered the building I came face to face with something which had been in my mind throughout. I had made up my mind that I would remain implacably determined not to take any part in the German war effort. I considered any willingness to work on my part would amount to just that. I knew that back home in England, factory workers of every sort were considered as much a part of the war effort as anyone in the Armed Forces, and I found a stigma in the thought of doing anything to further the German cause.

So I had decided on a policy of non-cooperation, that I would only work if I were pushed to it. I would stick to this policy as far as I dared and only give way if the situation appeared to be getting out of hand and danger seemed imminent. I did not know where this would land me, but I decided to see how things turned out. So now, as we entered the building, the moment of truth was about to arrive.

Inside the building all signs of any former machinery and equipment had been stripped out, leaving only the bare concrete floor and four high, white-painted walls with no windows. Along the centre of the floor a long row of tables had been aligned. Our work was to make panels for pre-fabricated buildings. The panels were the size of a normal door, one half consisting of solid concrete and the other half a section of solid plasterboard made of wood shavings set in a frame of concrete.

The line of tables allowed for us to work on an assembly belt system. The first two chaps, one either side of the table, received the previously used moulds and washed away all traces of concrete. Subsequent pairs of men then screwed the mould together again. It was then passed along, firstly for a steel wire reinforcing frame to be inserted, then the sheet of hardboard and finally, cement to be poured in to fill the mould. At that point the mould, which had two handles at each end like a stretcher, was carried to an area of the floor used as a drying area, where it was left for about four days to set hard. When the setting was complete each panel was taken out of the building on a little trolley and stacked outside.

It was extremely easy work compared with the labours of the chaps working in Anhalt and Concordia factories and their quarries. Although I knew I was fortunate in that respect, I was still determined to do the very least work I could get away with. So I teamed up with another fellow who also intended to show no enthusiasm and we worked as a pair on the tables. No matter which operation we were detailed to carry out each day, we were as slow and incompetent as we dared. This led to one tailback after another behind us, with everybody waiting for us to finish our task.

The work was overseen by a foreman named Friedel and three other civilian workmen. Friedel was a calm, business-like man not given to intolerance or displays of temper, although he made it plain he expected results. Two of the workmen showed little interest in the job or in our performance. The remaining workman, named Karl, was the one we had to be very careful of. Karl was a detestable character who hated every one of us. He was big-built, with a large paunch, a florid face and a large shaven head, the archetypal German of British caricaturists.

When Friedel remonstrated with us and commented that we could not be as clumsy as we seemed, we always solemnly promised to try to improve. Karl, on the other hand, would snarl and bawl at us. Although he never struck anybody, there was always the implied threat that it was about to happen. He showed his character on one occasion when one of our team remarked on a fledgling bird, a redstart, falling from its nest above us and floundering to the floor. On hearing the remark,

Karl immediately went over and picked the bird up. Bird in hand, he approached the nearby wall and, with a triumphant shriek, hurled it against the wall as hard as he could.

It was obvious that he disliked me more than most. I had to be very wary not to go too far with him.

He would watch me and then come screaming over to me, shouting, '*Deine Nummer, was ist deine Nummer?*' ('Your number, what's your number?').

I showed him the identity tag around my neck and answered, '*Zwei sieben und dreissig*' ('Two thirty seven') the last three figures of my PoW number.

On days when he was the duty escort to and from the factory he would always report on the evening handover, '*237 keine Arbeit heute. Immer keine Arbeit*' ('237 no work today. Never any work').

This was marked down against me. In this way Karl and I carried on our own private war.

On occasions the factory manager put in a brief appearance. He was a thin elderly man whose right hand was missing. He was short sighted, wore thick spectacles and was always dressed in a trilby and a long brown overcoat. When he watched our performance he always became frustrated and waved his handless right arm in a frenzy, babbling away in German, which we could never understand. From the moment he first waved his arm angrily at us, he was known as 'Wingy'. After one of his visits a team of two time-and-motion study men arrived to weigh us up. We tidied up our clumsiness and slowness a little but made sure we kept up some semblance of it. While they watched they did not speak to any of us, and after half an hour or so they left.

A short time after that I was taken off the assembly team and given a different task. This was to unscrew the mould frames in the drying area and take out the hardened panels. Then I used the small trolley to wheel each panel through the large metal sliding door of the building and stacked them up in lines against the factory wall. This was a more pleasant job, with some time out in the fresh air. Furthermore, the weather seemed always to be sunny, with no rain.

My first thoughts were that I would just carry on at my leisurely work rate, but I soon realized this was no longer necessary. The concrete on the factory floor and that on the ground outside had been laid separately. There was a dividing line in the two areas of separately laid concrete along the line of the sliding door. There was a small hole in the concrete along this line which I had not noticed. On one occasion one of the two small iron wheels of the trolley found the hole. The consequent jarring was too much for the unequal weight of the two halves of the panel and there followed a sharp crack as it fractured between the plasterboard and the concrete halves. There was no visible sign of a fault, but there was no longer any rigidity in the panel, so it had been rendered useless.

This altogether changed my attitude to the work, and the Germans must have been pleased to see the improvement. Now I could choose how many of the panels I wanted to fracture. The sound of the crack was sweet music to my ears. I made sure this did not happen any time there was a workman near me. One fortunate thing for me was that the panels must have been intended for some future project, because nobody ever arrived to collect any of them. Consequently, the faults were never discovered, so I carried on stacking panels most of which were probably useless.

*

About this time a very sad event took place. An Irish Guardsman, Tommy Brannan, had become highly distressed and confused. His conversation deteriorated into a nonsensical state and it was evident that he needed treatment. He developed anti-British feelings, with such outpourings as 'The British are so stupid they deserve to lose the war.' This was in direct contrast to the calm, placid and friendly demeanour he had always shown in the past. We approached the camp guard commander, and as a result, he was put on sick parade. When the doctor examined him, Tommy was earmarked for return to the *Lazarett*, the military hospital attached to Stalag XIA. On the day of his departure he was to leave at 3.00 am with an escort of two guards to catch an early morning train from Nienburg to Magdeburg. So we bade farewell before we settled down to bed.

The following morning all seemed normal and after the usual formalities the first group set off for work. On leaving the quarry they saw something which looked like a blanket across the path ahead of them. As they reached that point they realized to their horror that the blanket was stretched over Tommy Brannan's body. There was almost mutiny in the group. They refused to proceed and instead returned to the billet to demand an explanation. The consensus of opinion was that he would not have run from his close escort in the middle of hundreds of yards of flat open ground. Even if he had, two fit soldiers would have had no difficulty in restraining an underfed, overworked and demoralized prisoner.

It was confirmed that he had left with his guards, who claimed that, once out of the quarry, he had tried to run away and they had had no option but to shoot. He had been killed with a single bullet in his back. The man who had killed him was the most unpleasant guard of the bunch. He was known as 'Jackboots', because he was the only one who wore them. During the day a couple of our fellows brought back Tommy's body in a large wooden box on a handcart which was used as a hearse. They undressed him and washed his body. They also washed his blood-stained battledress jacket and hung it high on the barbed wire fence. The guards' balcony overlooked the spot and the jacket was high enough for them to see daylight through the bullet hole. We stood for a long time by the jacket chanting 'Jackboots, Jackboots', but no guard chose to show himself on the balcony.

A burial service followed, the pallbearers being his colleagues from the Irish Guards. Each man borrowed the best beret, battledress, belt, and boots available and turned themselves out so smartly that they put the German guards to shame. On a visit to Nienburg with my wife after the fall of the Berlin Wall, I called on the town's Registrar of Deaths. He showed me the record of the transfer of Tommy's remains after the war to the Commonwealth War Graves Commission.

*

Having the trolley job, I worked entirely on my own which gave me a fair time to disappear occasionally. I took the opportunity of exploring around the factory building. At the rear I found a heap of black slag running alongside and quite close to the building. It was about 9ft high, 15ft wide and 20yds long.

The factory grounds ended just behind the slag heap and gave on to a field as large as a small prairie, forming one huge potato crop. The plants looked ready for harvest and it was galling to see this potential food source so near and not be able to benefit. With no cooking facilities, it might as well have been a mirage. Hunger was an ever present spectre, but the thought of raw potatoes lacked appeal, even in those conditions. When I mentioned the slag heap, somebody said it was the waste from the furnaces of the former working factory, that it was still burning and that if I stood still by it I would feel the warmth. I wasted no time in testing this. Sure enough, I felt a gentle warmth. I took an iron bar and prodding it into the heap I found that about twelve inches into the slag it was glowing red and fiercely hot.

This was the answer to my prayer. I had found a ready-made oven. As soon as I was sure nobody was about, and as workmen had no call to go to the rear of the building anyway, I made a quick sortie to the potato field, went a couple of rows in and heaved out a plant. I scraped up half a dozen good potatoes and scrambled back to the slag heap. With the iron bar, I poked them into the slag about seven or eight inches in and all in a line. I then marked the end with the iron bar and retired to my trolley to work on a few panels. Soon after, I returned to the heap. I quickly established the optimum cooking time and finished up with some mouth-watering baked potatoes. The one thing missing was butter, but Hitler's slogan in his pre-war re-armament days had been 'Guns not Butter', so like the German population, I had to forego it. I shared them with some very grateful fellows in the building. As they were all committed to their assembly belt, I was the only one able to make my sorties, so the game was never overplayed.

There were occasional things to laugh about, including one comical incident when half a dozen personal parcels arrived. The six lucky fellows, of whom I was one, went along to the parcel room armed with a blanket. Three guards were there to inspect the contents. When my turn came, I held out my blanket and the contents of the parcel were emptied onto it. Then I had to spread it all on the table for inspection. On top of all was a chrome-plated tin opener of the type which had a cogged cutting wheel and a butterfly handle to operate the wheel. Two long handles gave a grip to hold the wheel in position.

When the guards saw it their heads went back and there was a loud, '*Also. Was haben wir hier?*' ('So, what have we here?').

They passed it among themselves, twisting and turning it all ways without any idea of what it was. We explained that it was a gadget for opening tins, but they would have none of it.

'*Nein, was ist's?*' ('No, what is it?').

We let them exercise their imagination for a little. Somebody then produced an empty tin and cut the base off it. They then agreed that it could open a tin but were still suspicious about what other illegal use could be made of it in an escape attempt, so my opener was confiscated. It had been a good idea on my mother's part but it was not one of the three permissible items for personal parcels. However, there was, in any case, an ingenious tiny tin opener in every Red Cross parcel.

*

In Germany the arrival of Red Cross parcels was a rare occurrence. We knew they were issued on a more frequent basis and wondered what happened to the missing ones. Each man had his own idea of how to eat the 10lbs of food in the parcel, in the knowledge that it might be a long time before the next one arrived. Some ate the contents as fast as they could and then existed on the meagre camp rations. These fellows were known as 'parcel bashers'. Others nibbled at the food each day and tried to spin it out as long as they possibly could. These were known as 'parcel mossers'. The remainder, which included me, would have a comfortable little meal each day and the parcel would last around two weeks. The habit of 'parcel mucking' which I had practised in Laterina, whereby two men would pair up, each drawing a parcel but first share one parcel and then open the second, was much less prevalent in camps in Germany.

I had always decried the parcel bashers, but I declared that I would bash mine when the hoped for Allied invasion of the continent started. That was a thing we were all praying for and looked upon as an occasion for great celebrations. Then one day a group of men began working in a nearby field. I took the opportunity of going over to chat and find out who they were. I learned they were Spaniards who had been brought to Germany as forced labour and were having a very hard life. The news they told me was so surprising it left me trembling with excitement.

It was what we had all been praying for. It was that the Allied invasion of Europe had started that day. The Spaniards had heard the news from Radio London on a clandestine radio that they had. We did not know it was to be called D-Day, but it was 6 June 1944.

I hurried back and spread the news. The rejoicing was unbounded, and for the rest of the afternoon we sang an endless chorus of marching songs like 'Roll out the Barrel', 'Run, Rabbit, Run' and 'There'll always be an England'. The German workers, who had not heard the news, were non-plussed at our behaviour. We began to pluck up courage and taunt them with 'America England Boom Boom. Deutschland *Kaputt*'. They did not believe us and came back with their usual '*Nein, Nein. England Kaputt*'. When we arrived back at our quarters that evening, we learned that the men in one of the other quarries had also learned the same news, so we took it as confirmed.

By an ironic coincidence, I was collecting a Red Cross parcel that very evening. I was being reminded of my long-standing promise to bash my parcel when the Allied invasion started. I spread the contents on my bed and pondered for some time. Then I thought, 'I've spread these things out for too long, I'm going to have a bash.' So I took a place at the table and began to eat. There were tins of bacon, salmon and cheese; there were raisins, chocolate and biscuits and no doubt other things I cannot now remember. I sat eating for ages until eventually all I had left was tea, some condensed milk and fifty cigarettes. I did not smoke and I always bartered the cigarettes for food. I was left with an ecstatic feeling, having been able to eat as much excellent food as I could manage, but I was quite knocked out. Then I just crawled between my blankets.

The next morning I was awfully ill. I could not think of going to work and put my name down for the sick parade that morning. That meant a march of a mile into Nienburg, which I could hardly manage. The surgery was in the town and a small group of us set off, escorted by a couple of sentries. The doctor was notorious for his habit of bluntly telling men to stop skiving and get back to work. This had happened in the case of a number of men who were obviously very ill. When my turn came, I did not tell him I had been gorging but just that I felt some great pain inside me. After prodding about a little, he surprised me by telling me that he was sending me to the *Lazarett*, the hospital back at Stalag XIA.

Chapter 18

The *Lazarett*

A visit to the *Lazarett* was good news, although I was too ill to be cheerful about anything. Escorted by two guards, I set off the next day at 3.00 am. Thinking of Tommy Brannan's fate, I was a little apprehensive, but I was relieved to find Jackboots was not one of the guards. We had to walk to Nienburg railway station, from where we took a train to Magdeburg. I was made to sit well away from the few civilian passengers. On reaching Magdeburg we had a long wait for our onward train to Altengrabow. It was still early morning but I was surprised how few people were about, some military personnel but hardly any civilians. I had to stand, very isolated, at the edge of the platform, while my escort sat some way behind me on a seat against a station building from which they could watch me. Nobody appeared to take any notice of me. When our train eventually set off, it was not long before we arrived at Altengrabow.

I knew from other fellows that all patients at the *Lazarett* were treated by Allied medical officers. Then German medical officers carried out a weekly inspection of the patients and decided who was fit for discharge and who should remain. The Allied medical officers knew which work camps suffered the worst conditions and did all they could to hold in the *Lazarett* any prisoners from those camps as long as possible. I was lucky in that prisoners from the three work places at Nienburg all got the benefit of this favourable treatment on account of the terrible reputation of the harsh working conditions at Anhalt quarry, even though the regimes at Concordia and Jesabruch were reasonably tolerable.

Although the feeling of sickness was still with me when I first arrived, my stay at the *Lazarett* could almost be described as enjoyable. I had first been taken to the Stalag, where my identity was checked, and soon after escorted to the nearby *Lazarett*. I was given food straight away, and it was so much better than at Nienburg. The accommodation comprised a number of large wooden huts. They were spacious and comfortable, with ten or twelve beds in each. Just being in such a place began to make me feel much better. I was seen by an English doctor and told him exactly what I had done to cause such a problem. He said I was lucky to have been sent to the *Lazarett* and I would probably be quite well in a day or two, but I should not worry about that. I took it that he meant that he would do what he could to delay my return.

I soon got to know my ward mates, who had been there for varying lengths of time. It was a motley company, each one of them hoping they would not be moved out at the weekend. One unfortunate fellow, a Londoner, had been aboard a PoW train at Aquila in central Italy which had halted at the town station at the moment an American bombing raid started on the town. The train had been hit and he had been blown out of the wagon. As he ran to get out of the area he realized his arm was missing. Although it had been blown right out of its socket, he had felt no pain.

Another fellow, an RAF man, was under great mental stress. Every night, he was convinced he was to face a firing squad the following morning. As men were calling goodnight to each other he would join in with the comment 'It's all right for you, you're not going to be shot in the morning.'

This was the time of the American 1,000-bomber raids. We frequently saw the Flying Fortress bombers over the *Lazarett*. When the first rumbles were heard there was a rush to the windows on the oncoming side and we saw squadrons of planes dotted all over the sky coming towards us. It was awesome to see the magnitude of the exercise, and there were shouts of encouragement and cheering as men were excitedly counting the numbers. It was a magnificent boost to our morale. As they passed above us, there was a rush to the windows on the other side of the ward and we sent up our good wishes and hopes for a safe return as they droned on towards their target. We saw no sign of anti-aircraft fire. That was the American effort with their carpet bombing, a whole squadron releasing their bomb load simultaneously. Then at night we heard the RAF planes. First came the pathfinders to light the target area with flares, and then the bombers came in singly for their precision bombing.

At the weekend the German doctors, accompanied by a British medical officer, arrived to carry out their assessment of each patient. When they got to the chap with one arm he was most vociferous about his unsuitability for discharge. Evidently this was a weekly routine, and the Germans, who were quite firm at the other beds, just nodded tacitly to the English doctor and passed on. It seemed the unfortunate chap was being allowed the comfort of the *Lazarett* for the duration of the war. At my bed they examined my chart and, after a little discussion, the Germans nodded and passed on. To my great surprise I had been granted another week, although there was no longer anything wrong with me. I was lucky to get this extension even though I worked at Jesabruch and not in either of the other factories or quarries at Nienburg.

During that week I developed a very painful toothache and decided I should see the dentist. This was easily arranged as there was a dental surgery in the *Lazarett*. When my appointment came I was shown into a large room in which there were two dental chairs alongside each other. A patient was in one of the chairs, attended by two dentists, and another prisoner was seated in the waiting area. I joined the latter and learned that both patients were Italian. The two dentists turned out to be Polish.

When the treatment began the Italian was protesting as loudly as he was able while his mouth was forced open. The two Poles stooped over him, but his legs were flailing wildly in front of him and he was obviously being restrained. To my horror, I realized they must have been trying to carry out an extraction without any anaesthetics. I thought this was no place for me, and my toothache was rapidly going. The Italian was eventually allowed to get out of the chair. I think the dentists wanted to finish off some documentation but, together with his colleague, he was off like a scalded cat out of the room.

The dentists then came over to me and told me that without anaesthetics it was too difficult for them to carry on and I would have to make an appointment for the following week. I did not look forward to that and hoped my toothache would disappear. However, at the end of the week the German doctors arrived and carried out their round. They decided I was fit enough to return to Nienburg. The awful effects of my parcel bashing had soon disappeared, and I had enjoyed my fortnight in the relative comfort of the *Lazarett*.

*

So I was taken back to the Stalag for an identity check and on to the station for my return to Nienburg. When I checked in at Jesabruch the following day I think Herr Friedel was most disappointed to see me back. To my dismay, my job on the trolley had been given to somebody else and I found myself back on the assembly belt making panels. However, I soon had another lucky break.

Alongside the Jesabruch building there was a large barn-like structure with a high pitched tiled roof. It had fallen into decay and it had now been decided to restore it and bring it back into use. It was quite high for a single-storey building. The roof was the first part of the job to be tackled, and a roofer was brought out from Nienburg to assess the job. After inspecting the building he said he would need someone to act as his assistant. To Friedel's ears this must have sounded like manna from heaven, and the man was told that just the right person was available. So I was detailed to be the assistant. I am sure that the rest of Friedel's team were also glad to see the back of me once again.

The job started there and then. The roofer was a pleasant fellow to be with and bore me no malice, so I was quite pleased. Together we set off on foot to Nienburg. When we reached the town, I got my first surprise. He told me that in town I could not walk on the pavement with him and that I would have to walk in the gutter. At first I was surprised, but in a way somewhat stimulated. I just felt that I did not want to mingle with Germans anyway, so it no longer felt like being made to walk in the gutter, but simply that I was choosing not to walk on the pavement. Eventually we reached his house and I was ushered inside.

My welcome was muted but no animosity was shown to me. Civilian rations were almost as meagre as those for PoWs, so I was not surprised that I was not offered food. I was offered some coffee but it was ersatz and, like most things in Germany, tasted awful. Afterwards I was taken to a yard at the back and told to load a number of ladders on to a handcart. Then began the return journey, with me pushing the handcart loaded with ladders. This time I was unable to walk on the pavement with the handcart, so the matter of feelings did not come into it.

On arrival at Jesabruch we unloaded the cart and assembled two ladders which would reach the roof of the building. At once it seemed to me as though the roof-line had doubled in height, and I swallowed hard. With a 'Come on, let's go' sort of expression on his face, my new boss indicated that we should each go up our ladder to inspect the roof. At this point the sense of freedom in my new found job came to a halt, and I told him that I could not go on the roof under any circumstances. So he told Friedel he wanted an experienced slater. A check around Jesabruch showed none was available there, so Concordia and Anhalt were consulted. My luck was out when it was found that the only suitable man was a Scots Guardsman named Macmillan from Inverness working in Anhalt quarry. He was available, but the quarry would need a replacement. Herr Friedel did not need a second thought about who the unfortunate person should be to take his place.

Concordia quarry had a relatively easy-going set-up, but Anhalt quarry was notorious for its very harsh working conditions. The Germans at Jesabruch were delighted to see the last of me. Herr Friedel had the last laugh after all. The thought of Anhalt frightened me, but Macmillan could not believe his luck. That evening in the billet he said to me, 'You're in trouble, Scouse. Anhalt's a place where strong men weaken and weak men die.' It proved to be not quite as bad as Macmillan had predicted, but it was about as hard a life as I could stand.

Chapter 19

Anhalt Quarry

T he change from Jesabruch to Anhalt quarry truly was a shock to the system. On the first morning I fell in with the Anhalt gang for the roll call. The walk to Anhalt was almost a mile, so we set off a little earlier than the normal 5.45 am start, in order to arrive by 6.00 am. Half way to Anhalt we walked past Concordia factory and its quarry, in which my friend Roy worked. On arrival at Anhalt the factory crew disappeared into the enormous brick complex of the cement factory while the quarry gang formed up at the top of the ramp leading down to the quarry floor. It was at this point that men were detailed for any special jobs to be carried out that day. I knew Anhalt quarry was going to be much harder than Jesabruch factory, but I was determined to keep up my policy of taking as little part as possible in the German war effort, no matter how difficult it might be. I knew I could not refuse to work but at least I would be doing as little work as possible, and I hoped I would be all right.

There were seven civilian staff at the quarry. Herr Klinge was the quarry boss, and his foreman on the quarry floor was Popeye, so called because, having only one eye, he wore an eye-patch. He also wore a hat similar to that worn by the cartoon character. Klinge was a rather short, stocky man, fierce and a committed Nazi. Popeye was scared of Klinge and was not strong enough to rule the quarry gang as Klinge would have liked. Three other men were there to keep an eye on the prisoners and guide them when necessary. There was Lugs, so called because he had the widest ears any of us had ever seen, the Rat, who earned his name through his generally despicable nature, and one known as the Mouse, because of his quiet demeanour. The remaining two were a locomotive driver and a digger operator.

The quarry floor covered a large area of ground, oval in shape and about 100yds by 80yds. Only a relatively short section of the face was being worked. It was worked in successive sections, each about 25yds long, of which two had been completed and now the third section was being worked. Between the top and the floor of the quarry face there were three ledges, each about 6ft wide, with a drop of about 7ft between each one. When the ledges were cleared of rock, three prisoners armed with heavy pneumatic drills drilled each ledge down to the level of the ledge below. These holes were then filled with sticks of dynamite, the series was wired up and the whole lot detonated.

The rock was thrown high into the air and settled in a sloping line from the top of the quarry down to the quarry floor. A heavy duty digger worked along the line of shattered rock and filled about six bogeys, each taking about a ton of rock. The bogeys were mounted on a narrow-gauge railway and were hauled around the track by a small, dilapidated locomotive to a point at which they could then be hauled by an endless chain up the ramp to factory level. There, in passing the rock crusher, a lever on each bogey was released, tipping the rock into the crusher. The bogey then curved round with the chain and descended once again to the quarry floor. That was the basic system of getting the rock from the quarry face up to ground level, where it then entered the cement factory via the crusher.

Once the crusher had reduced the rock to a fairly fine aggregate, it was transferred to two enormous storage silos and some other ingredients were added. Loads of plaster casts, brought by barge from crockery factories along the River Saale, were crushed in with the rock. The final mixture was piped to two huge cylindrical ovens, 5ft or 6ft in diameter, and many yards long, each fired by its own furnace. Both ovens contained hundreds of steel ball bearings, varying from tennis ball to small marble in size. When a furnace was loaded with rock and the fire going full blast, the whole cylinder began to revolve at great speed and the rolling ball bearings eventually ground the rock to the fine consistency of cement.

The cement was then piped through to the bagging section and made ready for bagging and despatch. At the rear of the factory there was a railway siding, where one track ran alongside the factory's despatch platform. It was a full-time job every day for two men to bag the cement and then, armed with trolleys, to load the railway wagons which had been shunted there overnight.

All was well so long as everything functioned properly. Sadly, this was all too frequently not the case. The equipment was all very old, long past its useful life span and in a deplorably dilapidated state. The three offending pieces were the digger, the locomotive and the chain on the ramp. Another item in the factory which could bring the quarry's work to a halt was the crusher. If the rock was rain-soaked, the crusher would often jam and, once jammed and out of action, no more rock could be hauled up from the quarry until the crusher was cleared, so all work had to cease.

Arriving at the quarry face that first morning, I was ignorant of all those things. I just stood among the group, wondering what was in store. After hearing a full explanation given to me by the quarry team, the one job I hoped to avoid was to be part of the gang working on the quarry face. From childhood I had always been uncomfortable with heights, and I thought that if I pleaded vertigo, it might keep me off the quarry face.

*

The work schedule was the same as that at Jesabruch: seven days a week, from 6.00 am until 6.00 pm, with every third Sunday free. There were two half-hour breaks beginning at 8.00 am and 12.00 noon. The first two stints were difficult enough to cope with, starting with a two-and-a-half-hour spell without any breakfast, often in the dark. Then, after a mug of awful ersatz coffee in the rest hut, having to go back on to the quarry face for another three and a half hours. The soul-destroying point came at 12.30 pm when, after the second break in the rest hut with a ladle of tasteless, watery soup, we had to go back to the quarry face for another five and a half hours. Every day the afternoon stint seemed interminable, and then there was still the exhausting walk back to camp.

The first job I was given, with two or three other fellows, was on the quarry face, but on the opposite side of the quarry from the current working at that time. Work had been carried out there in the past, and then that section had been abandoned and left in a very untidy state. Occasional rock-falls had been causing scree slides, which then blocked the rail track. So we were instructed to go on to the scree and clear the offending areas. I put in a plea about suffering from vertigo, only to be met with impatience from the German quarryman, who just indicated I should get on with it. I hesitated, stumbled and sat down, claiming I could not stand up on the slope. But it was to no avail. The other fellows meanwhile were getting on with the job, so I had no support.

When the quarryman failed to get me moving, one of the two armed soldiers who patrolled the quarry floor came over. His attitude convinced me that nobody was interested in vertigo. At that point I just had to give up and show that I was getting over my problem and start doing a bit of work. Apart from the two soldiers on the quarry floor, there were also two patrolling the ground at the top of the quarry, rifles over their shoulder and each accompanied by an Alsatian dog. They were there to see that nobody nipped over the top and slipped away across the fields.

*

After a couple of days that job was completed and I found that I was to be a regular member of the face gang. The timing was unfortunate, because a section had just been dynamited and the rocks formed a straight line sloping down from the top to the quarry floor. This meant that work had to be approached from the top instead of from the floor of the quarry. So at 6.00 am the next morning I was part of a group that assembled on the grass at the quarry edge. Every man had a large wooden stake and a sledgehammer. We each had to knock our own stake into the ground two or three yards from the quarry edge and three or four yards apart. Then we each attached a long length of strong webbing to the stake. The other end of the webbing had a hook which was then fixed to a fastener on a webbing belt which we had to wear around our waist.

At that point the job was ready to start. Now I really did have queasy feelings of vertigo, and this time I was not the only one. I knew I would get short shrift if I complained, so I approached the edge. Armed with a long-handled shovel, it was really difficult trying to keep my balance whilst I got one foot steady in the mass of shattered rock and then brought the other foot over the edge. Then, when I did find my balance, it had to be maintained while rocks, some of them quite large, were prised from the mass on which I was standing. So the work began very slowly, with occasional rocks clattering down the slope.

As we progressed, it became a little easier, because once the rock was cleared from the top couple of feet of the face, there was a wide enough flat platform of rock to stand on. Looking down at the mass of rock still to be cleared, it seemed that it would take a lifetime to get down to the quarry floor. It was a good feeling when eventually my shovel scraped the floor of the first ledge down, but I knew I still had two more ledges to go.

Once down to that first ledge, I was more confident and felt able to dispense with the safety belt. I no longer had to struggle to keep a foothold on the steeply sloping surface and I found that I could balance myself better. However, it was still desperately hard work having to prise a rock from the mass and then send it rolling down the slope. From then on I was able to scramble up the rock from the quarry floor when I was starting work.

*

High summer arrived and the heat intensified and seemed to surpass the desert heat we had experienced in Libya. Nienburg seemed to be in the centre of an enormous flat landscape. No matter in which direction one looked, there was no sign of a hill. But hot as the whole land mass was, the quarry took things to another level. This huge bowl with its whitish-grey rock face, and its floor almost the same, was like an enormous frying pan set in the ground. It made the midday heat almost intolerable. The sun blazed down every day, with the rock face reflecting the burning heat and even making it uncomfortable to stand on a ledge a couple of feet from the face.

The 240-strong party who had worked the two factories and quarries before the arrival of my contingent warned us of the conditions we would meet in the depths of winter and stressed the need to conserve whatever clothing we had. It was a warning to take note of, but, for the moment we were being fried in the quarry. Most fellows in the quarry face gang had very little clothing and, in the heat of that summer, the practice was to wear only a pair of woollen army underpants and army boots.

I was extremely fortunate in having received a clothing parcel from my mother only days before my escape from Laterina; so as well as shirts and underclothing, I had army shorts, battledress and my greatcoat. With my stock of clothing I could afford to wear my shorts as well, but I never bothered with a vest or shirt. Like everybody else, I developed a deeper suntan than I have ever had in my life. When I looked down at my torso and legs they were bronze and gave off a lovely purple sheen. However, the outward appearance of our bodies belied the very poor state of health that we were all in, being quite seriously undernourished and worked beyond our limits.

As had happened at Jesabruch, the German crew at Anhalt took a dislike to me. However, this time it was caused by different circumstances. My slow work rate there had been of my own choosing. Now it was a case of my not being capable of any sustained effort in tackling the heavy work at Anhalt. However, the effect was the same, and again it was the reason for my being drafted to any of the dirty and nasty jobs that came up.

In the summer months it did not matter much because, high up on the quarry ledges, we all looked fairly similar. Down on the quarry floor two armed soldiers patrolled the length of our workings and constantly called for more work from anyone they spotted leaning on their shovel. They seldom remembered who they were calling to, so it was rare that there was any recrimination against any one particular fellow.

However, things turned against me as the months passed and winter arrived. I have told how, following my escape from Laterina, Primetta and Iolanda had dyed my army greatcoat. My black greatcoat now differentiated me from the others on the ledges, and I became a sitting duck. In the cold weather, when the soldiers saw me wearing it, I was easily identified. I was immediately known by them as '*Schwarzmantel*' ('Blackcoat') and was regularly heckled and threatened. When we arrived back at the camp with our civilian escort, his day's report on the work was very frequently: '*Schwarzmantel hat keine Arbeit gemacht heute*' ('Blackcoat has done no work today').

*

One of those jobs which I all too often fell for was boulder smashing. When the dynamiting of the ledges was carried out, it did not always completely fragment the rock. As a result, large boulders of solid rock, sometimes almost waist high, could roll down on to the quarry floor. They were too large for the digger and would not have gone on a bogey anyway. So these boulders had to be dealt with by hand. This was a two-man job, each man wielding a heavy sledgehammer. The two men for the job were detailed when we arrived for work at 6.00 am and, any time Herr Klinge was present, I was one of the nominated two.

The job was controlled by Lugs, who was the boulder expert. He would scruti-nize the boulder closely, by torchlight when it was dark. When he found signs of a hair-line fracture, he pointed it out to us. Lugs stood aside and the two of us stood on opposite sides of the boulder. Lugs' first command was '*Druck!*,' and the first hammer fell. Then began an unbroken chant of, '*Immer druck! Immer druck! Immer druck!*', with each of us taking alternate swings. '*Immer druck*' seemed to mean, 'Keep hammering'. When I first picked up my hammer, it was so heavy I thought I would not be able to lift it, let alone swing it. In fact my efforts were a case of lifting it just enough and then letting it fall down on to the boulder. This just prolonged the agony, because a good swing would have done the job much quicker.

When my first effort hit the boulder, the shock wave went right through me and left me quivering on the end of the handle. Although the hairline crack in the rock always opened eventually, it often seemed an eternity before this was achieved. We had to keep on until it opened sufficiently wide to insert a metal wedge in the crack. We then had to aim at the wedge, and the boulder would divide faster. When it eventually fell into halves, one or both of those could still be too big for the crusher and once again Lugs would have to start looking for fractures. There could be three or four of these boulders to deal with each time and, by the time we were finished, I was good for nothing.

*

I was surprised one day to be given a responsible job. The three drillers had finished drilling a section of ledges which had been cleared, and the face was ready for dynamiting. One of the civilian crew told me to come with him and showed me how the job was done. He demonstrated how the drilled holes were stuffed with little tubular sticks of dynamite and the wires were attached. The process was fairly straightforward and the lesson lasted a very short time. Then he left me to it. Klinge and Popeye were both away at the time, or I am sure I would not have been chosen. I was by myself and I suddenly thought that dynamiting was not really my field. As the two bosses were absent, I decided I would not do it correctly. I connected some wires but I missed out one or two of the essential connections.

Then, when all was ready, we took cover behind the bogeys and the locomotive, and the warning whistle was sounded. One of the workmen operated the plunger, which should have blown every ledge up with a terrific roar. Instead there was a deathly silence. After a moment, the whole face gang burst out laughing. My instructor was pretty angry and demanded to know why I had not followed his simple instructions. I was very contrite and told him I was sorry but I thought I had done just as he had shown me. One of the drillers was called. He soon put matters right, and the blasting was done. I was lucky Klinge and Popeye were not present, and I did not get into too much hot water.

*

At the end of every day there was always a lot of rock lying at the foot of the quarry face. This was cleared by a night shift consisting of two Germans, a digger operator and a locomotive driver, supported by a few prisoners. On arrival for work one day we learned that the locomotive had broken down the previous night, so no rock had been cleared. As a result, the quarry gang could not operate. The addition of another day's shovelling down of rock would have been too much for the digger to cope with.

There was no prospect of an immediate repair of the locomotive. So it was decided the face gang should do the work of the locomotive. It was to be two men to a bogey and we would just have to push them round the couple of hundred yards to the chain that hoisted them up the ramp. I was paired off with a fellow named Adkins from Croydon to push one of the bogeys. The quarry floor was far from flat and consisted of a series of gentle slopes up and down. The bogeys were made of heavy metal. They were old and very battered by a ton of rocks being constantly dropped into them. The track on which they ran had never been firmly bedded in the ground. Altogether this led to very rickety progress round the track.

Like myself, Adkins was a slight chap. The prospect was not encouraging. It was still early morning, we had had no breakfast and there would be nothing for hours until we got a mug of ersatz coffee. Nevertheless, the work started and the first bogeys were being pushed along the track. Soon a line of spaced out bogeys was trundling round. There was a metal bar at each end of the bogey on which one could push. When it was our turn to go we gripped this bar and were glad to find the bogey moving. Once rolling, the bogey was easily manageable until the moment when we met an upward slope. It then lost its momentum and became a dead weight. From that point life became really hard work, with Adkins and yours truly struggling to keep up the pace.

After a number of uphill struggles the job was getting beyond us and, as our progress slowed, first one and then another bogey began to catch us up. Those fellows did not mind because they could not be blamed for the hold up. Among them were Scots Guardsmen, Irish Guardsmen and other hefty fellows who could manage much better than we could. As the hold-up grew, Popeye, the quarry foreman, spotted it and came over. Adkins and I were at the beginning of an upward slope and could not get the bogey started at all. Popeye was threatening and started to rail at the two of us, although we did not understand a word of what he was shouting.

We had had a rest while all the hassling had gone on and were eventually able to have another go. The morning progressed with a couple more hold-ups taking place, and on one of them the situation became serious. Adkins and I were now exhausted and could hardly manage the slightest upward slope. At that point Klinge, the quarry boss, appeared at the quarry edge above us. When he saw the column of bogeys below him he became almost manic. He was screaming abuse not only at us but also at Popeye. After a few minutes, still bellowing orders, he unbuckled his belt, which had a pistol and holster attached, and hurled them down in front of Popeye. At that point I felt that I couldn't take any more. I really thought that if Klinge had been down on the quarry floor he would have shot me himself.

Klinge was now almost apoplectic and Popeye was obviously very frightened. He made no move to pick up the pistol. Klinge's harangue continued, and eventually Popeye took the pistol but did not seem to know what to do with it. I thought, 'Here we go. I'm looking down the wrong end of a pistol and the finger on the trigger is frightened and twitchy.' Then something snapped, and in spite of the awful situation I found I was no longer frightened. There was nothing left in me and somehow I became calm. I was so totally drained and exhausted that I just thought, it doesn't matter anymore what they do to me.

At that moment the scene changed, with the appearance of Klinge's two small daughters. It was lunchtime and they had arrived with his dixie from the communal soup kitchen in town. As they had approached, they would have heard his invective. As they came into view on the quarry top, they stood one on each side of him and saw the scene below. They were obviously frightened by the situation and began to jump up and down, screaming in horror and shouting, '*Nein, papa, nein*'. This seemed to calm Klinge. He shouted something down to Popeye and walked away, one hand on each of his daughters' shoulders. Popeye was as relieved as I was and hurried away with the pistol and belt.

Later, during the lunch break, the rest of the gang were complimenting us for having held our nerve, but I could not follow their reasoning. It was not that I had been defiant but just that my spirit had gone and I was totally drained. At Jesabruch factory my causing of the hold-up on the assembly belt had been purposeful incompetence on my part. But the hold-up with the quarry bogeys was beyond my control because of my total inability to push such a heavy load up the slope. My partner, Adkins, was in much the same condition but, because I was Klinge's favourite whipping boy, most of the heat had been directed at me. After lunch Adkins and I were sent up to the factory to do odd jobs. The next day the locomotive had been repaired, so there were no more repeats of the bogey-pushing horror.

*

One day, when it was pitch dark and bitterly cold, we arrived at 6.00 am to find that the chain which hauled the bogeys up from the quarry and then controlled them down the ramp again had broken down during the night. We could tell from the way in which the chain was sagging from the bogeys standing at the top of the ramp that something was amiss. It was as bad as we could have feared. The chain had snapped near the top of the ramp, and the bogeys ahead of the break had careered to the bottom of the ramp taking the broken chain with them. Herr Klinge was supervising proceedings. I was the first of the chaps he detailed to deal with the matter. Each of the main links was five or six inches in length, with semi-circular ends, and the iron was as thick as my thumb. Each main link was joined to its neighbour by a small circular link of similar girth.

The top section of the chain had whiplashed back at the moment of the break. It was a mammoth task just to drag it downhill to its full length. The lower section of chain was lying at the bottom of the ramp and it really was at the limit of our ability to drag it up the ramp. Even Klinge joined in the effort and he was as hard and strong as an ox. The iron was so icily cold that it seemed to burn our fingers. I remarked that we should have gloves for such a job.

Klinge heard me and bawled, 'Meester Unveen wants gloves. He must write to Meester Churchill and he can have gloves.'

It took an age before the two ends of the chain were lying on the ramp near each other. Then the ends had to be lifted and supported while a new link was inserted to join them together. Lifting them and pulling them together was the hardest part of the whole exercise. It had all taken a long time. We had expended enough energy for a day's work, and it was not yet daylight.

Chapter 20

More Thoughts of Escape

L ife had become very difficult, and the intolerable, soul-destroying conditions in the quarry persisted. Even though any escape from a camp in
Germany seemed impossible, just the thought of getting out of the camp
and trusting to luck became worth considering. I talked it over with Tommy
Clifford, the Irish Guardsman from Liverpool, who occupied the top half of our
two-tier bunk. We decided to work on a plan to break out of the small exercise area
in front of our building, so started hoarding rations such as raisins, chocolate and
tinned food from Red Cross parcels, and bartering for more with our cigarettes.

It was a slow job, but the hoard mounted up and the question of where to store
it arose. The chocolate came in 2oz bars of a brand called Meltis, with the name
printed in red on the straw-coloured wrapper. The base of our bunks consisted of
a number of strips of wood stretched across the bunk. They were the same width
as the Meltis bars and were almost the same colour. We started laying the chocolate
bars along the strips so they were hidden under our palliasses. We stored the raisins in the cupboard alongside our bunk and hoped they would not raise suspicion.
After we had built up a considerable supply, we started working on how we could
remain in the exercise area after dark and then climb out during the night.

One day, when heading back to the compound, we arrived at Jesabruch quarry
and started down the path to the old powerhouse and our little compound. Before
we reached the level of the gateway to the compound, we were diverted on to the
narrow path that led to the catwalk towards the door into the guards' room on the
upper floor of the building. A guard emerged from the room calling, '*Zwei sieben
und dreissig. Wo ist er?*' ('237. Where is he?'). I had a sickening feeling, since 2, 3,
and 7 were the last three figures of my PoW number. I guessed something was
wrong but could not imagine what. When I raised my hand, the guard ordered
'*Hierkomm*', so I made my way across the catwalk.

When I entered the room the *Feldwebel*, the guard commander, was standing
with his back to the fireplace halfway along the wall on the right. He had a rolled
up newspaper tucked under his left arm. The wall in front of me contained the
door leading through to our quarters. Tommy Stewart, the German-speaking
'Man of Confidence', was standing against that wall. To his right the other three
guards were lined up. In the corner of the room on my left there was a wood-
burning stove.

I stood confused, wondering what it was all about. Then Tommy spoke. I could not believe what I was hearing.

'Scouse, you're in trouble. You've got to stand by that stove and, if you move, this guard has orders to shoot you.'

I was in a daze as I moved to the stove. At that point the end guard looked at me and slowly fumbled his pistol from its holster and pointed it at me. He was standing about 10ft away. I froze, to the extent that I would have passed muster in Madame Tussauds. The guard was the most timid of the four and he looked as frightened as I was. Once again I was looking down the wrong end of a pistol, and the finger on the trigger was frightened and twitchy. I felt sick and wondered how such a scenario could have arisen, not knowing what I had done wrong.

I did not know whether or not the party outside knew what was going on, but at that moment my colleagues were called to the door. Each one was brought into the room, searched and then sent through to our quarters before the next man entered. The process seemed to go on forever. All the time, the pistol was still pointing at me. I was afraid to look up at the guard's face in case he thought I was challenging him. At last the searches were over, and the last man went through to our quarters. There was silence in the room. Nobody moved. Then the *Feldwebel* motioned me over and I stood in front of him, relieved that I had survived the revolver threat. He did not bat an eyelid for some time, just staring at me, the newspaper still tucked under his arm.

Then suddenly he turned to his right and marched smartly to the wall, about-turned and marched back across the room. As he passed me he did a smart eyes-right and stared at me. On reaching the wall there was another about-turn and a repeat crossing of the room, now with an eyes-left as he passed and glared at me. One more turn followed and this time, on reaching me, he halted and faced me, staring fiercely into my face. By now my nerves were in a state of collapse because I did not know what this was all about.

The staring seemed to go on for a long time, and by now I had lost all feeling. Then at last he moved. His right arm came across and gripped the end of the newspaper. With a flourish like an army officer withdrawing his sword from its scabbard, he pulled the newspaper out and, swinging it in a high arc, brought the end down just in front of my nose. He left it there for a while then, with another flourish, drew it back, unrolled it, holding it flat, and once again pushed it towards me. Lying on the paper was a foot-long hacksaw blade. After letting me look at it, he shrieked '*Was ist der*'? ('What's this?'). I felt a little silly as I said it was a hacksaw blade, which Tommy Stewart then translated.

He demanded to know where I got it. I denied having seen it before. He asked who had put it there, without saying where it had been found. I denied all knowledge of the blade. This was repeated a few times before he asked for my seven roommates to be brought in. He lined them up alongside me and told them I had claimed the blade belonged to one of them. They all denied it vehemently. His next threat was chilling: he said he would condemn all eight to the cellar until one owned up. We all knew that the cellar was dark and rat-infested. It was an awful prospect.

He then changed completely and told us he would look into the matter further, but that we could go now. My nerves were shattered and I had never felt so relieved. I thought, the miserable bastards have found my chocolate, pinched it and used the hacksaw blade as substitute evidence of intention to escape. I was disconsolate as I entered my room. I went to my bunk and sadly flicked aside the corner of the palliasse. There, to my great surprise, I found row after row of Meltis bars. I thought the whole matter over and realized it was probably just a con by the guards, who had probably decided that in case anybody was thinking of escape, they would just put a damper on such thoughts. It seemed it was just bad luck that they had picked on me to use as their whipping boy. Tommy Clifford and I talked it over and decided that we should take this as a warning. We decided to end our careers as escapers forthwith. We were then able to sit down to a great chocolate feast.

Chapter 21

Personalities and States of Mind

Work at the quarry carried on, whatever the weather. If it rained all day we still had to remain on the face and push rock down. This meant that when we reached the compound that evening our trousers and boots were soaking wet. On our return, our trousers and boots were put in large baskets, six sets to a basket, and locked away for the night. This was an anti-escape strategy, but when we got them back at 5.30 the following morning they were still drenched, and we went to work in sopping wet clothes.

As winter came on, that situation worsened. The temperatures were well below zero, although we never knew just how much. The intense cold every morning caused our soaking trousers to freeze the moment we stepped outside. As we walked, the ice crackled and broke into small pieces which were held in the fabric of the trousers until they melted. In a spell of bad weather our boots and trousers could remain wet for many days. Snow was more tolerable than rain because we could shake dry snow off our clothing. I was luckier than many because I had an army greatcoat which kept a lot of rain off me, and as it did not have to be stored away with the trousers and boots I was able to dry it overnight by the stove in our room.

Although rain and snow never interfered with work in the quarry, there was one thing that did. That was an air raid warning. The sound of the sirens meant that we were at once shepherded from the quarry to the state-of-the-art metal-walled passages and safe rooms of an underground shelter. Air raid warnings at Nienburg were few and far between, and we never saw the bombers passing overhead. So there was none of the excitement I had had watching the planes at the *Lazarett* at Altengrabow, where we were on a main flight path and able to watch the raids day after day.

*

My friend Roy had been working at Concordia quarry and had landed the cushiest job possible. Unlike Anhalt, where the factory and quarry were alongside each other, at Concordia there were many hundreds of yards of narrow gauge single track railway between the two operations. For some reason I never understood, there was a set of points halfway along that stretch of rail, and someone had to sit there all day and change the points every time the locomotive passed pulling the rock-laden bogeys. Roy had been given the job and enjoyed several months of sitting, far from any hassling, just changing the points and waving to the driver each time the locomotive and bogeys passed.

Then his splendid isolation came to an end when it was decided that the points were no longer necessary and could be removed. So he was transferred to the Anhalt quarry face gang. When I heard this I advised him to try the vertigo claim. Soon after going on a ledge, propped up by his shovel, he purposely fell over, intending just to lie there. Instead he made too spectacular a job of it and fell off the ledge. The German workers were impressed by this and Roy saw no more of the quarry face, succeeding where I had failed so miserably.

Roy remained at Anhalt quarry, but as the food carrier. He had a dogcart-like contraption which he trundled in to the soup kitchen in Nienburg twice a day for the morning and midday breaks to bring us our coffee and later our soup. Everyone knew that Roy and I were pals, so with eagle eyes all around us there was no chance of any little extra ladles coming my way. I just had to ensure that at least the Klim tin, which I used as my receptacle, received a full ladle and I was not losing out.

On Sundays there was sometimes a small amount of meat in the soup. On one occasion we complained when the meat was off and inedible. The next time meat was due it was absent from the soup. When we asked the reason, we were told we had not wanted it. So we soon put a stop to that by saying we would have it and take a chance each week. After that it turned out to be edible.

One thing we could get was beer, which we had to pay for. Occasionally we had a pay day and received a small amount of marks. These were not real *Reichsmarks*, but *Gefangener* (prisoner) marks. They were like small Monopoly money, printed on a similar type of paper, and were treated with disdain by most fellows. Nevertheless, one could sometimes buy beer with them. It came in small barrels, which cost nineteen marks each. Just as the notes were not real money, neither was the liquid real beer. It was like sarsaparilla and was probably totally without any alcohol, but everybody was so desperate to get anything which might contain vitamins that they were willing to take whatever came along. An ironic point about that money, with which we bought the beer but generally considered useless and threw away, was that after the war it became a keenly collected item of militaria.

*

In the room next to mine was a tall Irish Guardsman from Liverpool, Harry Croft, who was a little older than most of us. Every time he filled his mug with beer, when we had any, he would groan, 'There's no bad beer; some's just better than others.' He worked in Concordia and every evening on his return to the compound he would flop onto his bunk and remark, 'Another day Churchill doesn't know about.' I knew he had worked in the Bryant and May match factory in Liverpool. Not long after the war I spent a few days in the grounds of the factory on Ordnance Survey work and I asked for Harry. He was still there but sadly Nienburg had affected his mind and he was no longer able to hold down any responsible job.

People responded differently to the pressures of PoW life. It all seemed to depend on one's outlook and state of mind. A Scots Guardsman known only by his surname, Barrie, was always the life and soul of the party, no matter how miserable the day. One day on the quarry face another Scot, from a Highland regiment, just known as Ginger, was working not far from me. The poor fellow had become so deformed that his back was permanently almost horizontal, and he was always in abject misery.

One particularly miserable day Barrie was working on one side of me and Ginger on the other. At one point Ginger turned his head towards Barrie and asked despairingly, 'Barrie, d'ye think the war wull end tomorra?'

Barrie stood for some moments pondering the question, with one hand leaning on the handle of his shovel and his free hand scratching his chin. Then, speaking as though he had given the matter deep consideration, he answered, 'Nae, Ginger, I dinna think it wull end tomorra.'

It seemed to display the difference between two souls, both in the same predicament, one in such deep despair and the other unworried and able to show such assumed solemnity.

It was up to each man how he coped with the pressures of life behind barbed wire. From the start I had chosen to think of an eventual escape. At Laterina every day I looked forward to talking to the sentries. This gave me an interest for the day and a sense of achievement that I was learning Italian, which would be of great use to me once I was able to escape. Then when I was offered a place in the tunnel team I had a real incentive to get up and be busy.

Germany was a more difficult place altogether in which to find any incentive to focus on. One thing which kept me occupied for quite a while was trying to sew an outline Artillery badge on my pullover. I had an army issue 'hussif', or housewife, containing needles, thread, thimble etc. I also had a skein of lengths of silk in a great number of bright colours. I cannot remember where this came from, but it gave me hours of concentration and took my mind off the conditions at Anhalt. I was not at all skilled, and the finished article was the crudest form of an Artillery badge, but it occupied my mind and I built into it a form of challenge to the Germans. This was how I used to try to keep my spirits up. On the whole, I think I succeeded. Possibly my own personal war that I was constantly waging against being part of the German war effort also further boosted my morale.

One thing which helped morale was any news from England. I used to receive reports of the football scene from Bob Prole, 'Ranger', the sports editor of the *Liverpool Echo*. During the war years there were no league tables and all matches were played as friendlies. Any player could volunteer for any team he happened to be stationed near. I used to read the reports sent to me by Ranger and then put them up on the notice board for all to see.

The most valuable and morale-boosting mail which I received were letters from my family. These were usually written by my father and gave me news of all the family, including my brother Les, who was serving in India with the Royal Air Force, and my sister Maude, who was serving with the W.A.A.F. at a radar station in southern England. My father also gave me news of his grocer's shop, of all his customers and any other general news.

When I had been in Laterina I used to receive letters quite frequently from my family. That changed after I escaped from Laterina and we were unable to correspond. I knew that my name would be on the missing list and my family would have no further news of me. It was ironic to think that shortly after my escape from Laterina, the villagers of Montebenichi offered me shelter and looked after my welfare to such an extent that I became as fit and healthy as I had ever been in my life. However during that period whilst I was posted as missing, my family would have been worrying about me, having no idea of my whereabouts, my welfare or even whether I was alive or dead. This would have been particularly painful and difficult for my parents. They were both already inconsolably distressed over the death of my sister Betty, who at the age of twelve was lost at sea in 1940 in the child evacuation scheme to Canada. My parents' grief was such that there was never any mention of Betty in their letters, and after the war when I returned to England, customers in my father's grocery shop told me, 'Your parents never smiled after Betty's loss, Frank.'

It was this that had eventually persuaded me to leave Montebenichi to try to reach the Allied Forces in southern Italy, believing that the Allies would soon arrive in Tuscany and we would be freed. Unfortunately the venture did not succeed, and we finished up in Germany, but at least I was once again in contact with my family, so in that sense the situation had improved for them.

Chapter 22

Factory Jobs

One day fortune smiled on me. The factory needed a lorry load of bricks but nobody in the factory gang could be spared for the journey, so the quarry was asked to supply two men. Since my transfer to the quarry I had maintained my unwillingness to work until pushed, and Popeye had no hesitation in naming me as one of the two to go. We reported to the factory, where a lorry was waiting. It turned out to be a coal-fired traction engine of the sort that, as a small boy, I had seen trundling past my father's grocery shop bound for Liverpool docks. It had a boiler with a coke fire below it and below that a large circular metal dish to catch the falling clinkers, the burnt-out remains of the coke. Behind the cab a pipe for smoke emission rose to a point higher than the cab top.

The two men in the cab told us to climb aboard and, as soon as we mounted, the driver set off. It was a rare treat to get away from the quarry. It was some distance to the brickworks and the traction engine was a slow vehicle. The weather was perfect and we settled down on the back of the vehicle to enjoy the journey. It was an undreamed of pleasure to stand leaning on the top of the cab, enjoying the sunshine, with a cool breeze fanning our cheeks. The sun was benevolent now and not the monster blazing down on us into the quarry.

When we reached the brickworks, the two Germans soon found the point from which we had to load the bricks and went off, leaving us to load. Our attitude to work was completely different now. We just set about the job at an easy pace. It was quite heavy work, with one man passing the bricks up to be stacked on the lorry. When the two Germans returned they checked what we had done. There were almost enough bricks on the lorry so it was not long before we finished loading, checked out of the brickworks and set off for the return to Nienburg. The afternoon was as good as the morning trip. This time we were sitting on top of the bricks, with the same cool breeze and a gentler sun.

Then we found there were even more pleasures to come. Passing through a small town, the lorry pulled up in front of a beer garden and the driver told us to get down. We were taken through the bar restaurant and found ourselves in a very long and rather wide garden. There were a few apple trees dotted about the garden, but the main thing was a great number of picnic tables, each with a family enjoying themselves on this lovely afternoon. Fortunately, although stripped to the waist, we were both wearing shorts and not woollen underpants as many fellows would have done.

We were taken to a table past the furthest family at the far end of the garden and soon were supplied with a plate of salami, a loaf of bread and a bottle of beer each. It was my first proper beer in two years. The label on the bottle told us it was *Sankt Klaus* beer. It really did seem that Santa Claus had come down the chimney to see us that day. There was more beer for us, and the happy air of the families with children playing began to make me feel more relaxed. But I knew that any such feeling would dissipate the next morning in the quarry.

Alongside us at the end of the garden there were a number of men practising on a small .22 rifle range. It was bizarre to have Germans blazing away with small-bore rifles while we sat alongside them enjoying salami and Father Christmas beer. If the scenario had been the Libyan desert, we would have been riddled with bullets. When our driver came for us, we walked back through the tables. All the families had been enjoying themselves, and a number of people nodded and smiled at us as we passed. We were not very far from Nienburg, so even in our old traction engine we soon arrived back at the compound. Convincing myself that it had not all been a dream was difficult. It was certainly my most enjoyable day in Germany, but it was unique amongst the many terrible days.

*

Alongside the crusher were two enormous silos. These were used for storing the crushed rock. They were cylindrical, very tall and maybe 12ft in diameter. Also towering above the factory were two chimneys reaching high into the sky. Fixed to the outside of each chimney stack was a metal ladder stretching from ground level to the very top. Many times I stood on a quarry ledge and thought that even if I were to be offered a return home the next day, I could not climb that ladder.

Once the rock had been crushed to a small aggregate, it was then transported to the top of the silo and poured into it. The lower part of the silo was a funnel-shaped cone which terminated in a release hole at the bottom. The hole could be sealed by a strong metal sheet which could be moved backwards and forwards to open and close the hole and so allow aggregate to be extracted from the silo. That material was then transported to two enormous furnaces for the final crushing to the consistency of cement. The process worked well when the crushed rock was dry. As the material was extracted from the base of the silo it was replaced not by stuff from the sides of the mass, but from the centre. This eventually led to a cone-shaped depression in the centre of the mass of crushed rock, as it drained down to the release hole.

However, in times of consistently heavy rain, the aggregate coming from the crusher was still so wet when it entered the silo that it would form a fairly solid mass. As this wet stuff tumbled into the silo and rolled down the slopes, it formed a solid block above the release hole and completely clogged it, thus bringing operations to a complete halt. With luck, probing through the hole with crowbars from below could settle the problem, but the blockage was usually not discovered until it was too late and it then had to be cleared from the inside of the silo. This was a two-man job and was given to two of the quarry face gang. The first time it happened while I was at the quarry, my reputation ensured that I was one of the unfortunate two to be chosen.

On the top of the silo there was a large upright tubular metal rod that had metal rings attached to it near the top. There was also a circular access hole in the centre of the roof. There were two of us up there and we each donned a harness. Then we were given a long length of stout rope, with a clasp hook at each end. One hook was attached to a ring on the metal upright and the other to a metal ring on the back of our harness. We were then each handed a heavy, spike-ended iron rod for prodding at the wet rock. We each climbed through the access hole and were lowered down into the silo.

It was a very eerie sensation being lowered into what seemed like an enormous cavern. I felt like a spider on the end of a strand of web. The silo proved to be hardly one third full, so it was a long way down, and the depth of wet rock blocking the release hole was not too great. We were both shocked when, as we spoke, our voices were thrown back at us from the metal sides of the silo in a loud booming echo, which made communication with the top difficult.

The upper edge of the rock was a circle around the inside edge of the silo wall, and the rock then funnelled down in a cone shape towards the release hole. Below the hole the sliding metal plate had been removed, so we had to attack the rock with our iron bars until we broke through that hole. When we got down to the level of the crushed rock we had to start swinging backward and forward until our boots could get a foothold on the sloping rock at the side of the silo. Then on opposite sides of the silo we made our way down the slope to the point where wet rock was blocking access to the release hole. There we had to attack the blockage, poking with the iron poles. Once we had cleared the problem and the aggregate was running again, we were hauled to the top and the job was done.

I have made no mention of how I got to the top of the silo and then down to ground level again. This is because, when I came away from the job, my mind had just blacked out on the experience. I just cannot imagine how the German crew got me to go up there. My mind must have just closed down, leaving me in a zombie-like state.

*

During major breakdowns in the quarry which brought work to a stop the quarry gang were sent up to the factory to attend to all the neglected jobs there. These were generally dirty jobs. Occasionally the furnaces were closed down to allow cleaning the inside of the ovens to be carried out. The powdered cement had all been drawn out by a power suction system and only the ball bearings and a useless residue remained. This task was one of the jobs given to us. While working inside the furnace we took the opportunity of stealing a couple of the larger ball bearings. These were later to prove useful for grinding wheat grains into flour back in our room at the compound.

A more unpleasant job with the cement arose after it had been drawn by power from the ovens. It was then blasted along pipes made of a zinc-like metal. The pipes passed along troughs almost a foot square sunk into the concrete floor of the factory, and the troughs were covered by lengths of iron plating. There were numerous right-angle bends as the troughs passed along the factory floor, and at these points there were always faults in the joints of the pipes. The resultant holes were infinitely small, but such was the power with which the cement was blasted along that it was inevitable some powder would escape.

This escaping cement came through each hole in a fine jet spray and was held in the trough by the iron cover. Eventually the trough became full of cement and we were called in at the next breakdown in the quarry. The escaped cement had to be extracted with a small scoop and carried away in buckets. It was so fine that each time we lifted a scoopful to the bucket it caused a cloud of cement to envelop us until we were covered with it. Back in the compound, despite the showers being cold and the shortage of soap, we could get most of the dust from our bodies. However, the worst problem was our hair, which became matted with cement dust and felt just like concrete.

The situation became so bad that it required drastic action. One of the ten people in my room was a New Zealander, Kiwi Mullen. Before the war Kiwi had been a sheep shearer, and we knew he had a pair of shears, though not the sort he used on his sheep. Those of us with the cementy hair problem asked him if he would shave our heads. He relished the prospect and offered to do it there and then. It was a daunting prospect because at the time shaven heads were not in vogue. He performed just as he did with a sheep, his left arm round me in a bear hug and the right wielding the shears. He started in the centre of my forehead and drove right up the centre and over the back. Once that was done, there was no going back. There was a mirror in the ablutions room, but I did not look at myself for weeks. It was certainly better when next I had to work with the cement ducts in the factory. It felt very strange, but I soon got used to it.

The ducts carrying the prepared cement finished up at the bagging point, which was alongside a loading bay alongside a railway siding. Two of the factory gang received the sealed bags of cement and wheeled them out on trolleys straight into the waiting wagons. There was a sad occurrence at that point one day. The two men arrived for work and, as usual, found some empty wagons waiting for them. On entering one they found beans spilt all over the floor. Feeling that their luck was in they could not resist eating some of them. Unfortunately, the beans had been laced with rat poison. Both men soon became very ill and later that day died a very painful death. I did not know them well, but I shared in the deep sense of sadness that was felt throughout the whole compound. There followed another burial service. As previously mentioned, many years after the war I called on the Registrar of Deaths in Nienburg who showed me evidence of the transfer of Tommy's Brannan's remains to the Commonwealth War Graves Commission. Unsolicited, he also showed me similar evidence of the transfer of the two men who died from rat poison.

*

An event which had caused mirth in the camp was when a marauding party of night shift men at the factory found a brick storage chamber in an earth bank between the factory and the quarry. When they explored it, they found that it contained a store of a variety of fresh vegetables. These were smuggled into the camp when the night shift returned that morning and were cooked and eaten immediately. That afternoon a furious Herr Klinge arrived at the factory threatening dire consequences for the thieves who had robbed his store. Needless to say, no trace of the vegetables was ever found.

The discovery of the vegetable store had been a lucky strike, but the main target of the night shift men going out on sorties was the railway siding. There were only a couple of German workers on duty at night, so it was a simple task for one or two fellows to slip away to the siding for a short time. Many of the wagons were left unsealed, and sacks of wheat were a common cargo. When their luck was in they were able to bring away enough wheat for everybody. Only enough for one cooking was ever taken, since if a store of wheat had been discovered in the compound it would have pointed to a connection with the thefts from the railway. However, one night the marauding group had a nasty shock when they opened up a wagon only to find a lot of dead bodies inside. That ended their marauding for that night.

The stolen wheat now brings in the ball bearings which were pinched from the cement furnaces. When wheat arrived in our room it was still whole grains and not at all suitable for cooking. Armed with a large steel ball bearing, however, we could use that as a grinding stone on the circular iron top of the wood stove in our room and crush the wheat into a state in which it could be mixed with water into something like dough. This was then rolled out and flattened into a shape resembling a sort of pancake. This was done as soon as the wheat reached us, so as to minimize the possibility of the it being found in a surprise search.

When the stove was lit and fully burning, the metal plate on top glowed red with the fierce heat. A two-man job then followed, one holding the pancake and the other armed with some implement to scrape it from the stove top. The scraping up had to be done the instant the pancake was dropped on to the stove top or the pancake was instantly incinerated. These half raw pancakes, made of loosely ground wheat and containing no other ingredients, were pretty unwholesome, and I do not know what they were doing to our stomachs. They were not even pleasant to eat, but the prospect of getting anything to eat overrode all else.

Chapter 23

The Salt Mine

L ife in the compound was normally calm and nobody wanted to make life worse than it already was. So everybody was generally peaceful and squabbles were few and far between. There were, however, occasional exceptions. One time a minor squabble in the compound yard, between a Cypriot and an Englishman, developed into a serious fight. It was not just a boxing match, but wrestling on the ground, locked in a combat that could have been fatal. Each man was using his hands trying to tear the other's mouth apart, bang his head on the ground and gouge his eyes out. A crowd gathered round, but the fight was so fierce that nobody could intervene. Only when a guard realized what was happening and came over and belaboured them with his rifle were others able to separate them.

The outcome was a hearing before a sort of court martial. The Cypriot was sentenced to be transferred to the salt mine, which was in the nearby town of Halberstadt. In any transfer there always followed a transfer in the reverse direction. The man we received in return was an Irish Guardsman. We already had a number of his battalion friends in the compound who had known the newcomer well. They were aghast at the state they found him in. He was broken in spirit, hardly able to help himself and barely fit for any sort of work. His friends helped him out but there was not much they could do. We wondered how many more in the salt mine were in his condition and just how awful the work conditions there must be. It worried me to think that if they did that to the Cypriot for fighting they could have done the same to me for my own constant intransigence. It might well have been my fate if the rows of ruined panels had been discovered at Jesabruch.

*

About this time we were surprised to see Klinge come down the quarry ramp with four or five civilians dressed in overcoats and trilbies. They were joined by Popeye. The group came along the quarry floor to where we were working on the ledges. They moved along slowly, stopping to discuss each person on the ledge, with Klinge making notes. We could not imagine what it was all about, but there was a nasty feeling about it.

The shock came the following day when we returned from work. On the notice board was a list of ten names for transfer to the salt mine. A number of our face gang were on the list and my name was at the top of it. I was sick when I saw it. I was not in a good state of health and it made me ill to think what the salt mine would do to me.

Part III

THE TIDE TURNS

Chapter 24

Welcome Glimmers of Hope

The day after I saw that my name was on the transfer list for the salt mine the quarry night shift was cancelled. Added to the recent appearance of the fighter planes this had to be a good omen, and we crossed our fingers. Then suddenly things were happening. We heard faint distant rumblings. They continued sporadically, and the general comment was that it could not be thunder on such a fine day. The magic word 'gunfire' was mentioned but was immediately dismissed as a rambling hope. However, the next day it continued, and now we were certain it was gunfire. We did not know whether it was American or British but we knew it had to be ours and we did not care which.

All of this was followed by what I considered to be a life-saver for me. A notice from Berlin appeared on the board stating that all movement of PoWs was forbidden forthwith. This was such a blessing, to know that my transfer to the salt mine was off. I said a prayer of thankfulness and cried with relief.

As spring 1945 approached, the military authorities in Berlin must have prepared themselves for the annual fever of hotheads trying to escape. A large notice appeared on the board entitled 'ESCAPING HAS CEASED TO BE A SPORT' in big capitals. It went on to say that there would be no tolerance shown in the future towards any escapes or attempted escapes, and that any offenders would be shot on sight. The text was dotted with sketches showing Alsatian dogs, armed soldiers and other deterrents.

When I saw this I smiled. For three years escape plans had been my whole focus. I had treated escape as a pastime, almost a sport, and it had played its part in getting me through the war. I had taken part in a series of escape projects which were played out like a game against the Italians and Germans. It started in Italy, where I began by learning Italian and stowing away food rations. I then went out from the work camp on a dummy-run, followed by the real thing. I had joined the tunnel team at Laterina, although my escape in the end was by climbing the wire. After that, whilst aboard the railway wagon bound for Germany, I had assisted in the attempt to hack out a side panel, although that escape was scuppered when German troops inspected the wagons. Finally, together with Tommy Clifford, I had made escape plans in Germany, but we gave up all thoughts of escape after the Germans played that trick on me with a hacksaw blade.

So I thought it ironic to see the notice, 'ESCAPING HAS CEASED TO BE A SPORT'. By this time, having heard the gunfire, we knew that the war was obviously nearing its end. I had no further escape plans. It seemed that the German authorities were panicking, and we for our part were living in hope of release within the near future. It was not long before we had to leave the camp, and I wish I had taken the notice from the board and kept it as a souvenir.

Then one day a most thrilling thing happened. Two Allied fighter planes roared out of the blue quite low and zoomed round the chimney stacks of the two factories for a minute or so. We could not believe our eyes, but we danced and cheered and roared, '*Deutschland kaputt*' from the ledges to the guards below. They pretended to ignore us. It almost seemed as if the pilots knew we were there and were saluting us. In the camp we had no means of collecting any war news so we never knew how things were going. We just had to keep hoping for the best, with blind faith. The only occasion we had picked up news was when I had learned from a group of Spanish slave labourers that the Allied invasion had started. Now, to see low-level friendly fighter planes flying in daytime in our own area was a heart-warming sight. The incident provided an enormous boost to morale.

*

The day shift at the quarry carried on as normal, so we were not spared that. However, there was a spring in everybody's step and everyone was perky. The guards were aware of it but showed no reaction. The gunfire became clearer, but it was still some distance off. We were now sure it would not be long before the Allies reached Nienburg. The thought came that the guards might want to move us away, and we decided to resist that. There were about 300 of us in the compound and we were sure the guards could not shoot us all, so we agreed to stand firm.

Our feelings were confirmed before many days passed. One morning the guards burst in at 4.00 am and ordered us out at once. The plan was to march away from Nienburg. A chorus of '*Nein, nein*' told the Germans we were not going. They surprised us by saying, '*Das geht doch! Bleibt hier, aber wir gehen jetzt*' ('All right, you can stay, but we're going'). They then explained that the River Saale was to be the Germans' next line of defence and that, if we listened, we would hear the tanks manoeuvring into position. When we opened the door we confirmed that this was so. We had to agree then that what they said made sense, and the sooner we were out of the place the better.

Chapter 25

The Long March to Freedom

Convinced by the guards that it would be foolish to remain at the work camp site, we reluctantly agreed to leave. We were given our boots and trousers and, dressed but unwashed, were hurriedly formed up by the guards in the yard outside. There was no formality of a roll call and, once on the road, it was just a case of ambling along at an easy pace. Roy and I were alongside each other, chatting away, as were most other men, with their particular friends. The few guards, rifles slung across their shoulder, were spread along the column. We had no idea where we were going and were not sure whether anybody else knew. It was just a fatalistic acceptance of something beyond our control. We had not eaten and had no idea where our next meal would come from. The one consolation was that the weather was fine and we would be walking beneath a sunny sky.

It was strange to think that I would not see the quarry again. I had been given a hard time there, though much of it was of my own making. The unpleasant jobs I had repeatedly been given were very hard for me to endure. Even the daily drudgery of shovelling rock off a quarry ledge was a soul-destroying task. I felt my conscience was clear, though, never having willingly done a stroke of work. Macmillan's dreadful description of Anhalt quarry, at the time I had to exchange jobs with him, had not proved quite accurate, but I was extremely weak and I felt lucky to have survived. Now I ambled along the road wondering what the future held for me. It seemed a miracle that the sudden change of fortunes had frozen any movement in the transfer of any PoWs, because I am sure that I could not have survived the salt mine.

The advancing spring of 1945 had brought good weather. After our early start, the day soon brightened into a beautiful morning. It was wonderful to know that I had left Nienburg behind forever and no longer had to worry about either the quarry or the compound. One of the most unpleasant things I had endured in the compound had been that the bunks were infested with bedbugs. It was always horrible to wake in the night and feel the creatures crawling around the blankets. Killing just one of the beasts caused such an unimaginably foul smell in the night that you were sorry at once that you had killed it. It was thoughts such as these that occupied my mind as we walked along. We did not know where we were heading, but it was good to feel the fresh air on our faces as we marched along the open road.

The column walked for a couple of hours before being given a break. After a spell sitting at the roadside, the march resumed, and that became the pattern for the day. During one of the breaks each man was issued with a small pack of raw minced meat. I was hungry and began to eat it, but it did not taste right. It was obvious there was to be no more food so I ate a little more until I found it really unpleasant. It was so obviously off that, hungry as I was, I threw the rest away.

After some time we met up with men from another work party. Shortly after that a third work party joined the march. By that time we must have been a column of 800 or 900 men. The guards had also trebled in number. We had been on minor roads since leaving Nienburg and had seen only small villages. There had been an almost total absence of traffic.

Towards late afternoon we were called to a halt alongside a large farmhouse. We were told that we could use the many barns and outhouses for sleeping. At once men were swarming all over the place. Lots of hens were pecking their way among the outhouses and there was a flock of ducks. In a matter of minutes there was not a chicken or duck left alive. Everywhere small fires were being lit to start cooking the booty.

I did not have a bird, but I went exploring the outhouses. At one of them I opened the door and found myself in a rather small room in the centre of which was an enamel bath. In the bath was a good quantity of milk that looked quite fresh. There must have been a great many gallons there. I scooped my Klim tin in and tasted the milk. It was beautifully fresh. Since my capture three years earlier, I had only once tasted fresh milk, and that was at Christmas 1943 when I was ill in my shack at Montebenichi and Corrada and Onelia had walked miles to a distant village where a farmer kept two cows.

So I drank my fill, which was quite a lot. Then I called loudly that there was milk available. At once men were milling around me to get into the place. The swarm grew and it was not long before the bath was empty.

*

The barns were full of straw and everyone made a soft bed for themselves. It was not possible for everyone to sleep under a roof, but it was a mild dry night and everybody slept well. The following morning we were roused early and were soon on the road again. Throughout our stay, we saw no one from the farm.

We started walking, without any breakfast. There was no indication of when we might next eat. We were being kept on small country lanes and walked through occasional small hamlets. The people in these places brought buckets and small baths of water to the roadside so that we could fill our mugs as we passed. This was a life-saver, and we were very grateful to them.

After a while I began to feel ill. I guessed it was the bad meat I had eaten the day before. Not only did my stomach feel bad, I felt generally unwell. Walking became difficult, and I was falling back towards the rear of the column. I was grateful that Roy was with me. A horse-drawn cart had been supplied from somewhere and was being used for those not able to walk. It was already packed with men and there was no room for any more.

As the column reached a small side road to the right that led through a wooded area, we were called to a halt. Without our noticing, the guards had all edged to the left of the column. At that point they turned their rifles on us and ordered the column to take the side road, so we took the road through the woods. When we emerged from the woods the flat plain seemed to stretch out in front of us forever.

Soon we could see that there was a major river ahead, far wider than the Saale, with an extremely strong current. It turned out to be the Elbe, and we had walked north of the confluence of the Saale and the Elbe. We then saw a ferry crossing. The ferryboat was a very large vessel, capable of carrying many vehicles on its wide flat deck. It crossed the river under its own power but was prevented from being dragged downriver by being linked to a massive chain stretching from bank to bank, presumably because of the strength of the current.

There was much unease among us at the prospect of crossing the Elbe. It was probably going to be a major problem to the advancing Allied forces behind us and would certainly delay our release. There was strong protest from the men being urged to go aboard the ferry, but the rifles were once again brought into action to put an end to any objection. Our hearts were heavy when we left the ferry on the eastern bank.

From that point on, we seemed to be pressed to keep up the pace. I was still feeling groggy and struggling to keep up. Having Roy walking with me was a great encouragement. We eventually arrived at the first town we had seen since we had started the march. It proved to be Zerbst. Most of the column did not enter the town, but when I saw the cartload of men unable to walk being guided into the town centre I followed and reported that I was unwell. To my relief, this was accepted and I accompanied them. Roy followed me and was also admitted.

We were led to a large one-roomed building that was a medical centre. It was built of green-painted metal and the walls were mostly glass panels. There was scarcely any furniture except beds. Those of us fortunate enough to be there were given our first proper meal in days. It was also my first night in bed since leaving the compound, so I slept well. The following day I felt much better.

*

There were many days when we had no food, and it was clear that the small villages we were passing through would be unable to supply food to a column of 1,000 men or more. The German population had also suffered. So we knew we had to find our food ourselves.

In spite of my having had a meal the previous evening, hunger was by now becoming a problem. It was plain that no organization ahead of us would have the facilities to supply food to such a large body of men, so the prospect was daunting. Unbeknown to us, however, fortune was to come to our aid. We were moving into an area of massive agricultural production and the chief crop seemed to be potatoes. We were soon to see the first field of them. It looked as large as a small prairie, and the crop had been harvested and buried in clamps 100yds long.

We saw the first one from some distance away. Immediately the pace quickened almost to a double march. As we arrived, men hopped across the roadside ditch and began frantically pushing away the covering soil and stuffing potatoes into their pockets. The guards were suffering the same privations as we were, so it was a mass of guards and prisoners side by side, all stealing potatoes. After the column had finally passed, there was not a potato left.

There was obviously never going to be food provided by any official source, so we just had to live on our wits. The potato clamps were to become a lifeline to us and were an almost daily routine. If we did not see one, we had no food that day. One other source of food was unwary chickens about the roadside as we passed through a village. Men had no compunction about leaping on these as the chance arose.

As the column moved along, every scrap of wood or small tree branch lying near the road was collected to be used to cook the potatoes when we halted for the evening. Some fellows tried baking them on embers, but they were not very successful. Mostly we used to boil them, though for this we had to have a supply of water. A rather unsatisfactory way to collect water was to fill our water bottles at the baths put out in villages. The narrow neck of the bottle meant that a great deal of the column passed you by. It also hampered others who only wanted to scoop up a drink. If there was no water available there was no cooking, and the only alternative was to eat the potatoes raw.

*

One day, shortly after we had crossed a railway line, we heard the rumble of a train behind us. At that moment a couple of Allied fighter-bombers flew over, spotted the train and launched an attack. We were close enough to see the havoc they caused. It was a goods train, so there would have been no great loss of life, but it appeared that the train itself was completely wrecked. I thought to myself that maybe this is why we did not receive Red Cross parcels regularly, and a wry smile came to my face. We were sufficiently far away not to be in any danger, but we were frightened that the pilots might not recognize us as Allied prisoners and come down to strafe our column. Happily that did not happen. Instead the pilots flew off, no doubt satisfied that their mission was successful.

Every day the walking was accompanied by a symphony of spoons clanking in Klim tins. These two articles were essentials, the spoon always kept in the tin. With many hundreds of men walking without any regard to keeping in step, the jangling din was incessant.

Well on into the march we were joined by a bespectacled, elderly German officer riding a bicycle. Nobody knew where he came from or why he joined us. From the start he attempted to instil some smartness into the column, although this was an impossible task. He could do nothing to stop the symphony of mugs and spoons, but he never gave up trying to get us to march in threes. He worked his way into the mass and then moved ahead, perched on the cycle, repeatedly calling '*Immer Dreien!*' Nobody took any notice of him. He was detested by all and became known as 'Immerdreien'.

It seemed as though the march was endless, as we trudged along day after day. Fortunately, it being April, we were blessed with a long spell of fine weather. Life would have been desperately miserable if it had changed for the worse. I was extremely fortunate that my boots were still in good condition. The elderly cobbler in Montebenichi had repaired them more than a year earlier, and I had good reason to be grateful to him. Other fellows were much less fortunate, their boots falling apart to the point where some were walking barefoot.

A moving experience was when the column twice walked past concentration camps. Neither camp was large, but the slogan above the wrought iron gates, '*Arbeit Macht Frei*' ('Work Sets You Free') was chilling to see. The people in the camp, presumably mostly Jews, were clearly in a dire state of malnutrition. Those able to stand came to the wire as we passed. All were dressed in the political prisoner garb, pyjamas with white and pale brown stripes. They looked like walking skeletons, their faces pallid grey in colour, with sunken eyes which seemed to be staring at us without seeing. Again we had the chilling thought that there were many others who had undergone experiences infinitely worse than we had suffered. We wondered how many of them could last until their release, obviously very near, eventually arrived. I never learned the names of the camps.

*

The nature of the countryside was changing and we were walking through large areas of pine woods. There was now a much greater military presence in the area. Some of the troops were ordinary units in grey-green, but the majority were SS, a much more menacing presence in their smart black uniforms. They obviously despised us and considered us no more than a rabble. The most forbidding groups of all, however, were the young fellows of the Hitler Youth movement. Standing at the roadside as we passed, they were highly antagonistic. It seemed as though they would have welcomed any excuse to turn their weapons on us. None of us spoke a word, and the mood in our column was very tense each time we passed groups of them.

It looked as though this area was being prepared as another line of defence. The woodland trees were plantations of pines about twenty-five years old. For quite a depth into the wood the trees had all been half sawn through, at the height of around 9ft, with the top section bent over to touch the ground. This left a mass of inverted V-shaped trees, firmly rooted, which the Germans obviously hoped would act as a barrier to advancing tanks. Massive logs of mature timber had also been used as anti-tank barricades at the point where the road entered the wood.

*

We learned that much earlier in the year the Russian advance into Poland had caused the Germans to move many thousands of Allied prisoners westward in a forced march. After some months of constant marching this column found itself approaching the advancing Allied forces. This caused the Germans to turn the column around, and it was not long before they linked with our column, making a total of many thousands of men. Many days we went without food, and we were all in a very weak state. The men from Poland had started marching several months before us, in freezing weather, and were in a very much worse state than we were. Many had worn out their boots completely and had to carry on barefoot.

This enlarged column carried on marching for a few more days, but then the situation became farcical. The German military presence in the area had become even greater, and it became clear to us that the Russians were not far away. Once again we heard distant gunfire, just as we had at Nienburg a fortnight earlier. It was plain that our guards had to choose to which army they would surrender. Their choice was the Allied forces, so we did an about turn and headed westwards.

The guards must have had some information on the tactical situation because they directed us on to roads a little south of the route along which we had come. This was in our favour, as we had cleared the previous road of food and firewood. We felt safer now that we were headed for Allied troops, and this made the marching easier. We passed a few more potato clamps and gathered bits of firewood on these new roads. The march carried on for several days with no significant change, except that the much larger number of prisoners made the task of scrounging for food far more difficult.

People in villages through which we passed were still putting out water for us. When we arrived at a village there were sometimes still some hens pecking away at the roadside. Men leapt on them whenever the opportunity arose. There were even instances of cats being grabbed. It seemed a poor way of showing thanks for the water people had put out.

One of the few good things during the march had been that rain had held off almost the whole time. Eventually we did have rain, but fortunately it was not heavy. Roy and I had some potatoes and we knew we had to find firewood before it became soaked. The rain was light but persisted most of the day. However, walking in the rain turned out to be not unpleasant. We had had almost no opportunity to swill ourselves down and we were by now really grimy, so to feel gentle water falling softly on our faces was a pleasant sensation.

We spent the night in a wood. The weather had cleared and it had stopped raining some time before we arrived, so the prospect was good. There were a couple of other fellows with Roy and myself. Between us, scouting around in the wood, we were able to collect enough fresh rainwater for our potatoes and to kindle a fire with our wood. So we were soon feeling much better. That evening we left the potatoes far too long while we were chatting and they boiled down to a thick stodge. It turned out to be not the best presented meal, but it was very satisfying and much appreciated.

The four of us chatted until the fire went out and we then prepared for sleep. I kicked away the last embers and scraped away the last traces of the fire. The fire had made a small area of ground much drier than the surroundings and it was so appealingly warm that I decided it would be a good place to spread my greatcoat. I was soon sound asleep but during the night I woke and could smell burning. I discovered that my overcoat was smouldering underneath me. That problem was soon put right. I moved across on to wet ground and was soon sound asleep again.

*

We had been on the go now for nearly three weeks since leaving Nienburg, and the next day started off just like any other. Then a small plane which we could see was American came quite near us, flying slowly and very low. We were cheered by the sight, taking it as a good sign. Spirits were sky high and there was a new spring in everybody's step. 'Immerdreien', the cyclist officer, was still calling for orderliness but he was getting short shrift and was continually being pushed off his bike.

Then, as the column moved on, we saw pieces of paper lying in the fields. Our emotions were overflowing when we reached these and began reading them. They were leaflets, printed in German and dropped from the plane we had just seen, telling German soldiers how they should surrender. It was too much to take in as we realized that the terrible ordeal of years must now nearly be over. We were certain now that Americans were very close. The guards were still with us but their mood was so different. The victory which they had so long taken for granted was now crumbling around them, and their shoulders drooped as they walked.

Events such as the American plane and then the leaflets sent the column's spirits soaring. But there was still more to come, and each incident seemed more dramatic than the one before. As we passed a village we saw that a window in each house was open and through the window a long pole protruded with a great white sheet attached, symbolising surrender. It was the most thrilling confirmation that our miserable life was about to change.

It was not so much a feeling of triumph as of relief, not so much a celebration that the Allies were winning the war as joy that we would soon be released from the bonds of captivity. I think my emotion then was the deepest feeling of the whole five years since I had sailed from England. Emotions were running high for everybody. The jubilation was beyond belief, and men did not know whether to laugh or cry, with a good deal of both going on.

*

We did not know how much further we had to go, but everybody was enjoying the walk now. Then the soft 'toot-toot' of a vehicle became audible some way behind us. There were short spells of silence, but it was gradually catching us up. Eventually it was at our heels and slowly edging its way through the mass of men. Then we saw it was a jeep-like German vehicle carrying four officers. They were not Germans, but although nobody recognized them, a voice called, 'These are Americans'. The speaker was told to keep calm and not get carried away. But then other voices joined in, claiming that the uniforms were American.

Most of us had never seen American troops and had no idea of the uniform. Roy and I had met the three Americans in the Fortezza da Basso in Florence, but they wore the Mediterranean-style one-piece combat suit, which was entirely different. It now became clear that the four were indeed Americans, and our celebrations began in earnest. Everybody wanted to greet them, shake their hands, salute them, kiss them, and the vehicle disappeared under a deluge of bodies. Men piled on top of each other until the four in the vehicle must have been in danger of physical harm. It was some time before they were able to continue.

*

Soon afterwards the road entered a stretch of woodland. When we emerged from the wood we saw a large bridge which must have spanned a very substantial river.

As we got nearer, we could see a great number of men gathered on our side of the bridge. On reaching it we saw that it had been supported by two sturdy columns rising from the river bed. However, the Germans had blown up the bridge to stop the Allied advance.

The whole of the bridge had not collapsed into the river. The near section had snapped in the middle and the two halves had broken in two, forming a V-shape. This was impassable to vehicles, but men could scramble down one half and up the other. That explained why the American officers had been driving a German vehicle. The scene was quite busy on our side of the bridge, and before crossing, Roy, George Hockham, another friend of Roy's from Concordia quarry days, and I decided to see what was going on.

On reaching the bridge, prisoners were being guided across it, but Germans, officers and men, were being held at a grassy area on one side of the approach ramp. There were quite a lot of Americans who had crossed the bridge and were organizing the Germans.

There was nothing brutal done to the Germans by the Americans, but one thing which angered our liberators was to see prisoners walking barefoot. They took the barefoot men over to the Germans, picked a likely looking officer, and said, 'Get your boots off, man.' Then to the fellow in need, 'Try these for size, son.' If they did not fit, another officer would be chosen, until the right size turned up. So, as barefoot men were arriving, there was a selection of boots waiting for them.

Eventually, we decided to cross the bridge and scrambled across the demolished section. As we climbed up on to the undamaged part we realized then that this was the moment that we could think of ourselves as truly free. With much back-slapping going on, Roy, George and I heartily shook hands. We spoke of Don, hoping he too had made it. Roy and I had met at Pietraviva in September 1943 and now in April 1945 we were free. It was a wonderfully exhilarating feeling.

*

As we arrived on the undamaged section of the bridge we found an enormous American tank stationed in front of us. An American officer holding a megaphone was sitting on top of it and continually calling out, 'We're mighty goddamned glad to see you guys.' He was not half as glad as we were to see him. The river was the Mulde, another tributary of the Elbe. The town on the far side was Bitterfeld, 30 miles south of our starting point, Nienburg, three weeks earlier.

The officer was telling us to go to the field on the left of the downward ramp, organize ourselves into groups of fifty, sleep in the field that night, and we would be looked after and fed as soon as possible. The evening was warm and dry, so that was no problem. A loud radio was now blaring from the tank and I heard a news bulletin announcing that the American President, Franklin D. Roosevelt, had died that day, 12 April 1945.

Soon the Germans were being brought over the bridge, now officially as prisoners, and our men, now ex-prisoners, went up to the ramp to see who they recognized. The men formed two lines down the ramp and the Germans had to run the gauntlet between them. As a man recognized a guard who had given him a hard time the guard received a thump as he was buffeted along. I saw 'Immerdreien' getting a hard time as he passed. His hat and his glasses were knocked off, and he was singled out as the one everybody wanted to thump. He was pleading for mercy and crying that he was old, but when everybody's life was miserable he had set out to make things even worse.

That was the moment of freedom that for three years I had prayed for, and now I gave thanks that I had managed to survive and had been spared.

Chapter 26

Home at Last

The thousands of former prisoners released by the Americans the previous day at the bridge awoke to their first day of freedom. As promised, early next morning a fleet of American trucks arrived, loaded with rations for men who were about to be issued with food for the first time in many weeks. We were all severely malnourished and in very poor condition, and this prospect seemed hard to believe. The rations were soon issued to the groups, each comprising fifty men as the Americans had requested.

Not long after, a fleet of large lorries arrived to transfer us to a very large and modern military barracks in the town which had been vacated by the Germans. We were to be kept there while the Americans adjusted our bodies from the rigours of the life we had been living to the healthy life we were now to get back to. Roy and I were billeted in the large spacious attic of the barracks. There were no beds in the attic, but we had mattresses on the wooden floor. Even with a great many men in the attic, there was plenty of room for everyone.

The first thing tackled was hygiene. During the three weeks we had marched around the countryside we had slept at the roadside and there had been no opportunity to wash. So the excellent shower rooms in the barracks were put to very good use straight away. Surprisingly, in spite of the conditions we had experienced, we were not lice-infested. However, the Americans paid no heed to that.

Soon after arrival, when everyone was in the barracks, two Americans dressed in protective clothing entered. One had a large metal cylinder strapped to his back and the other held a spray gun. They made no announcement but approached each man in turn. One grabbed the front of a man's trousers and pulled them forward while his colleague stuffed the spray gun down the trousers and blasted in a large amount of anti-lice powder. This carried on until every man had been treated. They then left without a word.

The Americans were concerned about our appetite and wanted to be sure that, after so long on a prison camp diet, we did not gorge on the food that was now available. The danger of over-eating was explained to us and we were given carefully monitored amounts of food for each meal. It took a couple of weeks before the Americans considered we were reasonably re-adjusted to a normal diet. Everybody was still very thin, but the feeling of improvement in our well-being was obvious.

*

News then came that repatriation was about to commence. This at once brought a buzz of excitement. Then the day arrived when lorries transported us to a nearby airfield. There we saw a great many Dakota DC3 planes. They were standing on the grass, one behind the other, four or five in a line along the edge of the airfield. An American was at each plane to control the number of men boarding. Scarcely anybody had flown in a plane previously. The one thing that worried everybody was that whenever a plane started up its engines, tongues of flame licked alongside the fuselage. This made it appear potentially calamitous for the plane to take off, but the Americans assured us that this was perfectly normal and we were in no danger.

When time for take-off arrived, all four planes in the line taxied forward at once and followed each other to the end of the runway. We watched the first plane take off and the others followed in quick succession. We waited for instructions to board our own plane. When our turn finally came, Roy and I walked forward. It was exciting to approach and be counted as we climbed aboard. There were between thirty or forty of us aboard. There was one long seat along each side of the cabin, so two rows of men were sitting facing each other. There was just one American crewman with us. He stood in the middle of the cabin all the time, just talking to us.

Then came the moment for our take-off. The plane rolled forward towards the runway with engines roaring, whilst everybody's hands were gripping the seat. When the nose tipped upward and we became airborne, everybody was turning their heads to look through the window and see the ground getting ever further below us. It was an unbelievable sensation. Everybody knew that, after all the years overseas, it meant that we were now within a few hours of setting foot on English soil.

The plane was very noisy, so to hear each other we had to shout at the top of our voices. The American was telling us about the flight. After a time he said we were approaching Cologne: 'If you look on this side you'll see the famous cathedral.' So we all got to the windows on the side he indicated and, sure enough, when the town came into view the outstanding feature was the cathedral. We also got a glimpse of the Rhine. Then we were pressing on towards home. His next piece of information was that we would see the Channel soon, so we were all squinting through the windows trying to see ahead and get a view of the water. All wanted to be first to see the white cliffs of Dover.

*

As soon as we saw the water we all got a big shock, because almost straight away the plane banked and began to lose height. We came down so low that we realized that we were not going as far as England. Then we saw a large grass area with a little control tower and a landing strip, confirming that we were about to land in France. This was a terrible frustration, and we objected loudly. The landing strip was at the edge of the cliffs on the French side of the Channel. We could see small white marquees erected in neat rows on the grass. When we touched down, a wagon came to the plane to take us to one of the marquees. We were told that we would not have to wait any longer than a couple of hours. None of the other marquees seemed to be occupied, and none of the other planes from Bitterfeld seemed to have come here.

It was a very frustrated bunch of men who were left to wait impatiently in the marquee. Nevertheless, we were eventually rewarded when a wagon arrived to take us back to our plane. Before long we were all aboard, the engines roaring, and once again we were airborne and banking towards the Channel. When we saw the white cliffs, there was much cheering and congratulating each other. Then the American surprised us. He stood in the middle of the cabin and shouted, 'Where do you guys want to go?' We had not expected to be given a choice. Immediately, a chorus of town names was shouted out, covering most of the country. He just said, 'We'll see' and went through to the pilot's cabin.

Then we crossed the south coast and were flying fairly low. The weather was fine, with clear skies, and so we had excellent views of the English countryside. It was exhilarating to see the pattern of small fields, woods, lakes, villages and an occasional town. The excitement only grew as we began to descend.

Then we landed at a large airport which was concreted and had large hangars. Once the cabin door was opened there was a scramble to get down. Men were dancing around and kneeling to kiss the ground. We had taxied to a spot far from the hangars and control tower and could not understand why we were so isolated. We then learned we were near Oxford but that this was not our final destination. So once again we had to re-board the plane, and this caused much frustration for all.

We took off for the third time, and this time our journey did not last very long. We touched down at a small airfield on which we could see a number of RAF huts. It turned out to be near Swindon. Once on the ground, the plane taxied to a point near the huts where a group of people were gathered. They turned out to be girls of the WAAF and one very young airman. Roy and I both had the same thought. It was another case of seeing somebody so clean and sparkling that we felt we could never again get to that state ourselves. His uniform and peaked hat were brand new, buttons sparkling, and his webbing belt gleamed white. His face looked scrubbed and his cheeks were rosy. Our worn old battledress must have looked awful to the welcoming party.

The welcome was very warm. Each one of us was taken by the arm by a WAAF girl and escorted to one of the huts. There tables were set for a meal, and our host-esses sat with us. At once I was given a telegram form to complete and address to my family, and it was collected and sent for despatch. We left the WAAF girls, but it had been really pleasant chatting with them. We were then taken to dormitory huts, the beds already made with clean sheets, and given soap and a towel for a shower. Once cleaned up, we were free to relax. It was a warm sunny afternoon with not a cloud in the sky. We could not have had a more perfect day to arrive back in England!

*

The following morning, after breakfast, Roy and I went off to the quartermas-ter's store. There we were issued with a complete set of new clothing, comprising uniform, boots, underclothing, the lot. There was also a civilian suit for every-body, with five different patterns to choose from. Each jacket and pair of trousers was properly marked with the size. There was none of the usual Quartermaster Sergeant's cry of 'What size d'you want, son? Too big or too small?' There were so many being issued to men being repatriated that those suits were rather like a uni-form. They became known as 'demob suits'. We were each given a kitbag to carry the extra stuff. It felt wonderful to take off all my old clothes and throw them away.

The paymaster issued a small sum of money, so I now had money in my pocket for the first time in years. I also received a railway warrant to Liverpool. Then I was free to go. It was strange to be able to walk wherever I wished and be able to talk to strangers. I found the busy traffic very peculiar and could not get used to it at all. Roy and I took a train to London and there we shook hands and congrat-ulated each other on having made it through all the adversities that we had faced. We also expressed the hope that Don, from whom we had been separated a year earlier, was still all right. We learned soon afterwards that he was, and that our little trio had survived. Then Roy set off for his home at Clapham Junction in London and I headed off to Euston station to get my train.

*

I was soon steaming out of Euston station on a train bound for Lime Street sta-tion in Liverpool. It was truly wonderful to see things and places once again that I could recognize such as the Ovaltine buildings, the twin towers of Wembley, the enormous railway sidings at Crewe and the bridge over the River Mersey at Runcorn. All these and, throughout the whole journey, the beautiful countryside with its small fields, woods and lakes, made every moment exhilarating.

Then the train was pulling in to Lime Street, and there was just the final lap to go. As I walked past people in the station it was so good to hear the Scouse accent. Amongst the crowd I felt like shouting, 'Speak up everybody. I can't hear you.' I might have lost a little of my own accent.

I now wanted to reach home as soon as possible so I went to the taxi rank in the station approach. It was a great feeling to open the door and say to the driver, 'Medlock Street, please, Number 41'. In hardly more than ten minutes the taxi was turning from Westminster Road into Medlock Street. A hundred yards further on we pulled up outside my father's grocery shop. We were underneath a great white banner stretched high across the street emblazoned with the message 'Welcome Home, Frank'. My father was out of the shop door at once and we greeted each other with an embrace in the street. It was nearly six years since he had accompanied me to the barracks in September 1939, when the Territorial Army had been mobilized. When we turned to pay the taxi driver, he would not take any money and just drove off.

*

I turned with my father and we went through the shop and into the living room beyond. I was expecting to find my mother waiting for me. But I was in for a surprise. My mother was there, but the room was also crowded with all my aunts and uncles. They all gave me a great welcome and then my mother came over to hug me. When she took her arms away she was gently crying and said, 'Frankie, you're so thin.' It was true. When I was able, I weighed myself. Even though it was quite some weeks since my release by Allied forces at Bitterfeld, I found I still weighed only six stone.

We all sat down and began to chat, but one thing was now embarrassing me. That morning I had been issued with a side hat, a type which is worn tilted on one side of the head. Not long before I left the compound at Anhalt quarry Kiwi Mullen, the New Zealander, had shaved my head. That was not many weeks earlier and my hair had hardly grown at all. A shaven head was not the fashion in those days, so I had pulled my hat down almost to my eye level on both sides to hide it. This left me looking rather comical, but eventually somebody said, 'Come on, Frankie make yourself comfortable, take your hat off, you're home now.' When I did so, my shaven head was exposed, looking like a worn out brush. It was greeted with howls of laughter from everybody.

Back in the Libyan desert three years earlier I had been with 234 Battery, facing the possibility of the three dangers I have mentioned in the opening paragraphs of this story: death, horrific wounds and capture. It had transpired that capture, to which neither my comrades nor I had given any credence, had proved to be the one that had befallen most of us. It had all been a tough test of endurance. But thankfully I had made it through.

Now that I was safely home I knew that I owed a great deal of thanks to the people of Montebenichi and the other villages and farmsteads of Valdambra, whose kindness and sacrifice had brought me to the peak of fitness. Without their help I would surely have found the hardships in Germany an even greater challenge to my survival.

Epilogue

As was the case for so many families up and down the country, life for the Unwins had been changed dramatically by the six years of the war. My parents had remained at their home in Medlock Street in Kirkdale, Liverpool, where my father had his grocery store. My brother Les was still serving in India with the Royal Air Force, and my sister Maude, having served in the WAAF as a Radar Operator, had married an American and was living in California. My parents were still utterly devastated by the loss of my youngest sister, Betty, aged twelve, who had been aboard the ill-fated SS *City of Benares* when it was torpedoed by German U-boats in September 1940. However, they were pleased to have me home, having lived with the uncertainty of my being a prisoner of war or being posted as missing for significant periods of time, during which they did not even know whether I was alive or dead.

I found that shaking off the rigid pattern of life in a German PoW camp was a slow process. I was granted six weeks' disembarkation leave, which I spent mostly at home with my family, settling down as best I could to civilian life. It was strange to see so many others scurrying around and carrying on their daily business. I was then recalled and spent a further year in the army, at a Royal Artillery camp at Lydd, Kent and later with the Pay Corps in Manchester.

Once back in England, my thoughts soon turned to all my friends in Montebenichi and the surrounding farmsteads such as Colli. I wondered how they had fared and what fighting had taken place in the area. I wrote to Giuliana and Corrada. Both replied, saying that all was well. The only war damage had been to the Landi house, which had been completely destroyed by shellfire. The remaining Allied prisoners had all been released by British forces. I wrote back to Giuliana and Corrada, promising that I would visit as soon as I was able to.

In July 1946 the army sent me to a Civil Resettlement Unit, whose aim was to introduce ex-PoWs to any trade or profession which they thought might interest them. During the war I had enjoyed doing artillery survey and wanted to pursue this line, so the Unit helped me join the Ordnance Survey, working in a division which was dealing with large scale plans. I found this work interesting and satisfying, and I was particularly pleased to be posted to Liverpool.

In September 1949 Roy Page joined me in a trip to Tuscany. We visited Montebenichi and Pietraviva, our two villages, and expressed our deep gratitude for all the kindness and bravery the villagers had shown. We also made new acquaintances in the nearby town of Montevarchi. We returned again in 1950 and 1951, cementing a lifetime connection for me with the people of Montebenichi and the Valdambra.

In 1953 I married my wife, Marjorie, and we set up home in Liverpool. We had a son, Peter, in 1954, and a daughter, Betty, in 1955. Life could not have felt better for me.

However, I found myself thinking of Italy, and in 1956, 1957 and 1958 I acted as tour leader for a party of tourists with Whitehall Travel, a semi-governmental travel agency. In 1956 the tour took in Viareggio and we were able to visit Montebenichi, so I introduced Marjorie to everyone in the village. In 1958 the tour spent a week in Florence during which we were once again able to visit Montebenichi.

During our week in Florence, Marjorie and I visited the British Consulate and saw the UK-based staff dealing with British subjects in need of assistance. On leaving the Consulate, Marjorie's comment was, 'Frank, these people are being paid to live here, you should get a job like that.' So the seed was planted for me to join the Foreign Office.

We then learned that the Ordnance Survey diagram of Liverpool would be complete by 1961, and I therefore faced the prospect of regular moves to different towns around the country. So I took an entrance exam for the Foreign Office, and in November 1958 we were sailing across the Atlantic, bound for Havana, Cuba. We landed one month before the conclusion in January 1959 of Fidel Castro's revolution. We had a very exciting and interesting two-and-a-half-year stay.

Further posts followed, to Tel Aviv (Israel), Vientiane (Laos) and Milan (Italy), followed by a tour in London, and then to Ottawa (Canada) and Lagos (Nigeria). We found all our posts absorbing, each with its own diverse cultures and interests. In Vientiane I was given my first consular job and was then a consular officer in all my subsequent posts. This culminated in my being awarded an MBE for my consular work in Nigeria.

During our posting in Milan between 1967 and 1971, Marjorie and I were able to renew our contact with our friends in Montebenichi. Through our friendship with Giuliana we visited nearby Siena and became interested in the Palio, the ancient custom of a horse race around the Piazza del Campo. Giuliana's husband was a member of the *contrada* (district) of Nicchio, which took in the prison where I had been held for some days in 1944. This introduced me to the people of Nicchio, who were interested that I had spent time in the prison. Marjorie and I attended several Palio races and also a victory dinner held by Nicchio after they had won the race. That was a truly memorable occasion, full of passion.

In 1970 I suggested to the villagers that we hold a party as a heartfelt gesture of thanks to everyone who had cared for me. They welcomed the idea. With so many villagers having left Montebenichi in the previous twenty-five years, invitations were sent to Florence, Siena, Turin, Rimini, Spain and Belgium. I booked all the rooms at the newly opened Hotel Ambra and invited fifty friends from Milan. Also included in the invitation list were four of the Nicchio leaders and their wives.

We decided to roast a calf and build the party around that. I ordered the calf from a butcher in Siena. The local wine producer gave me use of a large grassed area surrounded by woodland which was an ideal site for the occasion. We purchased three of his enormous straw-covered glass containers of wine. The wine was brought to the site on the back of a cart drawn by two of the great white oxen which were such a part of village life. I bought a large supply of charcoal and great quantities of bread, olive oil and other edibles.

The butcher had prepared the calf and brought it the day before. The villagers joined in, covering it with salt and garlic. Enrico, the village blacksmith, had made a wonderful spit 9ft long and two uprights on which the spit was rested, and Tomaso, the village carpenter, supplied trestle tables. The villagers dug a pit and filled it with charcoal. Enzo Capanelli supplied two very tall slender tree trunks which were planted one on either side of the barbecue pit, with a Union Jack on one and an Italian Tricolour on the other.

With the help of two friends from the consulate in Milan we got the fire ready and started roasting the calf by midnight, taking turns through the night rotating the spit for an even cook. We had a bucket of olive oil and a long-handled soft broom to baste the meat. As the day drew on, villagers and other guests began arriving. Soon there was an enthusiastic crowd, with everybody wanting to help.

When the Nicchio party arrived from Siena the four invited families brought with them fifty other members of the *contrada*, including two flag-bearers and two drummers dressed in the *contrada*'s Renaissance costume. To the beat of the drums, the flag-bearers gave an impressive display of flag waving, throwing their flags high into the air then catching each other's. This was a delightful touch, which added to a grand occasion and which was talked about in the village for many years.

On leaving Lagos in 1980, I retired from service abroad. Marjorie and I returned to live in UK, making our home in Orpington, Kent. After six months I re-engaged and was given an interesting job which drew on my consular skills. I then finally retired in 1985.

During our postings outside Europe, Marjorie and I had been unable to visit our friends in Tuscany, but that changed in 1980 when we returned to England. Marjorie loved driving and thought nothing of setting off to Tuscany to visit our friends in Montebenichi, Ambra and Montevarchi.

In the 1990s, as a result of my contact with Enzo Droandi, the historian for whom I had written an account of the story of the tunnel at Laterina PoW camp, I met various people at Laterina and became close friends with the Mayor, Signora Rosetta Roselli. In 1998 the town hall of Laterina hosted a convention on imprisonment. There were many speakers from various Italian universities and international organizations. Rosetta Roselli invited me to address the townspeople on life in Laterina PoW camp. The convention is recorded in a book, *Al di Là del Filo Spinato* [*Beyond the Barbed Wire*]. Some years later Marjorie and I attended the inauguration ceremony for a stone which commemorates the suffering of those in the camp at Laterina.

As the years passed, the older villagers of Montebenichi who sheltered me in the war eventually died. Two of the last to go were Giuliana and Maria Pia, marking the last of my wartime friends. It is sad to stand in the upper piazza and think of the many families who lived there during the war. Most of them have been buried in the cemetery which lies just below the village and, in the Italian way, the graves and headstones bear a porcelain photograph of the deceased. I remember so many of their faces. However, we have maintained our friendships with their children and grandchildren and have hosted members of various families at our home and at Peter's and Betty's homes, including as recently as the summer of 2016.

In my visits to Montebenichi, almost every year since 1980, I have seen many changes to the village and surrounding farmsteads. The population of Montebenichi and other villages dwindled. Whilst the older villagers died, the younger generations moved to Bucine, Siena or further afield, others marrying out of the village or moving for reasons of employment. However, many of the families have maintained their homes in the village as holiday and weekend retreats. The Landi shack, my home for the first couple of months after my arrival at Montebenichi, at that time had no front door and access was through a hole in the wall. It has now been converted into a lovely little villa with a swimming pool and a stunning view over the rolling hills of southern Tuscany. Other places have been bought and renovated and are now holiday homes for tourists, so the village is thriving in the twenty-first century.

Il Castelletto, the most attractive house of the former estate manager, has been converted into a four star hotel. The façade, with its many heraldic coats of arms, and the turrets and roof castellations had fallen into disrepair. These have all been renovated and now the façade is as vibrant and colourful as it would have been centuries ago. The inside is furnished and decorated with exquisite antique furniture, old paintings and beautiful statues. There is a very pleasant breakfast room, but unfortunately the hotel could not accommodate a hotel kitchen and dining room.

This led to negotiations between the owners of *Il Castelletto*, my friends the Giovannini family, and the local district authorities. Agreement was reached to convert the cellar of the Giovannini family home, resulting in the opening of an excellent restaurant. Maria Pia's husband, Gino Biagi, was already an accomplished chef who specialized in the very best of traditional Tuscan cuisine. Gino and Maria Pia and their son Simone, together with his Polish wife Ewa, and also Giuliana, have all shared in the running of the restaurant, such that it is now a thriving and renowned establishment.

The restaurant being housed in the cellar, it was given the name the 'Osteria L'Orciaia', with *orciaia* meaning 'cellar'. Whilst I was sheltered in Montebenichi, I can recall Valentino Giovannini taking me down to the cellar on various occasions. It seemed a huge expanse and was extremely dusty. I have a vivid memory of seeing, among the various articles stored there, two large terracotta urns approximately 3ft high. One bore the date 1872. Being only twenty-three, I was struck that this was almost a hundred years old. Such urns, traditionally stored in the *orciaia*, were used to keep wine or olive oil, *orcio* being the Italian for 'urn'. These same two urns are still now in the restaurant, giving me an extra nostalgic feel to the place.

In 2003, when Marjorie's dementia was very advanced, our 50th wedding anniversary was approaching. I could not think of any suitable way of celebrating such a special occasion. Then I had a brainwave and asked my family would they like to go to Montebenichi. It was my pleasure to host the venture and bring my family and all our various groups of Italian friends together for the first time.

Gino did us proud, serving an exceptional meal of the very best traditional Tuscan cuisine, accompanied by an excellent selection of wine. We invited our closest friends from Montebenichi, Ambra and Montevarchi. Most of my family speak Italian, so the conversation was lively and joyful. Moreover, Marjorie quietly enjoyed it, and the occasion was a resounding success.

Sadly, the most recent news is that Gino Biagi, who had made such a success of the restaurant, died in March 2017. However, it is wonderfully reassuring to know that his son and daughter-in-law, Simone and Ewa, have kept up the restaurant, living up to the reputation that Gino had established for offering a warm welcome and delicious Tuscan dishes, all in a most wonderful setting.

This book has been many years in the making and has frequently been left unattended for long periods. It began in 1989 after I received a letter from Enzo Droandi, a historian in Arezzo. He knew that there had been an escape tunnel at the PoW camp at Laterina but there was nothing about it in the archives at Laterina Town Hall. Could I help? And so I wrote the story of my time at Laterina, including the construction of the tunnel.

After I sent the tunnel story to Droandi, my son Peter, said, 'Dad, you've told us about the tunnel, but what about the prison camps?' At that point I decided to write the whole story. However, there were many years of inactivity during which I was caring for Marjorie when she was suffering with dementia. After her death in 2005 it took me some years to get back into the swing of writing the book. My increasing macular degeneration was then another block to its progress. However, encouraged by my family and friends, I resolved to complete it.

Retelling the story of my time in Italy was an easy task, with two escapes and the excitement of five months' freedom in Montebenichi and the Valdambra; but then came recapture, with the sound of cell doors clanging shut behind me. Writing about my time in Germany was hard and very painful, but my eventual release brought a happy ending.

My experiences and suffering as a PoW in Germany have always lived with me. However, there is no animosity in me. My elder grandson, Michael, is happily married to Dorothee, a lovely German, and they have given me my first great-grandson, Thomas.

My experiences in the war included many hardships, but they also expanded and enriched my understanding of life and gave me my love for Italy and travel. This resulted in my making various choices, such as the decision to join the Foreign Office. This brought, for Marjorie and myself and for Peter and Betty, many years of travel, adventure and enjoyment in many different countries and cultures. Now, aged ninety-seven, I treasure my life as having been truly privileged and, in so many ways, lived to the full.